THE SELF ILLUSION

Also by Bruce Hood

SuperSense: Why We Believe the Unbelievable

The Self Illusion
How the Social Brain Creates Identity

Bruce Hood

OXFORD
UNIVERSITY PRESS

OXFORD

UNIVERSITY PRESS

Oxford University Press is a department of the University of Oxford.
It furthers the University's objective of excellence in research, scholarship,
and education by publishing worldwide.

Oxford   New York
Auckland   Cape Town   Dar es Salaam   Hong Kong   Karachi
Kuala Lumpur   Madrid   Melbourne   Mexico City   Nairobi
New Delhi   Shanghai   Taipei   Toronto

With offices in
Argentina   Austria   Brazil   Chile   Czech Republic   France   Greece
Guatemala   Hungary   Italy   Japan   Poland   Portugal   Singapore
South Korea   Switzerland   Thailand   Turkey   Ukraine   Vietnam

Oxford is a registered trade mark of Oxford University Press
in the UK and certain other countries.

Published in the United States of America by
Oxford University Press
198 Madison Avenue, New York, NY 10016

Library of Congress Cataloging-in-Publication Data
   Hood, Bruce M. (Bruce MacFarlane)
   The self illusion : why there is no "you" inside your head/Bruce Hood.
   p. cm.
   Includes bibliographical references and index.
   ISBN 978–0–19–989759–9 (hardback : alk. paper); 978-0-19-998878-5 (paperback)
   1. Self.   2. Brain.   3. Cognition.   I. Title.
   BF697.H554 2012
   155.2—dc22
   2011047151

9 8 7 6

Printed in the United States of America
on acid-free paper

CONTENTS ■

PROLOGUE ■
The Reflected Self

Last night, I finished reading the biography of Howard Hughes—the tycoon, the aviator, the movie mogul, the socialite, and, finally, the reclusive billionaire, housebound by his pathological fear of dirt. At the time of his death, Hughes was worth $2 billion but he ended his days as an unwashed recluse, dressed in rags, with long, matted hair, curling nails, and the remnants of five hypodermic needles embedded in his arms. Throughout his life, he was a man of multitudes and paradoxes. He loathed social contact but then pursued and bedded hundreds or reputedly thousands of women. He would spend lavishly on fanciful movie projects and young starlets but then quibble over a few dollars on the expense sheet. He was a brash, fearless pilot who regularly placed himself at risk during the pioneering days of aviation, when he set and broke many speed and distance records, and yet his obsessive-compulsive disorder compelled Hughes to be terrified of dying from germs. His close confidant and advisor, Noah Dietrich, explained in his memoir, "There was more than one How-ard Hughes."[1]

This got me thinking. Are there people like that today? In recent years there have been Britney, Mel, Winona, and Tiger: they all seem to have skeletons in their closets, or at least dark sides to their personalities that are so at odds with their public profiles—erratic behaviors that seem so uncharacteristic. The gossip columns thrive on uncovering the hidden truths about celebrities, but are we mere mortals any different? Most of us believe that we are individuals making our own decisions and true to our self, but are we? We may not swing from one extreme to the next as Howard Hughes famously did, but are we more coherent? Is there a single you?

These questions may seem illogical to many. We are so familiar and comfortable with the experience of our self that to question it implies that we may be suffering from mental illness. Almost like asking if we are real or not. And yet, that is the question addressed here. Are we all mistaken when it comes to knowing who we are?

Each morning, we wake up and experience a rich explosion of consciousness—the bright morning sunlight, the smell of roast coffee and, for some of us, the warmth of the person lying next to us in bed. As the slumber recedes into the night, we awake to become who we are. The morning haze of dreams and oblivion disperses and lifts as recognition and recall bubble up the content of our memories into our consciousness. For the briefest of moments, we are not sure where we are and then suddenly "I," the one that is aware, awakens.[2] We gather our thoughts so that the "I" who is conscious becomes the "me"—the person with a past. The memories of the previous day return. The plans for the immediate future reformulate. The realization that we have things to get on with reminds us that it is a work-day. We become a person whom we recognize.

The call of nature tells us that it is time to visit the bathroom and en route we glance at the mirror. We take a moment to reflect. We look a little older, but we are still the same person who has looked in that same mirror every day since we moved in. We see our self in that mirror. This is who we are.

This daily experience of our self is so familiar, and yet the brain science shows that this sense of our self is an illusion. Psychologist Susan Blackmore makes the point that the word "illusion" does not mean that it does not exist—rather, an illusion is not what it seems. We all certainly experience some form of self, but what we experience is a powerful deception generated by our brains for our own benefit.

But there is a real difficulty in discussing the self illusion. Throughout this book, the terms *I, me, my, mine, you, yours, our, us,* and *we* are used, which all imply the existence of a self or multiple selves. (I also separate words such as *yourself* into *your self* and *ourselves* into *our selves* for the sake of emphasis.) You might conclude that the premise that the self is an illusion must be false because these terms already acknowledge the existence of the self in the first place. The problem is that there is no simple way around discussing the self without using these words that refer to this human experience most of us have.[3]

Second, understanding that the self could be an illusion is really difficult. It may be one of the most, if not *the* most, difficult concepts to accept. Our self seems so convincing, so real, so us. But then again, many aspects of our experiences are not what they seem. Take the most lucid experience that you are having right now as you read these words. As your eyes flit across the page, your visual world seems continuous and rich, but you are actually only sampling a fraction of the text one bit at one time, rarely reading all the letters in between. Your peripheral vision is smeared and colorless, yet you could swear that it is perfectly clear just like the center of your visual field. There are two blindspots, the size of lemons at arm's length, just off-center from your field of view that you do not even notice. Everything in your visual world is seamless and unbroken, yet your visual world is blacked out for a fraction of a second between eye movements. You are not made aware of any of these imperfections because your brain provides such a convincing cover story. The same deception is true for all human experience, from the immediacy of our perception to the contemplation of inner thoughts, and that includes the self.

In challenging what is the self, what most people think is the self must first be considered. If you were to ask the average person in the street about their self, they would most likely describe the individual who inhabits their body. They believe they are more than just their bodies. Their bodies are something their selves controls. When we look in the mirror, we regard the body as a vessel we occupy. This sense that we are individuals inside bodies is sometimes called the "ego theory," although philosopher Galen Strawson captures it poetically in what he calls the "pearl view" of the self.[4] This pearl view is the common notion that our self is an essential entity at the core of our existence that holds steady throughout our life. This ego experiences life as a conscious, thinking person with a unique historical background that defines who he or she is. This is the "I" that looks back in the bathroom mirror and reflects upon who is the "me."

In contrast to this ego view, there is an alternative version of the self, based on the "bundle theory" after the Scottish Enlightenment philosopher, David Hume.[5] Three hundred years ago in a dull, drizzly, cold, misty, and miserable (or *driech* as we Scots love to say) Edinburgh, Hume sat and contemplated his own mind. He looked in on his self. He tried to describe his inner self and thought that there was no single entity, but rather bundles of sensations, perceptions, and thoughts piled on top of each other. He concluded that the self emerged out of the bundling together of these experiences. It is not clear whether Hume was aware of exotic Eastern philosophy but in the sixth century BC, thousands of miles away in much warmer climates, the young Buddha, meditating underneath a fig tree, had reached much the same conclusion with his principle of *anatta* (no self). Buddha was seeking spiritual rather than intellectual enlightenment and thought that this state could only be achieved by attaining *anatta* through meditation.

Today, the findings from contemporary brain science have enlightened the nature of the self. As far as spirits are concerned, brain science—or neuroscience, as it is known—has found little evidence for their existence but much to support the bundle theory as opposed to the ego theory of the self.

If the self is the sum of our thoughts and actions, then the first inescapable fact is that these depend on brains. Thoughts and actions are not exclusively the brain because we are always thinking about and acting upon things in the world with our bodies, but the brain is primarily responsible for coordinating these activities. In effect, we are our brains or at least, the brain is the most critical body part when it comes to who we are. We can transplant or replace many parts of the body but most people would regard the patient to be essentially the same person after the operation. However, if a brain transplant were ever possible, then even though the patient may look the same as he comes out of the anaesthetic, most of us believe that he would be someone different—more like the person who donated his or her brain in the first place.

Some of the most compelling evidence that the self depends on the brain comes from studies of unfortunate individuals who have suffered some form of brain damage, either through aging or accident. Their personalities can be so radically changed that, to those who knew them, they become different persons. At the other end of the spectrum, many deliberately alter their brains temporarily with a variety of drugs that affect its workings. Whether by accident, disease, or debauchery, these studies show that if the brain is damaged, the person is different. If taking drugs that change functioning alters the brain, the person behaves and thinks differently. So, who we are depends on our brains. However, we are not just our brains in isolation. One of the messages that I wish to relay here is that each brain exists in an ocean of other brains that affect how it works.

The second major discovery is that there is no center in the brain where the self is constructed. The brain has many distributed jobs. It processes incoming information from the external world into meaningful patterns that are interpreted and stored for future reference. It generates different levels and types of motivations that are the human drives, emotions, and feelings. It produces all sorts of behaviors—some of them automatic while others are acquired through skill, practice, and sheer effort. And then there is mental life. Somehow, this 1.5 kg lump of tissue inside our skull can contemplate the vastness of interstellar space, appreciate Van Gogh, and enjoy Beethoven. It does this through the guise of a self. But the sense of self that most of us experience is not to be found in any one area. Rather it emerges out of the orchestra of different brain processes like a symphony of the self, just as Buddha and Hume said.

Some modern philosophers[6] argue that these brain facts alone are sufficient to deny the existence of the self at all. One can imagine all sorts of scenarios in which brain structures are copied or replaced cell by cell until none of the original brain is material left and yet people maintain an intuition that the self somehow continues to exist independently of all these physical changes. If that were true, then one would have to accept a self that can exist independently of the brain. Most neuroscientists reject that idea. Rather, our brain creates the experience of our self as a model—a cohesive, integrated character—to make sense of the multitude of experiences that assault our senses throughout a lifetime and leave lasting impressions in our memory.

Our brain constructs models of the external world. It can weave experiences into a coherent story that enables us to interpret and predict what we should do next. Our brain simulates the world in order to survive in it. This simulation is remarkable because much of the data that needs processing are corrupted. And yet, our brain fills in missing information, interprets noisy signals, and has to rely on only a sample of everything that is going on around us. We don't have sufficient information, time, or resources to work it all out accurately so we make educated guesses to build our models of reality. That working-out includes not only what's out there in the external world but also what is going on in the internal, mostly unconscious workings of our mind.

Who we are is a story of our self—a constructed narrative that our brain creates. Some of that simulation is experienced as conscious awareness that corresponds to the self illusion that the average person in the street reports. At present, we do not know how a physical system like the brain could ever produce those nonphysical experiences, like the conscious self. In fact, it is turning out to be a very hard problem to solve.[7] We may never find an answer, and some philosophers believe the question is misguided in the first place. Dan Dennett[8] also thinks the self is constructed out of narratives: "Our tales are spun, but for the most part, we don't spin them; they spin us." There is no self at the core. Rather, it emerges as the "center of a narrative gravity." In the same way that we can see a square at the center of the arrangement in Figure P.1, it is an illusion created by the surrounding elements. Take the context away, and the square disappears. In the same way, the self is an illusion created by our brain.

Occasionally, we get a glimpse of the illusions our brains create. We may mishear a comment, bump into things, or mistakenly reach for a shadow that looks graspable. This happens when we misinterpret the physical world. The same mistakes also happen in our personal world—the world that our self occupies. We reinterpret our failures as successes. We think we are above average on good attributes and not like others when it comes to behaving badly. We sometimes do things that surprise us or at least surprise others who think they know us well. This is when we do things that seem inconsistent with the story of our self. We say, "I was not myself" or "It was the wine talking," but we still retain a belief that we are an individual, trapped in our bodies, tracing out a pathway through life, and responsible for our thoughts and actions. Throughout this book, these assumptions are challenged by demonstrating that who we think we are is much more susceptible to outside influences than we imagine.

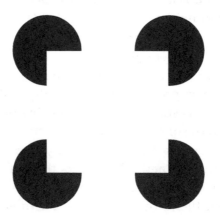

FIGURE P.1   An illusory square we experience that isn't really there.

These influences work from the very beginning. Proportionally, humans spend the greatest amount of time in childhood compared to any other animal. This is not only so that we can learn from others, but also so that we can learn to become *like others*. Becoming like others and getting on with them involves creating a sense of who we are—a participating member of the human species.

This development of the self emerges across childhood as the interplay between the modeling brain, constructing stories from experience, and the influences of other people. This does not mean that we are blank slates at birth and that babies are not individuals. Anyone who has reared children or encountered non-identical twins knows they can think and behave differently right from the very beginning even though they are raised in the same environment. Our dispositions vary from one individual to the next, a legacy of our genetic inheritance, no doubt. However, we all share a common goal to become part of the human race through our social interactions, and that can only take place when people construct a sense of self.

That process of constructing the self does not end with childhood. Even as adults, we are continually developing and elaborating our self illusion. We learn to adapt to different situations. Sometimes we even describe our self illusion as multifaceted, as if we have the work self, the home self, the parent self, the political self, the bigoted self, the emotional self, the sexual self, the creative self, and even the violent self. They seem to be almost different individuals but clearly there is just one body. We seem to switch effortlessly between these different selves, but we would be wrong to think that there is an individual doing the switching. That's part of the illusion. There is not one self or multiple selves in the first place. Rather, it is the external world that switches us from one character to another. This idea that we are a reflection of the situations is sometimes called the "looking-glass self"[9]—we exist as the reflection of those around us.

Initially, as infants, we are bundles of self-interested activity but evolution has preprogrammed our self to emerge and attend to others. Our greatest influence during childhood moves from the immediate family that looks after our needs to the competitive world of young children. We learn to interpret, predict, anticipate, and negotiate in the playground. Gradually, over late childhood and adolescence, we increasingly elaborate the narrative of who we are and eventually strike out to become a character differentiated from those who shaped us. For many adults, adolescence marks the turning point at which we "discover" our true self. We use groups, possessions, tastes, politics, and preferences to create the self—an individual who is different. At least, that is the story of self-formation in the West; other cultures provide a different framework that shapes a different type of self. Even hermits and outcasts from society are defined by their rejection of the principles that the rest of us accept. But whether we are distancing our self from the herd, or ingratiating our self as part of the herd, it is the existence of others that defines who we are.

If the self is largely shaped by those around us, what does that mean for our everyday lives? For one thing, it could change our fundamental outlook. Consider a modern-day miracle about the self. By the time she was 15 years old, Liz Murray's mother had died of AIDS and her HIV-infected father had moved into care. Liz found herself homeless and looking after her younger sister. In spite of all these obstacles, she excelled at school and won a scholarship to Harvard University, eventually graduating in 2009. Liz's "Homeless to Harvard" tale is an inspiring account of the triumph of the individual self over adversity. It is the epitome of the American dream, which is why so many love her story. But think again. What is the take-home message? Is it that if we try hard enough, we can all achieve our dreams? Clearly, that cannot be true. "Homeless to Harvard" is more a tale about the inequalities that exist in life. Liz Murray is remarkable, but that means that she is also the exception because most never overcome the hurdles that keep them from success. Many of us consider Liz to be one of life's "winners" but the flipside is that we all too easily regard others who fall down as "losers." When did this game of life become so unfair that we blame individuals rather than the circumstances that prevent them from achievement? This is known as the *fundamental attribution error* in human reason.[10] When other people screw up, it's because they are stupid or losers, but when I screw up it's because of my circumstances. The self illusion makes the fundamental attribution error an easy fallacy to accept. Also, putting all the blame on the individual self is tantamount to excusing all the policies that create inequality in our society. Maybe it's time to redress this imbalance by rethinking success or failure not so much as issues of the self alone, but more of society in general.

Knowing that the self is an illusion cannot stop you thinking that it exists, and, even if you succeed, as Buddha and Hume did, then maybe it is best not to try in the first place. But knowledge is power. Understanding that the self is an illusion will help to reconcile the daily inconsistencies that you may experience in the way you think and behave. We are all too quick to notice how others can be manipulated, but we rarely appreciate how our own self is equally under the influence and control of others. That is something worth knowing and watching out for.

1 ■

The Most Wondrous Organ

One of the strangest experiences we can have is to hold a human brain in our hands for the first time. It surprises us for so many reasons, but for me, it was the realization that I could hold something that was once a person not so long ago. Our brain, and the mind it supports, is what makes us who we really are.

As a scientist, the brain has always fascinated me, and yet it is not much to look at. When I first arrived at Bristol University, I used to organize a brain dissection class for my colleagues because, although we had all been taught that the brain plays the critical role in creating our mind, very few of us had ever had the opportunity to examine this wondrously mysterious organ. Some of us had measured the electrical activity of the brain as it goes about its business of thinking. Others had even worked with patients who had lost mental abilities through damaging their brains. But few had actually held another human's brain.

So, in December, just before we broke up for the Christmas holidays and after the medical students had finished their dissection classes, a group of about 20 fellow faculty members from the psychology department headed down to the medical school for a crash course in human brain anatomy. At the entrance to the dissection suite, we giggled nervously like a bunch of first-year students as we tried on ill-fitting lab coats. White lab coats—now this was real science! However, that jovial mood suddenly changed when we entered the large, chilled dissection suite and were faced with the stark sight of human bodies in various stages of advanced deconstruction on the tables. This was not some fake alien autopsy, but involved real people who had lived real lives. The nervous mirth so boisterous outside the suite was stifled. The faces of our group turned ashen and pale, with that tight expression that you often see at funerals as people try to appear dignified and composed when faced with death.

We split into groups and tentatively approached the lab benches, each of which had been furnished with a white plastic bucket. We put on rubber gloves and removed the lids. After the initial plume of formaldehyde fumes that stung our eyes and assaulted our nostrils had passed, we stared at the human brains inside each bucket.

At first sight, the human brain is rather unappealing. After it has been chemically prepared for dissection, it resembles a large gray walnut with the rubbery consistency of a firm mushroom. Like a walnut, it is obviously shaped in two halves, but beyond that much of the structures are relatively indistinct. And yet, we know that this small lump of tissue is somehow responsible for the most amazing experiences we can ever have in the universe—human thoughts and behaviors. How does this wondrous organ produce them?

■ The Matrix That Is Your Mind

In the science fiction classic, *The Matrix*, our hero, computer hacker "Neo," played by Keanu Reeves, discovers that his reality is not real. He thinks he is living in the United States in the year 1999 but, in fact, he is living in a post-apocalyptic future world hundreds of years later where humans have been battling intelligent machines. His mundane daily reality is actually a computer program called the Matrix that is fed directly into his brain and the brains of other enslaved humans who are imprisoned in pods and harvested for their bioelectrical energy by the intelligent machines. But because all experience is so faithfully simulated, the humans are blissfully unaware of their true state.

This plot may sound too fantastic to believe, but the movie is not that far off the mark when it comes to understanding the nature of the human mind. Of course, we are not enslaved humans controlled by machines—but there again, how would one ever know? These are wonderfully entertaining suppositions, and all students of the mind should watch the movie, but one thing is clear: each of us really does have a matrix in our brain. This is because our brains are constructing simulations or stories to make sense of our experiences because we have no direct contact with reality. This does not mean that the world does not really exist. It does exist, but our brains have evolved to process only those aspects of the external world that are useful to us. We only sense what we are capable of detecting through our nervous system.

We process the outside world through our nervous system in order to create a model of reality in our brains. And, just like the matrix in the science fiction movie, not everything is what it seems. We all know the power of visual illusions to trick the mind into perceiving things incorrectly, but the most powerful illusion is the sense that we exist inside our heads as an integrated, coherent individual or self. As a self, we feel that we occupy our bodies. On an intellectual level, most of us understand that we need our brains, but few of us think that everything that makes us who we are can be reduced down to a lump of tissue. Most of us think that we are not simply our brain. In fact, we are our brains, but the brain itself is surprisingly dependent on the world it processes and, when it comes to generating the self, the role of others is paramount in shaping us.

■ Brain Reductionism

Some people get awfully upset with statements such as "we are our brains"—as if this reduces or demeans the experience of life by making it material. Others point out that brains need bodies, and so the two are inextricably linked. Still others point out that brains exist in bodies that exist in environments, and so it is illogical to reduce experience down to the brain. All of these objections are valid but, ultimately, we need to start taking a stand on how we think these all concepts work together. The brain seems the most obvious place to start. We can change environments and replace most body parts, but our brain is pretty fundamental to who we are. And who we are includes a sense of self. That said, understanding where the sense of self comes from ultimately needs to involve the consideration of bodies and environments that shape the self.

Back in the dissection suite, it was the brain that had our full attention. This was no ordinary piece of the body. This was more than tissue. Somehow, each brain yielded the agony, the ecstasy, the confusion, the sadness, the curiosity, the disappointment, and every other mental state that makes us human. Each brain harbored memories, creativity, and, maybe, some madness. It is the brain that catches the ball, scores the goal, flirts with strangers, or decides to invade Poland. Each brain that we held in our hands that afternoon in the dissection suite had experienced a lifetime of such thoughts, feelings, and motivations. Each brain had once been someone who had loved, someone who had told a joke, someone who had charmed, someone who had sex, and, ultimately, someone who had contemplated his own death and decided he would donate his body to medical science when he was gone. Holding another's brain in your hands for the first time is the closest to a spiritual experience I have ever had. It makes you feel humble and mortal at the same time.

Once you have overcome the emotional shock, you are then struck by the absolute wonder of this organ—especially if you have an appreciation of what an amazing thing the human brain is. Although you cannot see them with the naked eye, packed inside this lump of tissue are an estimated 170 billion cells.[1] There are many different types of cells, but for our purposes, the nerve cell or *neuron* is the basic building block of the brain circuits that do all the really clever stuff. There are an estimated 86 to 100 billion of these neurons—the elements of the microcircuitry that create all of our mental life. There are three major types of neurons. *Sensory neurons* respond to information picked from the environment through our senses. *Motor neurons* relay information that controls our movement outputs. But it is the third class of neuron that makes up the majority—the *interneurons*, which connect the input and the output of the brain into an internal network where all the really clever stuff happens. It is this internal network that stores information and performs all the operations that we recognize as higher thought processes. By themselves, neurons are not particularly clever. When not active, they idle along, occasionally discharging an electrical impulse like a Geiger counter that picks up background radiation. When they receive a combined jolt of incoming activity from other neurons, they burst into activity like a machine-gun, sending cascading impulses out to others. How can these two states of relative inactivity and a frenzy of firing create the processing power and intricacy of the human mind?

The answer is that if you have enough of them connected together, this collection of interconnected neurons can produce surprising complexity. Like the legions of soldier ants in a colony, or thousands of termites in one of those amazing earth mounds, complexity can emerge if you have enough simple elements communicating with each other. This was discovered in 1948, by Claude Shannon,[2] a mathematician working at Bell Laboratories in the United States on the problem of sending large amounts of data over the telephone. He proved that any pattern, no matter how complicated, could be broken down into a series of on and off states distributed across a network. Shannon's *Information Theory*, as it became known, was not a dusty theoretical notion, but rather a practical application that revolutionized the communications industry and gave birth to the Computer Age. He showed that if you connect up a large number of simple switches that could be either "on" or "off," then you can create a binary code,[3] which is the communication platform for all digital systems that control everything from an iPod to the orbiting International Space Station. This binary code is the foundation for every modern computer language. It is also the same principle operating in every living organism that has a nervous system.

The neurons communicate with each other by sending electrochemical signals through connecting fibers. A typical neuron has lots of fibers connecting with local neurons next to it, but it also has a long-distance fiber, called an *axon*, that connects with groups of neurons much farther away. It's like having a bunch of friends you talk to regularly in your neighborhood, but also a really good connection with a group of friends who live abroad. The neurons are jam-packed into a 3–4 mm thick layer on the outer surface of the brain, known as the *cortex* (from the Latin for "bark"). The cortex is of particular interest because most of the higher functions that make us so human appear to rely on what's going in this tiny sliver of tissue. The cortex is also what gives the human brain its peculiar appearance of a giant walnut with many crevices.[4] The human brain is 3,000 times larger than that of the mouse, but our cortex is only three times thicker[5] because of the folding. Think about trying to cram a large kitchen sponge into a small bottle. You have to scrunch it up to make it fit. It's the same with the human brain. Its folded structure is nature's engineering solution to cram as much brain into a typical skull as possible without humans evolving heads the size of beach balls to accommodate the same cortical surface area. Ask any mother during delivery: she will probably tell you politely that it's bad enough giving birth to a normal-sized head without it being any larger!

Like some strange alien creature extending tentacles, each neuron is simultaneously connected to up to thousands of other neurons. It is the combined activity of information coming in that determines whether a neuron is active or not. When the sum of this activity reaches a tipping point, the neuron fires, discharging a small chemical electrical signal and setting off a chain reaction in its connections. In effect, each neuron is a bit like a microprocessor because it computes the combined activity of all the other neurons it is connected to. It's a bit like spreading a rumor in a neighborhood. Some of your neighboring neurons are excitatory and, like good friends, want to help spread the word. Other neurons are inhibitory and basically tell you to shut up. And, every time the neuron has such a conversation with its different neighbors or long-distance pals, it remembers the message either to spread the word or be silent, so that when the rumor comes round again, the neuron responds with more certainty. This is because the connections between the neurons have become strengthened by repeatedly firing together. In the words of the neurophysiologist Donald Hebb, who discovered this mechanism, synchronized neurons that "fire together, wire together."

These spreading patterns of electrical activity are the language of mental life. They are our thoughts. Whether they are triggered from the outside environment or arise from the depths of our mental world, all thoughts are patterns of activation in the matrix that is our mind. When some event in the external world, such as hearing the sound of music, stimulates our senses, this stimulation is transmitted into a pattern of neuronal impulses that travels to relevant processing areas of the brain. This, in turn, generates a cascading pattern of activation throughout the brain. In the other direction, whenever we have an internal thought, such as remembering the sound of music, patterns of neural activity similarly cascade across the relevant centers of the brain, reconstructing the memories and thought processes related to this particular experience.

This is because the brain deals with distributed patterns. Imagine that the neural patterns in your brain are like domino patterns in one those amazing demonstrations where you topple one domino and trigger a chain reaction. Only, these dominoes can bounce back up again, waiting for the next time they are pushed over. Some dominoes are easily toppled, whereas others need lots of repeated pushes from multiple sources before they activate and set the pattern propagating.

Now imagine that, rather than there being just one pattern of dominoes, instead there are trillions of different patterns of dominoes overlapping and sharing some of the same excitatory and inhibitory neurons. Not all the dominoes topple because the interconnectedness of certain clusters of neurons influences the path a neural activation takes. The fact that each neuron can participate in more than one pattern of activity means that the architecture of the brain is *parallel*. This is a really important point because it reveals a very crucial clue as to why the brain is so powerful. It can do several tasks simultaneously, using the same neurons. It's like the three-dimensional game of tic-tac-toe. Imagine that the zero or the cross is like the active or inactive state of a neuron. It can start or stop a line that we will use as a metaphor for a chain of neural activation (Figure 1.1).

Those chains can spread in many directions. If you place a cross in the bottom corner of the lower layer, it also activates the patterns on the middle and top layers simultaneously. If you only consider the layout on one level, you are likely to lose the game. Rather, to play the game well, you have to think of parallel activation on all levels at the same time. Likewise, activation of neurons produces parallel activation in other connected networks of patterns. That is just as well, because the speed at which neural impulses travel from one neuron to the next in real time has been calculated to be simply too slow for the speed at which we know the brain can perform multiple operations. The best explanation for our efficient brain speed at completing

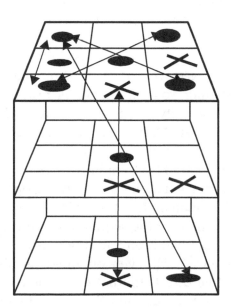

FIGURE 1-1   Parallel processing works like three-dimensional tic-tac-toe.

tasks is this parallel organization of the neural patterns.[6] Our brains really do multitask using the same hardware.

With such an arrangement, consider how a lifetime of experiences could operate as a multitude of fingers that topple different dominoes, creating different patterns of activation. In this way, the full diversity of what happens to us during our lives could be stored in the complexity of the neural circuitry as distributed parallel patterns. With billions of neurons, each with up to 10,000 possible connections with neighboring neurons, that arrangement has the potential to create an almost infinite number of different patterns of connectivity. The mathematics of brain connectivity is mind-boggling. For example, if you just took 500 neurons all connected together, so that each neuron could either be in a state of on or off, the total number of different patterns is 2^{500}, a number that exceeds the estimated total number of atoms in the observable universe.[7] Given that there are billions of neurons, you can understand why the human brain is considered the most complicated structure known to man—or, to be more accurate, rather *unknown* to man.

So, this is how the brain basically works. Just like Keanu Reeves' Neo, you have no direct connection with reality. Everything you experience is processed into patterns of neural activity that form your mental life. You are living in your own Matrix. Wilder Penfield, the famous Canadian neurosurgeon who reported how he could induce dreamlike flashbacks in his conscious patients when he directly stimulated their cortex during operations, most dramatically demonstrated this. He wrote, "They were electrical activations of the sequential record of consciousness, a record that had been laid down during the patient's earlier experience."[8] He even operated on his own sister and showed that direct stimulation of the cortex triggered motor actions, sensations, and thoughts. It's these patterns of connectivity that encode all the information we process, memories we store, and plans that we intend execute. Love, hate, the capital of France, the winners of the last World Cup soccer tournament, how to pitch a tent, how to divide by ten, the plot of your next novel, the taste of chocolate and the smell of oranges—every feeling, bit of knowledge and experience you have or plan to have is possible because of the cascading activation of neurons. Everything we are, can do, and will do is nothing more than this. Otherwise, we would need ghosts in the brain and, so far, none have been found.

■ How the Developing Brain Gets Organized

Of course, the human brain is considerably more organized than a chaotic jumble of overlapping circuits. Many areas have been mapped that correspond to different tasks or functions that the brain undertakes (Figure 1.2). There are brain regions that process information as it arrives from the senses. There are brain regions that plan, initiate, and control movements. There are brain regions where personal memories are stored. There are regions that perform calculations. There are centers for emotion, aggression, pleasure, and arousal—the fire in the belly of the machine that gets us out of bed in the morning and motivates us to act on the world.

One way to consider how the brain is organized structurally and functionally is to consider it like an onion. At the core of the onion is the brain stem that regulates the basic body functions that keep us alive, such as breathing and blood circulation. Above the brain stem is the midbrain region that controls activity levels, such as wakefulness and appetite. The midbrain also governs basic motor control and sensory processing. Arising out of the midbrain is the limbic system, a network that controls emotions and drives, such as aggression and sex. This has been called the

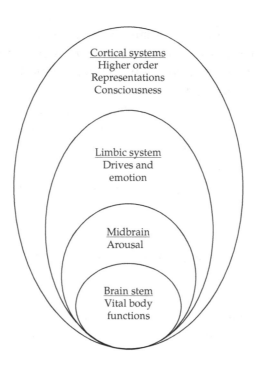

Cortical systems
Higher order
Representations
Consciousness

Limbic system
Drives and
emotion

Midbrain
Arousal

Brain stem
Vital body
functions

FIGURE 1-2   Illustration of structural and functional hierarchy of brain systems.

"reptilian brain" because it controls the sorts of functions we share with lizards and snakes.[9] These functions are simply triggered by the sight of a competitor or a potential mate—like a knee-jerk reaction. Deep in the history of our species, we behaved in this automatic way, but eventually we evolved higher levels of brain machinery that enabled us to control these reptilian urges. Sitting on top of everything is the cortex, a thin layer on the surface of the brain, packed with neurons that support higher-order processing for interpreting the world, generating knowledge, and planning actions.

One of the most surprising discoveries in recent years is that the cortex is not where the majority of neurons are found. Most neurons are densely packed into a specialized region in the base at the back of the brain, known as the *cerebellum*, which controls movement.[10] Only about a fifth of neurons are found in the remaining areas of the cortex that we usually associate with higher-level thinking. This is surprising as one would assume that the complex mental processes involving thought would benefit from having more processors. However, the power is not in the number of neurons but in the amount of connections. Like many performance issues in life, it's not how much you have, but what you do with it and who you know. Even though the cortex has fewer neurons than one might expect, it has much greater connectivity, with more extensive and longer fibers that join together different, widely distributed populations. This is the secret to the power of the human cortex—communication. By integrating information from diverse areas, the brain can generate rich, multidimensional experiences. Somehow, out of this richness comes our conscious self. Without cortical activity, you lose consciousness—you lose your self.

Not only does this multilayered model represent one of the major organizational layouts of the brain, it also illustrates the relative developmental progression that has taken place in the brain through evolution, with the lower systems being more mature and operational than the upper systems, which continue to develop into adulthood. Babies start out with functioning lower centers. With time and experience, these lower regions become increasingly interconnected with the higher centers that exert influence and control, so that the brain operates in a coordinated way.

You can see this coordination emerging throughout childhood. In fact, many scientists, like myself, believe that much of the change in early development can be attributed to not only the emergence of higher brain centers, but also the integration between these systems and their control over lower mechanisms. For example, something as simple as eye movement is controlled initially by lower brain systems below the cortex that are working from birth.[11] The problem is that these lower systems are fairly dumb. Those that control eye movement have evolved simply to direct your gaze to the darkest and brightest objects in the world. So, for very young infants, the brightest things usually get their attention, but the trouble is that they lack the control to look away easily. For example, below 2 months of age, they have "sticky fixation"— they get stuck on a particular visually compelling target.[12] The trouble is that if the most visible thing always captures your gaze, then you are going to miss everything else in view. In fact, when I worked at a specialized unit for children with visual problems, we used to get young mothers coming in worried that their healthy babies were blind because they did not seem to move their eyes a lot. They seemed to be in some sort of trance, staring fixedly at the window. They wanted to know why their young babies didn't look them straight in the eye.

The behaviors of these babies, like many of the limitations found in young infants, reflect the immaturity of their brains. During the early weeks, babies have very little cortical control. Over time, cortical mechanisms start to exert increasing control over the lower mechanisms through a process called *inhibition* that works like a vetoing system to shut down activity. Inhibition helps to rein in the lower centers to allow more flexibility. In the case of sticky fixation, the cortical mechanisms enable the baby to look away from highly visible targets, such as the bright light streaming in through the window, and to direct his gaze to less obvious things in the world.

It turns out that most human functions require some degree of inhibitory control. Here's a cruel trick to play on an 8-month-old baby who has developed the ability to reach out for toys. Show him a desirable, colorful toy that he really wants, but put it in a large clear plastic container. At first, he will bash his tiny little hands against the clear surface as he reaches for it. Even though he will keep bashing his hands against the transparent plastic, he will find it hard to stop reaching straight for the toy.[13] The sight of the toy is so compelling that he cannot inhibit his reaches. In fact, inhibiting our impulsive thoughts and behaviors is one of the main changes over the course of a lifetime that contributes to the development of the self. When these regulatory systems fail, then the integrity of the self is compromised.

It is as if our brain is a complex machine made up of many subdivisions that compete for control of the body—like a complex factory under the control of a senior manager who oversees production. It is this senior manager in our head office that we all experience as the self. You may be able to find your own senior manager by a bit of introspection—the process of focusing in on your mental state. Try this out. Find a quiet spot and close your eyes. Turn your attention to your self. Try to locate where that self is. With both hands, point with your index fingers to the sides of your head where you think your inner self is currently located. When both fingers are pointing to where you think you are having experience at this very moment in time inside your head, keep one finger pointing and with the other hand point to this same place from the front of your head, so that you can accurately triangulate the site of your consciousness. Now, draw the imaginary lines to find the intersection where "X" marks the spot (Figure 1.3).

You have just located your own "point zero"—where the "you" inside your head sits. Figure 1.3 is taken from a study to map out where people think their point zero is located.[14] It reveals that when we become mindful of our inner state, for most of us, it seems like we exist inside our heads, somewhere behind our eyes. We believe that this is the place where we are listening to a running commentary of thought, experiencing the sensations that the world throws at us, and somehow controlling the levers that work the action and motions of our bodies.

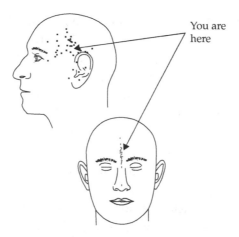

FIGURE 1-3 Plot of locations where individuals typically feel their "self" is located (based on study by Ferrari et al., 2008, with permission of the publisher.)

Take a further moment to experience your body in this quiet state. If you concentrate, you can feel its inner workings. As you read these lines, can you feel the subtle movements of your tongue bobbing up and down inside your mouth? Now that your attention has been drawn towards it, can you feel the pressure of the chair you are sitting on pressing against your backside? We can be in touch with our bodies, but we are more than just our bodies. We control our bodies like some skilled operator of a complex meat machine.

This internal self is sometimes called the *homunculus*, and this little chap is a real troublemaker. The homunculus is a problem because you are left none the wiser about the location of the self. In fact, considering the homunculus reveals why the reality of the self is a problem. There can be no single individual inside your head for the simple reason that, if true, then this homunculus would require an inner self as well. You would need a "mini-me" inside the "you" that is inside your head. But if the "mini-me" inside your head is a homunculus, then who is inside the head of mini-me, and so on, and so on? This would become an infinite regression leading to no end. Like an endless series of Russian *matryoshka* dolls, one inside another, the homunculus simply restates the initial problem of where the self is located in the mind. This is what philosopher Dan Dennett has called the *illusion of the Cartesian Theater*, after the famous French philosopher, René Descartes, who thought that each of us possess a mind that inhabits our bodies. Dennett described this like sitting in the audience inside our heads watching the world of experience unfold like a play on a stage. But who is inside the head of the person watching the play in the Cartesian Theater? Proposing an inner self simply does not help in solving the problem of where we are inside our heads.

Are we like a factory made up of lots of autonomous little workers inside our heads carrying out all the various tasks and functions that humans can achieve? To some extent we are, in that many of the subdivisions can operate independently. But there is not a worker army of homunculi any more than there is a chief executive in charge. Rather, our minds are a multitude of different processes and decisions that are often in conflict with each other, which often can occur below our level consciousness. This is why we will need to abandon the notion of internal individuals, which is inadequate to explain the complexity of our brain, and ultimately, discard the notion that an inner self exists.

■ Mapping the Mind Machine

If the brain is a complex machine organized into different processing subdivisions, where does this organization come from? Who sets up all the domino patterns in the first place? This question is one of the major battlegrounds in neuroscience. To what extent are we preconfigured for the world by our genes, and to what extent does that configuration emerge through our interaction with the world? It's the old "nature versus nurture" issue, but at the basic biological level. It all depends on what aspect of being human you are considering, but even the simplest features appear to combine biology with experience.

It is quite clear that we are born with many basic neural patterns in place. Many sensory and motor areas are well specified at birth, even though they have yet to reach their full adult potential.[15] But babies are not just passive sponges soaking up sensation from their environment—they can also act upon the world. For example, each human newborn is equipped with a repertoire of behaviors known as *reflexes* that play some vital role in development. Consider the rooting reflex, triggered by gently stroking the cheek of a newborn, which makes the baby turn her head and pucker up her lips in anticipation of a tasty nipple. If a nipple (or at least something of a similar shape) is touched to the baby's lips, this then triggers a sucking reflex. You might think that the baby has decided to feed, but the truth is that these behaviors are completely involuntary and automatic and do not require any thinking. In fact, you do not need a very sophisticated brain to execute them. Anencephalic babies, born without any cortex, can still execute sucking reflexes because these behaviors are supported by primitive neural circuitry that lies beneath the cortex. But anencephalic babies are never destined to experience what it is to be human. They do not learn. They do not get bored.[16] They simply respond. They will never develop a sense of their own self. Most die within days.

In contrast to the unfortunate babies born with brain damage, healthy infants are equipped with a brain that is designed to learn about its environment, and this learning starts very early. We now know that the unborn baby can learn the sound of his mother's voice, develop a preference for the food his mother eats while pregnant, and even remember the theme tune to the TV soap operas his mother watches while waiting for the big day to arrive.[17] All of this proves that the brain is already functioning and storing patterns of connections that represent the outside world. This is one reason why separating the relative influence of nature from nurture is always going to be hard and contentious. When do you start measuring? From conception, or from birth?

Neuroscientists argue about how much of the adult brain structure is already evident in the infant, but it is quite clear that even if much of the blueprint for brain architecture has been passed on in the genetic code we inherit, there is still considerable scope for making amendments and building extensions to the original plan. This is where the environment shapes the brain, by sculpting the matrix of neuronal connectivity that generates our minds.

■ Plastic Brains

I once bought a "Grow Your Own Brain" gimmick toy, which was basically a compressed tiny plastic foam brain that you put in water, and it eventually expands to a much greater size. It's amusing but not really a useful teaching aid. It is true that as babies grow their brains expand, but they are not simply swelling. The human newborn baby's brain weighs about a quarter of the weight of an adult brain, but within the first year, more than half of the difference in weight is made up. What may surprise you is that this weight change is not because the brain is growing more neurons. In fact, newborn babies have almost their full complement of neurons, which will remain with them throughout the rest of their lives. Rather, most of that weight change is due to the rapid expansion of communications between the neurons.[18]

As you can see in Figure 1.4, a diagram of the cortex taken from newborns through to 15 months old, the human brain undergoes a massive explosion in connectivity between neurons during infancy.[19] For example, during peak activity, the rat pup brain is generating neuronal connections at the rate of 250,000 every second. That's 15 million connections every minute. We do not know how fast the process occurs in humans. If anything, it may well be even faster.

These structural changes reflect the way that biological processes interact with the world to shape the brain to fit into its environment. Two complementary processes create this sculpting.[20] First, genetic commands tell the neurons to start growing more and more connections. This creates an initial overproduction of connectivity between the neurons. That's why the diagram looks like the underground root system of weeds growing in your garden. Second, this bout of overproduction is followed by a period of *pruning*, during which connections are lost between neurons.[21] Around four out of every ten connections are lost, with about 100,000 lost every second during the peak rate. This loss of connectivity is particularly interesting and at first surprising. Why would nature put in all the effort to build bridges between neurons only to knock them down almost equally as fast at a later date?

It turns out that the overproduction and subsequent culling of connections may be a cunning strategy to shape the brain to its environment. A massive connectivity means that the brain is wired up for every potential pattern of activation that it may encounter from experience. But remember, only neurons that fire together wire together. When neurons are not reciprocally activated, nature prunes their connections through inactivity. Returning to the metaphor of our extended neighborhood, "If you don't return my call, I am not going to bother contacting you later." Or, for those of you familiar with social networking on

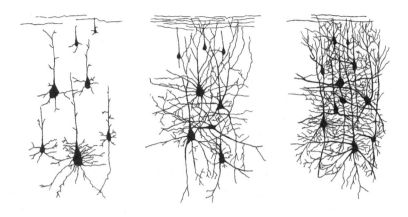

FIGURE 1-4   Illustration of neurons increasing connectivity during development.

Facebook or Twitter, then it's the case of "unfollowing" followers who do not follow you back.

Reciprocal communication enables experience to change the brain's architecture. We know this from animal research, in which the effects of early environments have been shown to influence the connectivity of the brain. For example, if you raise rat pups in isolation, without much to see or do, their brains are lighter and have few cortical connections compared to the brains of pups raised in an enriched environment where there are lots of other rats with which to play. Nobel Prize winners David Hubel and Torsten Wiesel found that the activity of cortical neurons in the visual area was impaired in cats and monkeys raised in deprived visual environments during early development. Moreover, specific types of visual deprivation produced selective impairments. For example, animals raised in a stroboscopic world had relatively normal vision for objects but could not see smooth movement, in the same way that you cannot see continuous motion in a bad 1970s disco when the strobe light is on. One unfortunate woman who acquired damage to this part of her visual brain late in life described how difficult it was for her to cross the road because she could not judge the speed of approaching cars. When she poured a cup of tea, it looked like a series of snapshots or still photographs with the cup empty, half-full, and then overflowing.[22]

Sometimes, the ability to see certain patterns is lost. Animals raised in environments without straight lines end up not being able to see straight. In short, early deprivation studies reveal that the punishment fits the crime.[23] If you remove some experience during early development, it has long-term effects later in life. Children raised with faulty vision grow up with permanent visual loss known as *amblyopia*. Amblyopia is not a problem of the eyes but of the brain regions that produce vision. That's why putting glasses on someone with amblyopia late in life makes no difference. It's also why amblyopes cannot fully appreciate 3D movies because they have lost stereovision, which needs good input from both eyes early on in life. If you want to make a difference, you have to correct the problem when it first arises, so that the developing connections in the brain are not permanently ruined.[24] This leads on to discussion of another fundamental principle of brain development—sensitive periods.

■ Windows of Opportunity

Timing is everything, be it golf, sex, or comedy. This turns out to be true for many basic aspects of brain development when input from the environment is required. Our brains have evolved to be malleable through experience, but some experiences are required and expected at certain times during our lifetime. As noted above, deprivation can lead to permanent problems in later life, but it turns out that these effects are most pronounced at certain times.

Once the connections have been pruned due to inactivity, it is increasingly difficult to reestablish communication between the relevant parts of the brain. The window of opportunity has slammed shut.

These episodes of time-limited brain development are sometimes called "critical periods" because no amount of remedial exposure after the window of opportunity has passed can reinstate the lost function. In truth, "sensitive period" is probably more accurate as the brain has a remarkable capacity to recover, although it is worth noting that sensitive periods apply only to some of our human abilities and not others. Natural selection has evolved brains to expect certain experiences at certain times in development.[25] Why would nature hedge her bets that way? Surely, blank slates are the best solution for uncertain worlds.

The reason is quite simple—like any successful manufacturer, nature always seems optimized to cut the cost of production. Nature prefers to build machines that are tailored to work without being overspecialized. For example, there is no point in building an all-purpose machine when some purposes are unlikely or redundant—that would be too costly. It is much better and more efficient to anticipate the most likely world, rather than having the machine specified in advance. This is how evolution selects for the best fit. Those with systems that are not optimized for their environment are not as efficient and will eventually lose the race to reproduce. This explains why babies' brains are prewired loosely to expect certain worlds they have not yet encountered and then become streamlined and matched to their own world through experience.

Although the modern world appears complex and confusing, the basic building blocks of how we see it are fairly predictable and unchanging from one generation to the next. Experience simply fine-tunes the system. However, if you remove the experience during the critical time when it is expected, then this creates permanent problems. One of the first demonstrations of critical period loss comes from the Nobel Prize-winning work of Konrad Lorenz, who showed that newborn goslings would follow the first moving thing they saw—even if that happened to be an elderly Austrian bird expert.[26] The early movies of Lorenz show this bearded gent walking around smoking his pipe, being loyally followed by a line of goslings. Their bird brains were equipped with a built-in mechanism to *imprint* on and follow the first big moving thing, whatever or whoever that was. For many animals, nature has produced a similar strategy to get them up and running as fast possible and to follow the important others in their gang. In the case of geese (and many other birds), nature gambled that the first moving thing was usually Old Mother Goose, so there was no need to be too discerning. Austrian ornithologists would do fine. However, if the goslings were raised so that they did not see any large moving thing at all for the first ten days, then they did not later imprint because the window of opportunity had passed. In their natural state, with no one to follow, these goslings would have perished as their mother moved on.

Humans are more complicated than birds, and our period of growth and nurturing is the longest in the animal kingdom, so there is less pressure to adapt as quickly. Nevertheless, there does appear to be evidence that we too have windows of opportunity and are preconfigured to attend to certain information from the environment. For example, human language development is usually trumpeted as one of the best examples of a brain-based ability that is both uniquely human and biologically anchored. In *The Language Instinct*,[27] Steven Pinker points out that just about every child, irrespective of where he is raised, learns to speak a language almost effortlessly at roughly the same time, whereas his pet hamster, raised in the same household, does not. It doesn't matter how much you talk to your pets, you won't get them answering you back. The only sensible explanation for this is that the human brain is preprogrammed to learn a language, whereas pet hamsters' brains are not. Any infant raised in any environment can learn the language to which he is exposed. This proves that there is a built-in, uniquely human capacity to learn language, which must be genetically encoded, but that the actual language acquired is determined by the environment.

The human baby's remarkable ability effortlessly to acquire language is only one line of evidence for the biological basis of language. Have you ever noticed how difficult it is to learn a second language as you get older? For example, I do not seem to be readily able to learn a foreign language, and it is not through lack of trying. Despite hours of effort with Linguaphone learning tapes, I am unable to break the British stereotype of only being able to speak English. This is because the plasticity in the neural circuits in my brain that support language learning has been progressively lost. Some of us do not have such a problem, but it may be related to whether we were exposed to other languages at a young enough age. This is one of the reasons that foreign-language learning is much easier when you are younger than 7 years of age. For example, when Korean immigrants to the United States were tested on their ability to learn English, individuals had no problem if they arrived before they were 7. For older immigrants, it became increasingly hard for them to learn English, even though they attended night classes and were highly motivated to learn.[28] This indicates biological limits exist to learning languages.

For many, just hearing the difference between languages becomes hard. In a classic study, Canadian infant researcher Janet Werker demonstrated that all babies could hear the different sound structures that exist in spoken Inuit and English languages before the age of 10 months. However, the longer they were immersed in their own language environment, the more difficult it was for them to hear differences in the structure of other languages.[29] As we age, we lose the ability to detect the subtle differences between spoken languages. The best explanation is that our brains are tuning into the experience from our environments and losing the ability to process experiences that we do not encounter. Our brains are becoming less plastic for language learning. This is why, for Japanese speakers, English words that have "l" and "r" sounds are often confused, which can lead to comical miscommunication. Pinker wrote about his visit to Japan, where he described how the Japanese linguist Masaaki Yamanashi greeted him with a twinkle in his eye when he said, "In Japan, we have been very interested in Clinton's *erection*." (This was several years before the U.S. President would face impeachment in 1998 due to the Monica Lewinsky scandal.)

Windows of opportunity exist in language and, as we shall see, even extend into other human qualities. But before we do, we should exercise some caution against overinterpreting the research on brain plasticity and critical periods described so far. This is because the discovery of critical periods in many animals led to some extreme beliefs and practices about human plasticity, especially when it came to how we should raise our children and what was the best parental practice. During the 1990s, there was a general panic that we were raising children in impoverished environments. The fear was that if we did not expose our children to a stimulating early environment, especially during the first 3 years, they would end up brain damaged. Suddenly, there was a public appetite for infant brain training, and every parent and grandparent felt compelled to buy brain-enhancing devices from jazzy mobiles to hang over the crib, videos and DVDs to stimulate the brain, tapes of Mozart to play to pregnant mothers,[30] and every other kooky notion that was "proven by research" to improve your child's chances of getting into one of the Ivy League or Oxbridge universities. The marketers even had the audacity to name their various products *Baby Einstein* and *Baby Bach*. John Bruer, then director of the James S. McDonnell Foundation that supported much of the neuroscience research behind the original animal work, even wrote a book, *The Myth of the First Three Years*, to try to counter this hysteria based on the overinterpretation of animal deprivation studies to human development.[31]

The truth is that deprivation has to be quite severe before permanent loss occurs because most daily environments are sufficiently complex to provide enough input for hungry young brains to process. Parents should not be conned into thinking that they can enhance a process that has taken millions of years to evolve. In fact, some products, such as baby training DVDs to enhance language, have been found actually to impair language development because parents were relying on the television rather than on the richness of normal social interaction.[32]

Concerned educators and shrewd companies have either naïvely or deliberately misinterpreted the extent to which brain plasticity operates during sensitive periods. More importantly, there is little evidence that we can improve upon Mother Nature to supersize the early learning environment for a better intellectual outcome. But, such messages fall on deaf ears. When it comes to doing what's best for their kids, most parents err on the side of caution, and so I suspect that the baby brain-boosting industry will always flourish. If only they would understand that the human brain has not evolved to absorb information from technology, but rather to absorb information from other people—much more complicated and yet so familiar.

■ The Gossiping Brain

At around 1.5 kg, the human brain is thought to be around five to seven times larger than expected for a mammal of our body size, and it has an especially enlarged cerebral cortex.[33] If our brain had the same architecture as a rodent's, it would weigh just 145 g and hold a meager 12 billion neurons.[34] Why do humans have such big, complicated brains in the first place? After all, they are very expensive to run, and although they only account for 2% of typical body weight, they use up 20% of metabolic energy.[35] It has been estimated that a chess grandmaster can burn up to 6,000 to 7,000 calories simply by thinking and moving small pieces of wood around a board.[36] What could justify such a biologically expensive organ? An obvious answer is that we need big brains to reason. This is why we can play chess. After all, a big brain equals more intelligence. This may be true to some extent, but evolutionary psychologist Robin Dunbar has been pushing a less obvious answer— one that has to do with being sociable. He makes the point that big brains are not simply useful for solving any problems, such as when playing chess, but rather seem to be specialized for dealing with problems that must arise out of large groups, in which an individual needs to interact with others.[37]

This is true for many species. For example, birds of species that flock together have comparatively larger brains to individuals of those species who live more isolated lives. A change in brain size can even occur within the lifespan of an individual animal, such as the locust. Locusts are normally solitary and avoid each other but become "gregarious" when they enter the swarm phase of their life cycle. This swarm phase is triggered by the build-up of locusts as their numbers multiply and threaten the food supply. They swarm to move en masse to a new location. As they rub against each other, this tactile stimulation sets off a trigger in their brains, and they start paying attention to each other. Amazingly, areas associated with learning and memory quickly enlarge by one-third as they begin to swarm and become more tuned into other locusts around them, becoming a devastating collective mass.[38]

Larger brains facilitate social behavior. The link between brain size and sociability is especially true for primates, in which the extent of the cortex predicts the social group size for the species even when you take body mass into consideration. For example, gorillas may be big primates, but they are fairly solitary animals with small, close-knit family units, and so their cortex is comparatively smaller than that of chimpanzees, which are much more sociable and like to party.[39]

If you are a member of a species that has evolved to coexist in groups, then you are faced with some challenging decisions about how to spread your genes. To make sure that you have enough resources for your self and any offspring, you need to get sneaky. This is particularly true of primates who engage in deception and coalition formation, otherwise known as Machiavellian intelligence,[40] after the medieval Italian scholar who wrote the rulebook about how to govern through cunning and strategy. Primates in highly social groups try to outsmart and outflank fellow competitors for both the attention of potential mates and the distribution of resources. They need the mental machinery to keep track of others and second-guess their intentions. To do that, they need big brains with large areas of cortex to keep track of all the potential complex behaviors and information that large groups generate. For example, consider the number of interactions that exist between a dozen friends. Not only do you have to keep track of every relationship between each pairing, but you also have to work out all the potential combinations between subgroups within the group.

Using analysis based on all the major primate groups, Dunbar has shown that the cortex-to-group-size ratio can be used to predict the optimum group size for humans. According to Dunbar's calculations, humans should coexist best in groups of up to 150. Any larger and the demands on social skills exceed our best capacity. It is a radical claim, and still very contentious, but there does appear to be evidence to support the hypothesis, especially when one considers preindustrial societies. Over the course of human civilization, technology and industrialization have changed the ways in which we form groups. But keep in mind that the post-agricultural age began around 10,000 years ago and, with it, human behavior changed as our species shifted from roving hunter-gathers to sedentary subsistence farmers. When you consider only those remaining hunter-gather societies that did not adapt to agriculture, the analysis reveals that Dunbar's ratio exists among traditional societies. Even early religious settlements in the United States, such as the Hutterites, seem to have been most successful when their communities contained no more than 150 individuals. When a Hutterite community grows larger than 150, a new breakaway community is formed. Finally, analysis of modern companies reveals that large workforces operate and are managed best when employees form subdivisions of around the magic 150 workers. When Malcolm Gladwell was researching Dunbar's ratio for his bestseller, *The Tipping Point*, he reported that Gore-Tex, the company that manufactures the high-tech material found in many sporting clothes, expanded its operations by forming subdivisions of 150 workers each time there was a need to open a new division.[41] Dunbar's number is an intriguing idea, especially as technology develops to change the way humans interact and keep track of each other. However, what worked for earlier societies may still be operating today in the modern, socially networked world.

In line with the growing field of social cognitive neuroscience, Dunbar is correct in arguing that the human brain has evolved specialized capacity and processing capability dedicated toward social functions. We know this because why else would humans have evolved into a species whose individuals spend the longest proportion of their lives as children dependent on adults? The simple answer must be that, as a species, we have evolved a strategy to pass on as much information as possible from one generation to the next through our storytelling and instruction. Our ability to communicate means that our offspring can know more about the world they are to embark on by listening to and learning from others, without having to rediscover everything for themselves. In short, our extended human childhood means that we do not have to reinvent the wheel with each generation.

■ Baby Bat Brains

Now that you know that the basic architecture of the developing brain is one designed to learn from others, I expect you are wondering what it must be like to think like a baby. To answer that, let's consider this problem from the perspective of what it must be like to be an animal.

The philosopher Thomas Nagel[42] famously asked, "What is it like to be a bat?" Most of us with vivid imaginations can contemplate being much smaller, having fur and even wings (who has not dreamed of being able to fly?), but we cannot really know what it is like to be a bat. A bat would not have the mind of a human, because its brain is different, and so you cannot use your human mind to experience being a bat. As a bat, you would not be able to see in the way that humans do because your vision is so poor. You would have to rely on echolocation, which is why bats squeak when they fly; echolocation serves as a way of mapping out the air space in front of them and identifying tasty insects to eat. A bat probably has more in common with a dolphin than a bird. The list of differences goes on, but the point is that you can never know what it would be like to be a bat for the simple reason that you have a human brain and a mind. The same applies to human babies.

Developmental psychologist John Flavell once said that he would trade all his degrees and honors to spend 5 minutes in the mind an infant—just to experience what it must be like to be a baby again.[43] That would probably be a waste of his academic accolades. Just think about it for a moment. How could you see inside the mind of another person, let alone a baby? Human babies have human minds, but those minds are very different from one that we could appreciate as adults. If you had an adult mind inside the body of a baby, it would not be the same as thinking and experiencing the world as an infant. You would have to abandon all the knowledge and reasoning that you have built up as an adult. You would have to think like a baby. So, you would not have an adult's mind thinking like a baby. You would be a baby. As much as we might try, we can never get a true sense of what it is to have the mind of an infant. Every parent falls for this trick. When we stare at our infants in their cribs, we try to second-guess what they are thinking. We try to imagine what it must be like to be them, but for all our wishful thinking, they might as well be a bat.

An infant's mind may be very alien to us, but it is one that will eventually become an adult mind. Nature has built into humans the capacity to learn, and to learn very quickly from others. It is not only doting adults who focus their attention on their offspring; each baby is wired to pay attention to others. It's how our species has evolved a remarkable ability to transfer knowledge from one generation to the next, and no other animal on the planet can do this as well as humans. But do babies know who they are? Babies have conscious awareness, but does a baby have a sense of self yet? We cannot know for certain, but I suspect not. Beginning the process of creating the self illusion requires early social interactions.

2 ▪

The Machiavellian Baby

> The development of the child's personality could not go on at all without the constant modification of his sense of himself by suggestions from others. So he himself, at every stage, is really in part someone else, even in his own thought.
>
> James Mark Baldwin (1902)[1]

Hitler was one—so was Mother Teresa. Every monster or messiah has been one. We were all babies once. We have all been cherub-like angels, blameless and innocent of any crimes and, in most cases, the apple of someone's eye. But somewhere along the way, some of us lost our innocence. Some of us became evil. Some of us became good. Some of us became bankers. However we turned out, we all discovered our sense of our self along the way. How did that discovery happen?

People used to think that the infant's mind was completely empty at birth, and then filled up with information from the world around. The 18th-century English philosopher, John Locke, described the mind of a newborn infant as a blank piece of paper upon which experience would write itself.[2] William James, the 19th-century American philosopher, thought the newborn's world was a chaotic jumble of confusion.[3] Both were wrong in assuming that a baby has no built-in abilities and that all experience is total chaos. Natural selection has been busy creating human brains ready for certain information. Like your laptop computer delivered through the mail, babies come with a brain operating system that has evolved to learn certain things about the world and ignore other stuff that is not of use to them. And the most important things to a human baby are other humans. Human infants are wholly dependent on others and, as mentioned, spend the longest proportion of their lives in this state of dependency compared to any other species. Why?

Approximately 250,000 years ago, a few thousand *Homo sapiens* migrated out of Africa aided by a brain that was sophisticated enough to adapt to new environments, but also one that had evolved the capacity for the transmission of knowledge from one generation to the next. We were born to learn. Long before writing and the Internet were invented, humans had the capacity to communicate with each other in ways that no other animal could. With communication came an explosion in technology and skills. This was not information in our genes but rather knowledge gleaned from others. Our parents, and their parents, and their parent's parents before them, had thousands of years of knowledge passed down from each generation. That's why every newborn baby does not have to reinvent the wheel. This is such an obvious fact about human civilization that we often forget that we are the only animals on this planet that retain skills and knowledge that we pass on to our offspring. Other animals can learn about their environments, but no other animal has the human capacity for acquiring thousands of years of experience within a lifetime.

The best way to tap into that knowledge is to pay attention to others, which is why humans spend so much time as children. Other species that spend comparatively longer periods as juveniles also end up smarter than their cousins who reach adult maturity more quickly. For example, crows are a remarkably clever family of birds that are capable of solving many more of the complex problems that behavioral bird experts throw at them compared to other birds, such as chickens. After hatching, chickens are up and pecking for their own food much faster than crows, which rely on the parent bird to bring them food in the nest. However, as adults, chickens have very limited scavenging skills, whereas crows are much more flexible in foraging for food. Crows also end up with bigger and more complex brains, which is why they are sometimes referred to as the "feathered apes" because they are as clever as chimpanzees. Their extended fledging period enables them to develop intelligence. Across various animals, childhood has been compared to the research and development (R&D) phase of the life cycle.[4] Those species that spend longer in R&D end up with a larger repertoire of skills and, not surprisingly, also end up the most sociable.

In humans, not only do we learn from others about the world around us, we also learn to become a self. In the process of watching others and trying to understand them, we come to discover who we are. During these formative years, the illusion of the reflected self we experience is constructed by those around us through our social interactions.

■ On the Face of It

Brains got bigger as a way of coping with the processing demands of increasing group size. You need big brains to think about people, so that you can negotiate the best path through the social landscape. You have to be cunning and that requires the ability to anticipate what others are thinking. In order to be a successful Machiavellian primate,[5] as another famous Italian, Don Corleone, would say, "You need to keep your friends close but your enemies closer still." In other words, you have to be vigilant for those who wish to take advantage of you.

One of the first things you need to do is identify important individuals in the group. You have to be choosey. It's no good trying to apply the same interactions to everyone. Imagine the problems you would create if you were a sexually active male and could not distinguish between your mother, sister, and your girlfriend when it came to sexual advances. It is important from an evolutionary point of view (not to mention social cohesion) to distinguish between individuals, and one of the most important ways that humans identify others is to rely on the uniqueness of faces.

Faces are an unusual class of patterns because they all share the same basic structure of two eyes, a nose, and a mouth. Yet, despite the similarity, the average human can recognize thousands of separate faces. This facial expertise is supported by neuronal circuitry in a region known as the *fusiform gyrus*, a cortical region located just behind your ears.[6] It is active when we look at faces, and if you are unfortunate enough to have this area damaged (especially on the left side), then you may suffer from a condition known as *prosopagnosia*, a kind of face-blindness. Prosopagnosics can no longer tell faces apart and fail to recognize those that were once very familiar.

Our love of faces begins very early. Like Lorenz's goslings that followed the first moving thing they saw, human newborns have built-in brain circuitry for following faces.[7] Even though their vision is bad enough to qualify them as legally blind, faces are like magnets to young babies. They can hardly take their eyes off a human face, even if it is just a rudimentary pattern made up of two dots for eyes and a third for a mouth. This initial preference for face-like patterns is quickly replaced by a system that learns to recognize specific faces. By 6 months, if you show infants a face they have never seen before, they easily remember it much later. They are learning who's who. But it's not just human faces. Six-month-old infants recognize both human and monkey faces. However, by 9 months, babies lose the ability to tell the difference between monkey faces, much as we do as adults.[8] It's another example of a sensitive period with brain plasticity that becomes increasingly tuned in to experience. What is remarkable (but not if we remember that we, too, are primates) is that baby monkeys also seek out any face, either monkey or human, but become more tuned into those to which they are exposed. We know this from studies of monkeys raised without seeing faces in laboratories where the human handlers wore blank masks to cover their faces.[9] If monkeys never see faces, they lose the ability to tell any faces apart. If they see only human faces, they get good at telling humans apart. This selective responding to faces is another example of the "use it or lose it" principle, in which the neural networks are tuning into early experiences to create a permanent record.

Early face experience also shapes human brains. For example, children born with cataracts never see faces clearly as infants. When their vision is surgically corrected later in life, they still have problems with recognizing faces even though they can now see clearly.[10] No matter how much training and practice you have later in life, some early exposures are important for shaping brain development. So, when Tarzan returned from the jungle to take up his position as Lord Greystoke, he would have had a problem telling the difference between the cook and the scullery maid, having never seen a human face as an infant. His recognition for ape faces at the zoo, on the other hand, would have been just fine.

The same goes for telling the difference between individuals from another race. Unlike most adults who think members of other ethnic groups look very similar, babies initially have no problem. They can tell everyone apart. It is only after exposure to lots of faces from the same race that our discrimination kicks in. However, you can train babies not to become tuned into their own race if you keep exposing them to faces from other races.[11] So, the next time you think that other races all look alike, don't worry, it isn't racism—it's your lack of brain plasticity.

■ Smile and the World Smiles With You

Brain development requires more than just mere exposure. Having found a face as a newborn, what do you then do? Because we human infants are born so immature, we cannot waddle toward our mothers like birds can for at least another 10 months or so. Yet, it would appear that young babies are naturally inclined to get a rise out of adults by copying them—or at least responding in a way that adults think is an attempt to imitate. That's right—if you stick your tongue out at a newborn baby, sometimes she will stick her tongue out right back at you.[12] Even baby monkeys do this.[13] It's not the same as bratty children in the rear window of a bus giving you the finger or pulling facial grimaces, but if you wait patiently, a newborn may try to copy your expression. The reason that this is so remarkable is that it means humans enter the world ready for social interaction.

After tongues comes the smiling. By 2 months, most infants will readily and spontaneously smile at adults. This is a magical moment for any parent. Brain imaging studies reveal that when mothers look at pictures of their own smiling baby in comparison to those of other babies, the circuits in the reward centers deep in their brain, an area known as the *nucleus accumbens*, light up.[14] These are the same circuits that get turned on by flowers, chocolate, orgasms, and winning the lottery. No wonder social smiling is considered intensely pleasurable.

I vividly remember my own utter surprise and joy when my eldest daughter smiled at me for the first time. It wasn't so much a smile but a burst of laughter and giggling (she has been laughing at me ever since). Even as an expert on infant behavior who knew that social smiling can be expected around this time, nothing could prepare me emotionally for my daughter's first smile, which thrilled me and sent me hurrying off to tell anyone who would listen. In some cultures, such as the Navajo of North America, this first social smile of a newborn is a time of celebration, and the person who sees this is considered enriched and should hand out gifts to all members of the family. They say the individual has arrived in the tribe.[15]

With a simple pull of 12 facial muscles, our Machiavellian baby can control the adults around him with a smile. When a baby smiles at us, we smile back and it feels great![16] This is because smiling triggers the correspondingly happy feelings in the emotional centers of our brain that are usually associated with this facial expression. Even forcing a smile by getting someone to bite down on a sideways pencil makes them they happier than if they are asked to suck the pencil, which makes them pout.[17] Copying each other's expressions makes us feel differently, which is one reason why emotions can become almost contagious between people. In fact, we tend to only smile when there are others around. In one study, players in a ten-pin bowling alley were found to smile only 4% of the time after a good score if they were facing away from their friends but this increased to 42% when they turned around to face them, thus indicating that this expression is primarily a signal to others.[18]

Smiling is linked to the development of those brain regions that support social behavior, and these regions are located toward the front of the brain in a cortical area known as the *orbital cortex* because it sits over the orbits of the eye sockets. Although smiling has been observed using ultrasound in unborn babies, indicating that it is a hard-wired behavior, at around 2 months it operates in combination with the higher-order centers of the brain that are recruited for social interaction.[19] At 2 months, the baby is already using a smile to control others.

The built-in capacity for smiling is proved by the remarkable observation that babies who are congenitally both deaf and blind, who have never seen a human face, also start to smile at around 2 months. However, smiling in blind babies eventually disappears if nothing is done to reinforce it. Without the right feedback, smiling dies out, just like the following instinct does in goslings. But here's a fascinating fact—blind babies will continue to smile if they are cuddled, bounced, nudged, and tickled by an adult[20]—anything to let them know that they are not alone and that someone cares about them. This social feedback encourages the baby to continue smiling. In this way, early experience operates with our biology to establish social behaviors. In fact, you don't need the unfortunate cases of blind babies to make the point. Babies with sight smile more at you when you look at them or, better still, smile back at them. If you hold a neutral or worse, a still, impassive face, they stop smiling and get quite distressed. By the time the baby is 6 months' old, he will cry at angry faces and frown at those that look sad. Babies expect and prefer adults to smile at them. Who doesn't? It's a universal expression first recognized by Charles Darwin as one of the core components of human social interaction.[21]

■ Laughing Rats

Laughing and smiling are not just signals for others that we are like them—they are strong emotional drives that bind us together as a social species. They are just some of the mechanisms that begin to integrate the individual into a group. When my infant daughter burst into laughter, she was demonstrating one of the most powerful primitive needs to make contact. Without the ability to laugh and smile, we would be isolated individuals. We use laughter to lubricate awkward social interactions, as a way of signalling that we are easy-going, not aggressive, and potentially someone worth investing time and effort in. In short, we use laughter to generate our reflected self because our sense of self depends on what others think of us, and being funny is considered by many in our culture as an important measure of who we are. It is one of the reasons that most of us think we have a better than average sense of humor—although statistically, that cannot be true. Very few people would readily admit that they do not have a sense of humor. It's one of the main attractive features that singles use to describe their attributes in personal ads. People who take themselves too seriously are regarded as cold and distant, whereas those who make us laugh are more likely to be considered warm and approachable.

Without the ability to laugh, it is difficult to imagine how we could ever endure life's challenges. Even during the worst imaginable atrocities of the Nazi concentration camps, there was laughter. Viktor Frankl, a psychiatrist who survived the Holocaust, wrote how laughter was the one thing that helped many survive.[22] In his memoir, Terry Anderson, who was held hostage in Lebanon for 2,455 days during the 1980s, wrote about how his fellow prisoners coped by using humor.[23] One captive told shaggy-dog stories. Another mimicked the guards. The laughter made the unbearable situation bearable. Maybe this is why in the wake of every shocking world event where lives are lost, someone comes up with the inevitable "sick" joke. It's as if we need laughter as a release mechanism for pent-up anxiety. Freud coined the term "gallows humor" and described how it operated as a defence mechanism when confronted with the prospect of death. In such times, laughter can afflict us like a sneeze that cannot be suppressed. I know this because as a teenager at my own father's funeral, I was overcome with a fit of giggles that I could not stop—something that I felt guilty about for years until I realized that this was a common reaction to stress.

Psychologist Robert Provine, who has studied the science of laughter,[24] reminds us that the mechanisms that generate laughter are largely unconscious and that we do not choose to laugh, in the way that we choose to utter a sentence. It is more of a reaction that is triggered by others around us. When others in our group laugh then we laugh, too. Laughter is an emotional state—a feeling that arises from systems that work unconsciously deep in the brain and produce the arousal. But what we find funny depends on how these emotions are triggered, which is the output of the cortical systems that process content. Laughter can be triggered by a joke, or it can be caused by something less intellectual and more bodily, such as tickling. Even as an infant, we can share laughter with others, and this appears to be one of the primary social mechanisms with which we are equipped. When you tickle your baby and she laughs, she is displaying an ancient evolutionary mechanism—one that is shared by other animals.

Animal laughter has been a controversial claim. Until fairly recently, laughter was considered uniquely human. However, most human behaviors have evolved, and so we should not be too surprised to find primitive versions in other species. As many pet owners already know, their animals display behaviors that looks like they are having fun during rough and tumble play. Puppies and kittens seem to engage in behavior that has no obvious rewards other than the joy of play. Initially, it was argued that these behaviors were precursors to adult aggression—a means of developing survival skills for hunting. Even the interpretation of animal behavior was misguided. For example, chimpanzees who bare their teeth in a smile are generally regarded as displaying a threat or fear response.

However, animal laughter during play had to be rethought when Jaak Panksepp made an amazing discovery with rats.[25] First, he noticed that rats that had been deafened for experiments on hearing did not engage in as much rough-and-tumble play as normal rats. There was something missing in these deaf rats. It turns out that it was the squeals of delight. When Panksepp placed a sensitive microphone in the cage that makes high-frequency sound audible to human hearing, they discovered a cacophony of 50 kHz chirping during the play sessions—the rat equivalent of laughing. He soon discovered that rats were also ticklish and would chase the experimenter's hand until they were tickled. Apparently, rats are most ticklish at the nape of the neck. They would play chase with the hand and engage in all the other familiar baby tickling games like "coochie-coo." Baby pup rats laughed the most, and as the play activity declined with age so did the laughing.

What is it about tickling that is so enjoyable? There is a tactile element to it, but that is not enough to explain the behavior because it is well known that you cannot tickle yourself.[26] There is something about being tickled by someone else that is necessary to induce the experience. It turns out that it is the absence of self-control that creates the pleasure of tickling. Whenever we touch our selves, our brains keep track of our movements. We need this self-monitoring in order to guide our movements but also to know whether changes in sensations are due to our own actions or changes in the external world. We are not aroused when tickling our selves because the action is totally under our own control and predictable. However, researchers at the Institute of Neurology in London found that you could tickle yourself with a tickling machine when there was a delay inserted between the action of operating the lever and the probe that did the tickling.[27] When the self no longer seems in control, we surrender to the illusion of an external agent. This also explains why schizophrenic patients can tickle themselves: their self-monitoring is believed to be disrupted, and they attribute sensations and experiences generated by their own brains and bodies as coming from somewhere else.[28] No doubt losing this sense of self during tactile stimulation extends beyond tickling into other areas of sensual pleasure, which is one reason why getting a massage can be so enjoyable!

Laughter has been considered one of the primitive universal emotions recognized in every culture. Of all the different emotional expressions, laughter is one of the few that adults who have been deaf and blind from birth can generate, indicating that it predates other emotions in our evolution. If it is so old and shared with other species, this suggests that it may have a really important function. Although we all have moments of solitary mirth, private jokes that make us smile, laughter is predominantly a social phenomenon that has its roots both early in human development and also early in the development of our species.

We like to laugh and make others laugh. Not only does laughter have a multitude of benefits in terms of coping with stress and illness, but it works to bind individuals together in social coalitions. It is a deeply emotional response activated by the emotional regions of the amygdala and associated brain networks, but it operates in conjunction with higher-order processes related to social cognition—thinking about others. We use laughter to signal our willingness to be members of the group, and we also laugh at others to ostracize them. In this way, laughter is a powerful weapon of group coalition and identity. However, sometimes this weapon can go off on its own. We know this because various disorders that disrupt the connectivity of the different brain regions associated with laughter can lead to impulsive and socially inappropriate outbursts.[29] Multiple sclerosis, strokes, Alzheimer's disease, Parkinson's disease, and other forms of brain lesions can damage the communications between different parts of the brain that control social behavior. Even in healthy adults, the stress of highly emotional situations (such as funerals) can cause us momentarily to lose the capacity to suppress our giggling. It's also one of the reasons that alcohol and comedy go hand in hand. When you drink, you are partially disinhibited because alcohol impairs cortical suppression. We are more at ease and less concerned about our behavior in public. We become louder, sillier, and find jokes funnier, or at least laughing at them more acceptable. Socially appropriate laughter requires not only interpreting complex social situations but also regulating impulses that may be inadvertently triggered. This is why children must learn to control laughter. We may be born to smile and laugh, but eventually our cultures take over and tell us when it is appropriate to do so. This may explain why comedians are continually pushing the boundaries of socially acceptable humor and yet, deep down, we are egging them on. We take delight in testing the boundaries of our own self-control.

■ Securely Attached to Apron Strings

Initially, most babies are party animals—staying up all night and willing to be friendly with anyone. They find all adults fascinating. It may be true that, in comparison to other women, a young baby prefers to look at his own mother's face, listen to her voice, and prefer the taste of her breast milk as well as her smell.[30] But when it comes to socializing, young babies initially don't care who the adult is so long as they interact with them in a meaningful way. Meaningful for a young baby means attentively. So long as our interactions are timed to the babies' activity, they pay attention to us.[31] As noted, babies have been shown to copy adult facial expressions but, in reality, most of the copying goes in the other direction. That's why they don't like adults who hold impassive faces.[32] On the other hand, adults who engage in an overly animated manner, too much "in your face" as it were, are equally upsetting.[33] The perfect combination is one of harmony, with infant–adult interactions coordinated in a synchronized ballet of behavioral exchanges.[34] For babies, it is as if the first 6 months have all been about discovering that they are human and paying attention to other humans. Now the task switches to constructing their unique sense of self.

This is where our early relationships seem to play a critical role in shaping our self. Initially, babies like everyone but that changes somewhere around the first half-year of life. Now babies become increasingly discerning. Not only do they restrict their preference to their own mother, they can become terrified of strangers. This fear will increase over the next year until they start daycare school. You can even gauge the age of an infant if he bursts into tears when you approach him. This phase of social development marks the beginning of mother–infant attachment and the corresponding appearance of stranger anxiety.[35] Of course, most parents, especially mothers, have already formed a strong emotional bond with their infants from birth. For a start, our babies look cute because of "babyness," a term coined by our bird expert, Lorenz, to describe the relative attractiveness of big eyes and big heads that is found throughout the animal kingdom.[36] Big-headed, doe-eyed babies are adorable to adults, which explains why we think that puppy dogs, pop star Lady Gaga (who manipulates the size of her eyes), and even cartoon characters such as Betty Boop or Bambi look cute. They all have relatively big heads and big eyes. It's one reason why women (and some men) from every culture around the world have used makeup to emphasize the eyes for beauty. Babyness also explains why prepubescent girls prefer to look at pictures of adults, but when they hit puberty, they prefer to look at babies.[37] Nature has wired in baby love for those ready to have them.

Social bonding with babies is a chemically coordinated event that engages the reward centers of both brains—mother and child.[38] The potent hormonal cocktails that flood the reward centers generate the feelings that accompany our thoughts. Just as hormones regulate social bonding, they are also released in times of social stress. This is why most mothers and their offspring cannot be easily separated. If you try to take an infant rhesus monkey away from its mother, you get *maternal rage*, a violent reaction typified by extreme aggression, arousal, and the release of cortisol.[39] Cortisol is the hormone that floods the body to motivate and prepare it for action. It breaks down fats and proteins to generate extra energy while putting other systems on temporary hold. Combined with other hormones, such as adrenaline, our arousal system is activated to prepare us for life's three big Fs: fighting, fleeing, and fornication.

When it comes to fighting, people can rarely be more aggressive than a mother separated from her child. During a routine security check at an airport, my wife Kim was traveling with our first daughter and nanny through immigration. At one point, she handed the baby to the nanny in order to retrieve the necessary documentation. However, the nanny and baby were ushered through security to the next stage of processing and a glass barrier slid across to separate mother and baby. Realizing the situation, Kim attempted to push through the barrier, whereupon the security guard raised an arm and told her to wait. Kim, with her cortisol raging, threatened to overpower the armed guard and smash through the barrier to retrieve her newborn if the gate was not opened immediately. The male guard recognized the maternal rage and crazed look and immediately let the young mother through. This is why most animal experts caution against approaching young offspring when the mother is about.

At about 6 months, babies start to show the same strong emotional reactions to separation from their mothers. Now they do not want to be held by others and will scream and wail if you try to separate them from their mother. As their cortisol levels spike,[40] they unleash that piercing wailing on separation that is almost unbearable until the infant is consoled and returned to the comforting arms of his mother. This is no laughing matter. There are few things more distressing to a mother than the sound of her own infant crying. This "biological siren"[41] ensures that, even if they are not yet mobile, the Machiavellian baby can still control the movements of their mother from within the confines of the playpen. When she does actually begin to crawl and toddle toward the end of her first year, a baby will literally hold onto her mother's apron strings as she goes about her routines. A colleague of mine, Annette Karmiloff-Smith, made a television documentary[42] in which she filmed a young toddler and his mother as the mother went about the house doing her daily chores. When speeded up, it was as if the toddler was attached to his mother by an invisible elastic band, never letting her get too far away.

John Bowlby, the British psychiatrist, was one of the first to describe this early social attachment behavior.[43] He had been very influenced by Lorenz's imprinting in birds and reasoned that attachment was a similar evolutionary mechanism that ensured that mother and infant remained in close proximity. In Bowlby's view, children are a bit like batsmen in a game of baseball or cricket—they feel secure when they are touching the bases or while behind their creases, but become increasingly anxious and insecure as they step farther and farther away from them. The mother serves as a secure base from which to explore the world.

Bowlby predicted that children not given the opportunity to form a secure attachment as infants would end up as maladjusted adults. Much of this was based on his observations of children separated from their parents during the Second World War and relocated to institutions that did not provide the nurturing environment for attachments to form. He found that children separated early in life failed to develop normally, and many exhibited antisocial behavior as adolescents. In France, a similar picture emerged out of war-torn Europe when children were separated from their families.[44] How children were treated during early development had influenced the way they behaved as adults. Their reflected self, which had emerged in a chaotic, uncontrollable social world, had led them to shun social cohesion and conformity as adults.

In the 1960s, one of Bowlby's colleagues, Mary Ainsworth, invented an experiment to reveal the nature of young children's attachment using a temporary enforced separation from the mother in a strange environment.[45] It began with the mother and her infant in a waiting room. A strange woman would come in and begin a conversation with the mother. At this point, the infant was usually happy playing nearby with the toys in the room. After a couple of minutes, the mother would leave her infant in the company of the stranger as she left the room for 3 minutes. The stranger would try to interact with the infant until the mother returned. This sequence was then repeated. What Ainsworth discovered was that infants reacted to their mother's separation in different ways.[46] Most would start crying when their mother left but would settle again when she returned. These infants were described as securely attached, demonstrating the appropriate strategy of raising the alarm when the mother was too far away but settling on her return. Other infants were insecurely attached because either they did not care if their mother left, which was described as "avoidant" or they were inconsolable and "resistant" even when she returned to try to settle them.

There are two important limitations of the attachment account of the developing self. First, emotional attachment to the mother is found across the world, but it is displayed in different ways, depending on the individual child and the way he or she is raised.[47] Second, as any parent will know, especially those who have raised twins, children come with a whole batch of dispositions and tempers that shape how they interact with others. Some kids are just clingier than others, and this temperament reflects how they respond to stress and uncertainty. Their emotional brain centers are trip-wired to overreact to uncertainty, and they probably inherit that part of their personality from their parents. My former Harvard colleague, Jerry Kagan, called this natural disposition *inhibition*, which reflects the reactivity of the amygdala. In his research, Kagan found that around one in eight children were born inhibited and destined to respond fearfully to new situations.[48] At the other extreme, around one in ten infants are born *disinhibited*, which makes them more fearless and able to cope with uncertainty and new situations. The remaining babies lie somewhere in between. Kagan found that he could identify the temperament of the infant at as early as 4 months of age, and this would predict the child's personality 7 years later.

The emerging social behavior of the child must reflect the interaction between the child's disposition and the environment. Parents instinctively adapt to the temperament of their children, but this can be shaped by cultural norms. For example, some cultures, such as in Germany, seem to encourage independence, whereas Japanese children traditionally spend more time with their mothers and do not cope with Ainsworth's strange situation so well. This indicates that both the natural disposition of the child and the environment work together to shape the emotional and social behavior of the child.

Remarkably, studies of infants followed-up as adults reveal that the way we respond as infants to social separation stays with us to some extent as adults. Our infant attachment patterns appear to influence our emotional attachment to partners later in life.[49] Those infants who develop a normal pattern of wanting their mother and then settling easily back in when they are reunited are more likely to go on to form relatively stable relationships as adults. They find it relatively easy to get close to others and are comfortable being dependent on others and having others depend on them. They do not worry about being abandoned and are comfortable in intimate relationships. In contrast, those who had formed an insecure attachment to their mothers are either too needy and clingy for fear of being abandoned or, if they were avoidant as infants, they typically do not want to get too close to others or allow others to get close to them.[50] Of course, if these adults go on to have children, then it is easy to see how adult attachment can influence the shape of the environment for the next generation.

Who would have thought that our first love would be the deepest, having long-term effects on how our romantic relationships work out as adults? You can just hear Freud tutting in the background, "I told you so." However, not everything is cast in stone. Relationships come and go and can change over the course of a lifetime, and some may have more impact than others. Circumstances and environments are constantly changing and unpredictable. The early attachment effects, like other individual differences, are more likely to be dispositions that interact with the multitudes of factors that shape our personality over a lifetime. These early attachment effects may reflect temperaments, cultural variations, parenting styles, and all of the above, but it seems unlikely that they will determine how we turn out with any certainty. One thing that is certain is that whatever may be the role of early factors, it is critical that they play out in some form of social environment. We need others to develop, not just for nurturing and care, but to become socialized.

■ Babes in the Woods

In 1798, a naked boy, aged somewhere around 10 years, wandered out of the forest in the province of Aveyron in France.[51] The villagers had periodically spotted him, but no one knew who he was. More likely than not, he was one of the many abandoned children left to die in the woods during these hard times when infanticide was commonplace during the French Revolution. But somehow "Victor," as he was later called, managed to survive. When the local villagers eventually caught him, news of Victor reached Paris, where his plight became a cause célèbre. In the spirit of the Revolution, the philosopher Jean-Jacques Rousseau had argued that man was born inherently good but that society corrupted the *noble savage* within all of us. Victor was the first test case of this argument, and so the Parisian intelligentsia was eager to meet him. As a child uncorrupted by society, Victor could be the living embodiment of Rousseau's noble savage.

However, Victor was far from noble. He was violent, made animal noises, and defecated indiscriminately. At first, it was thought that he might be deaf and mute, so he initially spent time in the National Institute for the Deaf and Dumb, but it soon became apparent that Victor's problem was more than simply not being able to communicate. A young Parisian doctor, Jean Itard, who had been treating children at the Institute, described Victor in his memoirs as:

> [A] disgusting, slovenly boy, affected with spasmodic, and frequently with convulsive motions, continually balancing himself like some of the animals in the

menagerie, biting and scratching those who contradicted him, expressing no kind of affection for those who attended upon him; and, in short, indifferent to every body, and paying no regard to any thing.[52]

Itard believed that, with patient training, Victor could be integrated back into society. At first, progress looked promising as Victor started to understand spoken commands. He even managed to wear clothes. However, his ability to communicate did not develop further, and after 5 years of intensive training, Itard abandoned his attempt to reintegrate Victor into society. Victor remained in the care of Itard's housekeeper until his death in 1828.

Wild or feral children like Victor have periodically cropped up to stimulate public interest. What would a child without any parenting or experience of other humans be like? Would they ever acquire a language? It is reported that, in 1493, James IV of Scotland ordered two infants to the island of Inchkeith in the Firth of Forth to be raised by a mute woman because he wanted to know what language the children would end up speaking if they never heard another human talk. According to the diarist, Robert Lindsay of Pitscottie, who reported the incident some years later, "Sum sayis they spak goode Hebrew."[53]

Clearly, feral children have been sparking the imagination of intellectuals interested in nature and nurture for centuries. It makes good fiction—remember the young boy Mowgli raised by wolves in Rudyard Kipling's *The Jungle Book* or Edgar Rice Burroughs' *Tarzan of the Apes*? We are interested because we want to know the natural dispositions of humans and what they learn from the environment. What is their self like in the absence of parental influence?

One problem in answering this question is that many of these cases come from poor, isolated, rural communities, and so it is difficult to get sufficient background information and details. In one of the better-documented cases from the 1970s, psychologists studied "Genie," a 14-year-old girl who had been kept in social isolation from infancy in the back room of her psychotic grandfather's condo in Los Angeles. Like Victor, she had limited communication and understanding, despite the concerted attempts of speech therapists and child psychologists to rehabilitate her.

The case of Genie has been used as evidence to support the critical period of social development, but without knowing the initial state of these children, it is still difficult to draw firm conclusions.[54] Maybe they were abandoned because they were already brain-damaged. In reviewing the case of Victor, child development expert Uta Frith observed that he displayed many of the characteristics of severe autism.[55] We also do not know whether and to what extent early malnourishment of feral children contributes to potential brain damage. Maybe it was not the lack of social interaction so much as the damaging consequences of not being cared for by others who provide children with the necessary nutrition to develop normally. However, the fall of a Romanian dictator in 1989 would reveal that both physical and psychological nurturing is essential for long-term social development.

■ What's Love Got to Do With It?

The tiny faces peering out between the bars of the cribs shocked the Western world back in 1990, as the full atrocity of the Romanian orphanages came to light. Romania Marxist leader Nicolae Ceauşescu had outlawed birth control and ordered women to bear more children in an attempt to increase the country's population. In an already poor economy, many of these children were simply dumped in institutions because their parents could not cope. Children in these orphanages were not only malnourished; they were also socially abandoned, with no interaction with their so-called caregivers. On average, there was only one caregiver for every 30 babies. The babies lay in their own feces, fed from bottles strapped to their cots, and were hosed down with cold water when the smell became unbearable. Some babies had been left lying on their backs for so long that their heads had flattened abnormally. Harvard psychologist Chuck Nelson, who headed up the U.S. team that studied the Romanian orphanages, described the conditions as "breathtakingly awful."[56] Colleagues who arrived to evaluate these children were instructed not to cry in front of them. Nelson said, "One of the eeriest things about these institutions is how quiet they are. Nobody's crying." The normal social bonds had been broken.

When the plight of the orphans came to light, the world descended on Romania to rescue these children. Families determined to give them a better start in life brought around 300 orphans to the United Kingdom. In the United States, Nelson and his colleagues studied 136 of them.[57] How would they fare? British psychiatrist Sir Michael Rutter led a team that would study 111 of these children who were less than 2 years of age when they first came to the U.K.[58] There were no medical records for these orphans, and there is always the problem of knowing if an individual child suffered from congenital disorders, but the research revealed some amazingly consistent findings.

When they arrived, the orphans were mentally retarded and physically stunted, with significantly smaller heads than normal children. However, by 4 years of age, most of this impairment had gone. Their IQs were below the average for other 4-year-olds, but within the normal range that could be expected. These children seemed to be largely rehabilitated. Some had done much better than others. Orphans who were younger than 6 months of age when they arrived were indistinguishable from other normal British children of the same age. They made a full recovery.

Their window of opportunity had not yet closed when they arrived in the United Kingdom. The longer they had been in the orphanage after 6 months of age, however, the more impaired their recovery was despite the best efforts of their adopted families.

The orphans were followed up again at 6, 11, and 15 years of age. Again, as a group, they fared much better than expected given their poor start, but not all was well. Those who had spent the longest time in the orphanage were beginning to show disturbed behavior, with problems forming relationships and hyperactivity. Just as Bowlby and others had predicted, the absence of a normal social attachment during infancy had left a legacy of poor social attachment as an adult. Rutter concluded that infants younger than 6 months recovered fully from social deprivation, but older infants were increasingly at risk of problems later in life. Although malnutrition played some role in their impaired development, it could not be the only reason. When they looked at the weight of babies when they entered the United Kingdom, it did not predict their development. Rather, it was the amount of time that they had been socially isolated that played a greater role. Their ability to fit in socially had been irrevocably ruined by their isolation as infants.

Can you survive without others? Possibly. Some people have survived years in isolation. But would you want to? And what about the need for others when we are children? The Romanian orphanage studies reveal that there is something deeply fundamental about our need for interaction with others that makes social psychological development essential for our well-being. Those orphans lucky enough to be rescued in time proved that with nurturing homes and care, we can recover from the misery of isolation. However, what is shocking is how quickly isolation can permanently impair our social development. It would appear that within a year of birth, each of us needs others in order to be happy for the rest of our lives. This suggests that the sense of self that emerges over the developmental course is one that carries the legacy of early social experiences because the processes that construct the individual during this sensitive period are disrupted. In other words, the developing human brain critically expects input from others and, if this is not available, it has lasting impact on the epigenesis of normal social behavior.

■ Monkey Love

The Romanian orphans responded similarly to the rhesus monkeys in Harry Harlow's infamous isolation studies during the 1960s.[59] Harlow had been inspired by Bowlby's theory of why children raised in orphanages develop antisocial behavior, but he wanted to rule out the alternative explanations that these were children from poorer backgrounds or that poor nutrition in the institutions had led to these effects. To test this, he raised infant rhesus monkeys in total social isolation for varying amounts of time (these studies would never be approved today, now that we know how similar monkeys are to humans). Despite feeding them and keeping them warm, those monkeys that spent at least the first 6 months of life in total isolation developed abnormally. They compulsively rocked back and forth while biting themselves and found it difficult to interact with other monkeys. When they became mothers themselves, they ignored or sometimes attacked their own babies. The social deprivation they had experienced as infants had left them socially retarded as adults. If they were introduced to the rest of the monkeys before the 6 months was up, then they recovered more social behaviors. Monkeys who were isolated only after the first 6 months were not affected. Clearly, from birth, monkeys and humans require something more than sustenance. It isn't food and warmth they need, it is love—without the love of others, we are lost as individuals, unable to form the social behaviors that are so necessary to becoming a normal social animal.

What is it about social isolation that is so destructive for the developing primate? There is no simple answer and one can speculate about different mechanisms. For example, babies who are born extremely prematurely can spend several weeks isolated in an incubator to provide a suitable breathing and sterile environment for their immature lungs. Not only are they born too early, but they are also very small and have a low birth weight. However, if you interact with them by stroking them and massaging them while they are still inside the incubator, this minimal contact significantly improves their physical development. They grow and put on weight much faster than do premature babies who are left alone. The most likely explanation comes from animal studies that show that grooming and tactile contact stimulate the release of growth hormones in the brain. These growth hormones affect metabolism and the calorific uptake, so that these little guys can absorb more nutrients from their food. In the United States, psychologist Tiffany Field[60] has shown that simply stroking premature babies for 15 minutes each day for 10 days leads to significantly increased body weight, an earlier discharge from the hospital and an estimated saving of around $10,000 for each infant. It may all seem a little too touchy-feely, but massaging babies makes sound financial sense—on top of all the health benefits.

It's not just weight gain; brains also thrive with social interaction. As noted above, rat pups like a bit of rough-and-tumble play. In the 1940s, Donald Hebb[61] looked at the effects of raising baby rats in complete isolation, compared to those raised in social cages containing lots of other rats with which to interact. He found that not only were isolated rats significantly slower on problem-solving, such as running around a maze, but their brains were not as well developed as the social rats, which had heavier brains and thicker cortical areas. If you remember back to the wiring illustration in chapter 1 (Figure 1.4), this thicker cortex was due to increased connectivity between the neurons. So, being raised in isolation is not healthy for a social animal.[62] We now know that loneliness stunts growth and impairs the health of humans, monkeys, rabbits, pigs, rats, mice, and even the humble fruit fly *Drosophila*[63]—and the *Drosophila* does not even have much of a cortex, let alone brain!

In addition to physical growth, for humans, one of the real problems of social isolation is not having access to those who know more about the world. Adults usually look after—and look out for—the child. Even if an infant manages to survive, not having older and wiser individuals around means uncertainty. Without the ability to understand, control, communicate, regulate, navigate, or negotiate the world, an individual is helpless. And without others to help, these uncertainties create stress and anxiety, which in the long term are corrosive to our health and mental well-being.

It's not just love and attention children need: they also require order and structure. They seek out adults who behave predictably. Paradoxically, they will even form strong attachments to parents who are abusive, just so long as they are reliably abusive.[64] This is because the abuse creates anxiety in the child that, in turn, increases their need to attach. This becomes a vicious dysfunctional cycle of love and hate that sets the scene for abusive relationships later in adult life.[65] Infants need adults who respond reliably to them because they are attentive and predictable. That's why most babies love "peek-a-boo"—it's more than just a game—it's a way for infants to identify adults who are prepared to invest their time and effort.[66]

Of course, sustenance and nutrition are vital, but infants require other people in order to discover who they are.

Without others, we cannot develop the sense of self that most of us have—an integrated, coherent individual existing independently as a member of a larger social group. Who knows what kind of self, if any, would emerge in a child raised in total isolation? One can only speculate that such an inhuman situation would produce an inhuman self.

■ Copy Me

It is said that imitation is the sincerest form of flattery. By the time infants reach their first birthday, they are always looking for opportunities to imitate. Their social brains, percolating with explosions of connectivity, are on the lookout for useful information from others. By watching others, babies are making use of thousands of years of evolution that has equipped them to learn rapidly by observation— which is so much easier and better than trying to figure stuff out for themselves.

It would appear that most of us like to be imitated, or at least we like people who copy our behaviors. Have you ever noticed how people in love do this? The next time you are in a park where couples hang out or maybe a popular restaurant where romantic, candlelit dinners are common, take a look at the actions of people in love. Even though you may not be able to hear the sweet nothings they exchange, you can immediately tell when two people fancy each other by the amount of imitation they share just by looking at their body postures and nonverbal communication.

To be able to copy others is one of the most powerful skills with which humans are born.[67] From the very beginning, babies are sophisticated people-watchers, following adults around and copying their behaviors. No other animal has the same capacity for copying the way we naturally do. This ability probably existed before we evolved language, as it would have been really useful as a way to pass on knowledge about tools. No other animal makes or uses tools as conspicuously as humans do, and despite the isolated reports of nut-cracking or termite-prodding with sticks by chimpanzees, these pale into insignificance compared to what babies spontaneously learn from watching others.

This is because humans have been programmed to imitate. If an infant watches an adult perform some new action on a never-before-seen object, a 1-year-old will remember and copy the behavior 1 week later.[68] The child knows what the goal of the action is even when the adult is thwarted by some problem. In one study,[69] a female adult looked and smiled at 14-month-old infants and then leaned forward to activate a light-switch on a box by bending over and touching it with her forehead. When presented with the light-switch box, the babies produced the same bizarre movement. However, if the woman had her arms wrapped in a blanket and did exactly the same movement with her forehead, the babies did not copy the head movement but activated the light-switch on the box with their hands. The babies must have reasoned that, because the woman's hands were restricted, her goal was simply to press the switch. When her hands were not bound, however, babies must have reasoned that using your head was important for activating the light-switch.

Many animals can copy but none does so for the pure joy of being sociable. Copying is not an automatic reflex. Babies do not slavishly duplicate every adult action they see.[70] If the adult does not smile and get the babies' attention from the start, then babies don't copy. Also, babies only copy adults who seem to know what they are doing. Initially, babies will copy the actions of an adult who is wearing a blindfold. The baby does not know that the adult cannot see. However, if you give the baby the blindfold to play with, then she doesn't make the mistake of copying the blindfolded adult again. Babies know that a blindfolded adult can't possibly be looking at anything worth paying attention to. In other words, babies will only copy adults when they are led to think that something is worth doing. Babies will even copy robots that seem to behave socially. My colleague Shoji Itakura, in Kyoto, has shown that if a robot initially looks at an infant, then the infant will copy the robot's actions. If the robot does not react socially to the child, it is ignored. By simply looking at the baby, the robot is assumed to have a purposeful mind worthy of attention.[71]

■ Monkey See, Monkey Do

Have you ever wondered why you wince when you see someone else being punched? After all, it's not you who is taking a beating but you copy their reaction. Neuroscientists have been studying the neural basis of this social copying phenomenon following the discovery of brain cells, aptly named "mirror neurons," that appear to fire in sympathy when watching other people's actions. Mirror neurons can be found in the cortical regions of the brain, toward the front and top of the head, in an area known as the *supplementary motor area*, which is active during the planning and execution of movements.

The mirror neuron system was originally discovered by accident in the laboratories of the Italian neurophysiologist, Giacomo Rizzolatti, in the 1990s.[72] I remember attending an early lecture given by Rizzolatti, in which he explained how he and fellow researchers had implanted an electrode into the brain of a monkey, in a region that controls movements to study the firing of neurons while the monkey reached to pick up a peanut. As predicted, the neuron fired when the animal reached out to pick up the reward. But what they didn't expect was that the same neuron also fired when the animal watched the human experimenter pick up the peanut. How could that be? This was a cell in the motor area of the monkey's brain, not in the human's brain. It was as if the cell was mirroring the behavior of someone else. The monkey mirror neurons did not fire to just any movement of the human, but only to the actions that led to retrieving the peanut. The neuron seemed to know the experimenter's goal. Whether mirror neurons are a distinct class of specialized neurons is still hotly debated,[73] but they do appear to resonate with other people's actions and therefore could reveal what is on other people's minds.

The discovery of mirror neurons spread through the academic community like wildfire. Some likened their discovery as having the same impact in neuroscience as unravelling the structure of DNA had in biology.[74] This was because mirror neurons seemed to provide a way of knowing other people's goals and intentions. Mirror neurons operate like a direct link between minds, in the same way that computers can be networked so that when I type a sentence on my laptop, it will appear on your screen. This possibility was a big leap forward for neuroscientists working on how we establish that others have minds similar to our own.

If my mirror neurons fire when watching someone else's actions, then, because my actions are already linked to my own mind, I simply have to know what is on my mind to know what you are thinking. As we noted earlier, if you smile and I automatically smile back at you, this triggers happy thoughts in me as well as a good feeling. By mirroring your behavior, I can directly experience the emotional state that you are experiencing. When we mimic someone else's expression with our own muscles, we can readily access the same emotion that is usually responsible for generating that expression. This may be why people who have their own facial muscles temporarily paralyzed following a Botox injection to remove wrinkles are not as good at reading other people's emotional expressions because they are unable to copy them.[75]

Mirror neurons are part of the reason that we enjoy watching movies and plays. When we watch others, we can experience their emotions directly. When we empathize with the emotions of others, we feel their pain and joy. In a condition known as *mirror-touch synesthesia*, some individuals literally feel the pain of others. These individuals, for example, could not watch *Raging Bull* or other movies involving boxing. Brain imaging reveals that when these individuals watch other people, they experience overactivation of the mirror system associated with touch.[76] Another region, known as the *anterior insula*, is active when we are making self versus other discriminations. In individuals with mirror-touch synesthesia, this region also "lights up," thus they find it difficult to distinguish between what is happening to them and what is happening to someone else.

According to synesthesia expert Jamie Ward just over 1 in 100 individuals have mirror-touch synesthesia, but many more of us have a milder experience when we wince watching someone being hurt.[77] Other people's emotional displays similarly trigger the same emotional circuits that are active during our own traumatic experiences. That's why tear-jerkers work. They plug straight into the same brain regions that are active in our heads when we feel sad. TV producers have known this for decades and have used canned laughter to prompt the same response in viewers because laughter is emotionally contagious. We cannot help but smile when others do so. This effect is enhanced if the laughter is interspersed with the occasional shot of a studio audience member cracking up in hysterics.

Mirror neurons can also explain other aspects of social behavior, including our tendency toward mimicry—that involuntary human behavior in which we unconsciously duplicate another's movements and actions. When people queue up, they space themselves out equally from each other and often adopt the same postures. People in rocking chairs unintentionally end up rocking in synchrony when they watch each other.[78] During conversations, people will cross and uncross their limbs, nod their heads, and mimic all manner of movements in synchronization with the other person, although it is worth noting that this depends on whether they like or agree with each other in the first place. This issue is discussed in more depth in Chapter 6 because it turns out that mimicry has important consequences on how we respond to others we consider to be like us or different.

What about yawning? Have you ever had that involuntary urge to yawn after watching someone else stretch open their mouth and bellow out that wail to slumber? Around half of us will yawn if we watch someone else yawning. No one is quite sure why we do this as a species. One theory is that it is a behavior that helps to synchronize our biological clocks. However, a more intriguing possibility is that yawning is a form of emotional contagion—like a rapidly spreading disease, we catch the urge to copy others as a way of visibly bonding together. This may explain why contagious yawning is not present in young babies but develops somewhere between 3 and 4 years of age, when children sharpen their awareness of others having thoughts.[79]

And what about vomiting? Just the sight of someone else being sick can induce an involuntary gag in those around them—in the movie *Stand By Me*, there is some truth in Gordie's campfire story about the "barf'o'rama" where the protagonist, Lardass, induces mass vomiting in a crowd attending the village pie-eating competition. It is not just sights. In one survey of what sound people find the most horrible, the noise of someone vomiting was considered the most disgusting.[80] Such emotional contagion would be a very useful way of learning important information from others about what's safe to eat. After all, what we find disgusting can be shaped by what others around us think. It's as if all of our systems, designed to pay attention to others, appear to be set up to resonate with what others are experiencing.

If we smile, cry, yawn, winch, wretch, rock, nod, synchronize, and basically mimic others all the time, to what extent are these the actions of an autonomous self, independent of others? Of course, as soon as our attention is drawn to these mirroring behaviors we can resist the urge to produce them, but that is not the point. Normally, it is in our nature to resonate with others, which is why these examples reveal our inherent dependence on others, and this is part of the self illusion. These findings reveal a whole host of external, extrinsic factors vying for control of us. If we resist, then we do so by exerting effort or alternative actions. Some would regard that as a self being in control—an internal agent who does not want to do what others in the group want. I would contend that we are often capable of vetoing the influence of others but that it is not our natural disposition. Second, most of us can redeploy actions to achieve different outcomes but that is simply a readjustment of internal states and drives. We can do this often, but not always.

Mimicry binds us in an intimate relationship with others, but imagine what would happen if you mimicked every person you encountered. Imagine if you could not redeploy your actions and stop yourself from copying others. With so many people doing different things, it would soon overwhelm you. You would lose your self because you had been replaced by the identity of others. Oliver Sacks, the neurologist, described how he once encountered a woman on the streets of New York who was compelled to copy everyone she passed in the crowd. The woman, in her 60s, was mimicking the movements and expressions of every passerby in a quick-fire succession lasting no more than a second or two. As each passerby responded to her overt display with irritation, this in turn was mimicked back to them, thereby increasing the ludicrous display. Sacks followed the woman as she turned down an alley-way:

> And there with the appearance of a woman violently
> sick, she expelled, tremendously accelerated and
> abbreviated, all the gestures, the postures, the
> expressions, the demeanours, the entire behavioral
> repertoires of the past forty or fifty people she had
> passed. She delivered one vast, pantomimic
> regurgitation, in which the engorged identities
> of the last fifty people who had possessed her
> were spewed out.[81]

The unfortunate woman had an extreme form of the condition known as *Tourette's syndrome*, which is characterized by involuntary movements, thoughts, and behaviors. Whereas most people can voluntarily copy others even though they are often unaware of what they are doing, for her, mimicking others had become a compulsion. Luckily, Tourette's is a rare condition, but it reveals how each of us has to regulate our behaviors to be socially acceptable. Normally, when we have an urge, we can voluntarily control it. We may not be aware of it but we are constantly fighting a battle with our impulses and urges that, left unchecked, could make us socially unacceptable. Most of us have had socially unacceptable thoughts about others, but we can usually keep these to ourselves. Imagine how difficult life would be if you acted out every thought or told everyone exactly what you were thinking.

It might make for compulsive viewing, but all hell would break loose as social conventions collapsed, and this is why we need to control our selves in public. This control is achieved by mechanisms in the front part of the brain that regulate and coordinate behaviors through inhibition. These frontal regions are some of the last to reach maturity in the developing brain, which is one of the reasons why young children can be so impulsive. They have not yet learned how to control their urges.

For the Tourette's sufferer, somewhere along their developmental path, something has gone wrong with aspects of their impulse control. Their tic symptoms are like spasms that seem to be automatically triggered. Some tics are just simple twitches, but others are more complex and disruptive, such as *coprolalia*—the urge to shout obscenities. Many of us have felt like swearing out loud on a number of occasions, but some with Tourette's syndrome are unable to stop themselves from doing so. Drugs that influence the activity of inhibitory neurotransmitters can alleviate many of the tics but, so far, there is no cure for Tourette's syndrome. Those with Tourette's syndrome have to fight a constant battle to control their tics, and these battles are worst when there are other people around. As the pressure to behave normally in a social situation increases, the urge to tic can be like an itch you can never scratch— and the more you try to stop the tic, the more the urge builds up, just like a sneeze. Not surprisingly, social encounters can be extremely stressful, making the condition worse as the person with Tourette's syndrome tries to control himself in the crowd. I expect that many of us have these impulses in social situations, but why?

I think the answer is related to the problem faced by those with Tourette's syndrome. The presence of others triggers anxiety as we become self-conscious in public. We feel that we are being monitored and evaluated, which makes the need to appear normal more critical. This fear in turn increases levels of anxiety. As our anxiety increases, we lose control over impulses and urges.

Where does that self-consciousness come from if not from others? Babies are not initially self-conscious. After all, who can be if they have little control over bowel movements? Somewhere along the path of childhood, we start to develop a sense of self-identity and pride. As we discover who we are, we come to value our self, based on what others think. Earning respect and social acceptance from others is probably one of the major preoccupations that we can have. But, you might argue, who is in control of these antisocial thoughts and actions if not the self? The answer is that others both trigger those reactions, as well as suppress the need to express them. On our own, there is no need to conform but we did not evolve to live on our own."

Early social development begins by copying others, and we continue to do so throughout our lives. The self illusion ensures that we are either oblivious of the extent to which we mimic others, or we think that we deliberately copy others. When we act socially, we think that we are calling the shots and pulling the strings but this belief in autonomy is part of the illusion. We are much more dependent on others than we appreciate. We want to be part of the group but that, in turn, means we have to control our behaviors. We cannot just do whatever we want and be accepted. We want to be valued by others but before we can fulfill that obsession with self-esteem, we have to be able to gauge what others think of us. That requires developing an awareness and appreciation of what others think—something that takes a bit of experience and know-how.

3 ■
The Looking Glass Self

After his career has faltered, über-male model Derek Zoolander, protagonist of the 2001 movie *Zoolander*, looks at his reflection in the muddy puddle next to the sidewalk and asks himself, "Who am I?" To answer this, he decides that he must embark on a journey home. It's a familiar story of self-discovery—where we seek to find the answer to who we are by following the trail of evidence right back to our childhood. Most of us, including superstar male models, have this sense of origins. We think of our self as travelling a path in time from childhood to adulthood, punctuated by life events and the people along the way who have influenced us and shaped who we are.

Our self exists in the reflection that the world holds up to us. In 1902, American sociologist Charles Horton Cooley coined the term, "the looking glass self" to express the way that the self is shaped by the reflected opinions of others around us.[1] People shape themselves to fit other people's perceptions, and these vary from one person and context to the next. Spouse, family, boss, colleagues, lover, adoring fans, and beggar in the street each hold a looking glass up to us every time we interact, and we present a different self. Each person or group may think they know us, but they cannot because they are not privy to the all the different contexts in which we exist. This is the familiar lament of celebrities who complain that the persona they present to the general public is not the true personality they hold privately. More than that, Cooley argued that no real identity exists separately from the one created by others. We are a product of those around us—or least what we believe they expect from us. He summed up this notion of the self illusion in this tongue-twister of logic, "I am not what I think I am and I am not what you think I am; I am what I think that you think I am."

Consider the different questions and implications raised by Cooley's looking glass self. How do we develop a sense of self in the first place? How do children develop an understanding of what others think and, more importantly, what they think about them? This must be especially important during that most difficult time of adolescence when children try to find their true self. How is our identity shaped by the characteristics that are imposed on us by biology and cultural stereotypes? All of these questions reflect upon the sense that the self is defined by those around us.

■   Man in the Mirror

When Derek Zoolander looked in the puddle and saw an incredibly good-looking face, he immediately knew who it was staring back at him in the reflection. However, this seemingly trivial ability to recognize one's self is not something that everyone can do. As we age, brain death can progressively destroy everyday functions that we take for granted—including those that generate our sense of identity. Take TH, a 77-year-old Australian man who would look in the mirror and describe the gentleman staring back at him as a "dead ringer" for himself, but it was definitely someone else.[2] TH had normal intelligence and was not crazy, but he could not appreciate that the reflection in the mirror was his own. When asked where this man in the mirror had come from, TH replied that he must be a neighbor in an adjoining apartment. He confabulated a bizarre story to fit with his experience of the stranger in the mirror, but the truth is that TH has a rare neurological condition called *mirror misidentification*, in which patients think their own reflections do not belong to them. They appreciate the likeness, but there is no self-recognition. Something in the face-processing circuitry of their brains has failed to register their own outward identities. There is no flicker of familiarity.

Mirror misidentification is one of the dissociation disorders in which individuals do not feel connected to reality. Their sense of self and identity within the world is distorted. Sometimes people even believe that they are dead and that the world around them and all their experiences are an illusion. This death delusion, known as *Cotard's syndrome*,[3] is rare but I got an insight into the condition from a colleague whose own father had Cotard's syndrome and described it like living in an artificial world where nothing was real. Experiencing the here and now as real is part of being consciously aware of your present surroundings, but disconnection disorders such as Cotard's syndrome remind us that we need a healthy brain to keep us in touch with reality. Occasionally, we can all experience a disconnection or depersonalization in which we feel a sense of unreality and detachment from our self. Symptoms include dreamlike states, loss of empathy, and a sense of disconnection with our bodies.[4] It can seem like we are actors in a play or that we are watching the world from behind glass. It is surprisingly common. Estimates vary, but up to three out of four of us have felt like this at some time in our lives, especially after a stressful life event. Over half the combat troops returning from tours of duty are thought to experience depersonalization. Clearly, if brain disorders and stressful life events can distort the personal experience of self such that an individual does not feel that he is really himself anymore, then these episodes reveal the fragility of the self in the first place.

Even mirror misidentification may not be all that rare. Many of us have had that fleeting experience when the face we observe in the mirror does not seem to be our own—especially when we have be under the influence of various recreational drugs that can distort reality. You can even induce mirror misidentification with hypnosis.[5] But you don't have to be wasted or in an altered state of consciousness to experience a temporary disconnection between your sense of self and your own reflection. Try this out. Turn the room lights down or, better still, light a candle. Now have a good look at your self in a mirror. Stare into the eyes that are reflected back at you. Scrutinize the features of your face. After a minute or two, you will experience a strange sensation. You will start to experience depersonalization. Within a minute of staring, most people start to see their face distort to the extent that it no longer looks like their own but rather that of a stranger.[6] Whatever the self is that we experience when looking in the mirror, it is one that is easily disrupted when we look at it more closely.

What do babies or, for that matter, animals make of their own reflections when they see them for the first time? Following an observation by Charles Darwin that an orangutan did not seem to recognize itself in a mirror at the London zoo, psychologist Gordon Gallup[7] developed a way of measuring self-recognition in animals by placing a small dab of odorless red rouge makeup on their foreheads while they were asleep and then seeing how they responded when they saw themselves in a mirror. If the animal noticed that something about its appearance was not quite right, Gallup argued it had a self concept—an idea of who it was (Figure 3.1).

Gallup found that many animals, including some adult apes, could recognize themselves since they tried to remove the makeup, but that other animals failed. Numerous other studies have shown that those animals that pass the mirror test are those that live in social groups. It is surprising then that human infants do not typically recognize themselves in the mirror test until well into their second year.[8] They simply treat the baby in the mirror as another baby. In effect, very young infants are experiencing mirror misidentification when they see the other baby in the mirror. Some would argue that without this self-recognition in the mirror, they have not yet constructed their own sense of their self.[9]

FIGURE 3-1   At somewhere around 18 months, human infants pass the rouge test.

■ Why We Lose Our Self in Reflection

Why can't we remember what it was like to be a baby? Why can't we remember our infant self? What's the earliest memory you have? If you are like most people, it will be from some time around your third to fourth birthday, and it will be really patchy. There are always the odd few (and, indeed, they are odd) who say they can remember being born—passing down the birth canal and being slapped on the bottom by the midwife. Most have no memory of self before their second birthday and, even then, the memories from around that time are fragmented and unconnected.[10] It's not that you have forgotten what it was like to be an infant—you simply were not "you" at that age because there was no constructed self, and so you cannot make sense of early experiences in the context of the person to whom these events happened. You can look at photographs and recognize your self, but you cannot get back inside the toddler you once were. Why is this?

Has the passage of time worn out the trace of your memory, like a photograph fading? This seems unlikely. An articulate 12-year-old is equally oblivious to her own infant memories as a 40-year-old who can remember events from when she was 12, almost 30 years later.[11] The lack of memory cannot be because too much time has passed. Is it the case that babies do not form memories in the first place? Without the ability to form memories, your sense of self would be utterly shattered. This loss happened to Clive Wearing, an eminent musicologist at Cambridge University, who was struck down with herpes simplex encephalitis in 1985. Herpes simplex is the same infection that produces cold sores, but for Clive it had infiltrated the protective tissue that protects the brain, causing it to swell and crush the delicate structures of the hippocampus—a region where the neural circuits encode memories. Even though he survived the encephalitis, Clive was left with severe amnesia and is now unable to remember from one moment to the next. In her 2005 memoir, *Forever Today*, Deborah Wearing describes her husband Clive's tormented existence:

> It was as if every waking moment was the first waking moment. Clive was under the constant impression that he had just emerged from unconsciousness because he had no evidence in his own mind of ever being awake before... "I haven't heard anything, seen anything, touched anything, smelled anything," he would say. "It's like being dead."[12]

Probably the most harrowing aspect of Clive's condition is that he still remembers fragments of his previous life and knows exactly who Deborah is—each time he sees her, he runs tearfully into her arms as if it is the reunion of long-lost lovers when in reality she may have only left the room minutes earlier. Without the ability to store new memories, Clive is permanently trapped in the here and now. He maintains a diary in an attempt to keep track of existence but this makes for painful reading: "2.00 p.m.—I am awake for the very first time. 2.14 p.m.—I am now conscious. 2.19 p.m.—have just woken for the first time." Each previous entry is crossed out as he asserts that he has only just become conscious. Deborah describes how, one day, she found Clive holding a chocolate in one hand and repeatedly covering and uncovering it with the other hand as if practising a magic trick.[13] Each time he removed his hand, he was amazed by the appearance of the chocolate. Without the ability to form new memories, everything that is out of sight is out of mind for Clive Wearing.

The child psychologist Jean Piaget believed that infants begin life just like Clive—unable to remember anything that cannot be immediately perceived. He thought that infants lacked the capacity to form enduring memories of the world around them.[14] However, we now know that

Piaget's vision is not entirely accurate because infants can form memories. Babies learn in the womb, and that requires forming a memory in the neural networks of our brain. Hundreds of experiments conducted on young infants over the past 30 years require them to possess memory that can be surprisingly enduring. For example, a 3-month-olds who learns to kick his legs to activate a mobile that is tied to his foot by a ribbon will remember that experience 1 month later.[15] If you bring him back into the lab, he starts start kicking much faster compared to infants who never had the initial training. So it can't be the case that young infants do not have any memories. Whatever memories they may possess, however, do not become part of the self story that most of us rehearse and recall when we are much older and asked to reminisce.

Rather, the question is what kind of memories do infants form? One possibility is that they only have memory for events when you place them back in the same situation, which is why they can learn and remember things they have encountered before. For example, in 1999, memory researchers contacted a dozen students who had taken part in a memory test in which they saw fragments of pictures presented for 1–3 seconds to test if they could remember them. Even though they saw them only briefly, students could recognize the pictures. Not too amazing, you might say, until you discover that this memory test took place 17 years after the original study! The students were now full adults with busy lives, and some could not even remember taking part in the original study, back in 1982, at the University of Minnesota. Yet, stored somewhere in their memory networks were traces of the original experience because they identified pictures that they could not remember having been shown.[16]

Even Clive Wearing seems to have this ability to learn, but he can't remember that he has learned. It's like unconscious knowledge. Both Clive and young babies may not have the ability to consciously recall or reflect upon previous experiences. In contrast, most of us can recall what we had for breakfast yesterday by actively reconstructing the event in our minds. That requires a different kind of memory, one that psychologists call *episodic*—it reflects the actual experience of remembering the episodes that punctuate our lives.[17] Memories of these episodes are crucial for constructing the self story, and those that are particularly personal are known as *autobiographical memories*—those events that we can recall in which we are the main player.[18] One might be tempted to assume that our autobiographical memories are accurate recollections but, just like any memory, they are not like photographs or recordings. One of the greatest discoveries in psychology is that human memories are reconstructed and malleable. We do not have a recording of our own personal experiences in our head like some video archive. There are no microfilms in our memory banks.

Memories are constantly active—like a story being retold over and over again. Moreover, when we encounter related new experiences, we interpret them in terms of our existing memories, which in turn are transformed by the new experiences. We are constantly integrating the here and now into our past. Consider the following powerful demonstration. Read the following list of 15 words and try to remember them as best you can. Take a couple of seconds on each word to memorize it well.

thread
pin
eye
sewing
sharp
point
prick
thimble

haystack
thorn
hurt
injection
syringe
cloth
knitting

Now, turn to the end of the chapter and answer the questions to see how good your memory is. Most people fail this test[19] and yet they are pretty sure that they got the right answer, which makes the effect all the more dramatic. How can most of us be so convinced and yet so wrong?

The neural networks encountered earlier show how all information is stored as a pattern of activation across networks of neurons. You falsely remember the occurrence of the word that was never presented because it was related in meaning to the other words in the list. In the neural networks that process language and meaning, the pattern representing the word you believe you encountered was triggered as part of the collateral activity of all the other words that were processed and encoded. When one considers that memory is constant neuronal updating, it is remarkable that we remember anything at all with good clarity.

In 1932, the British psychologist Sir Frederic Bartlett, one of the few psychologists ever to be knighted, demonstrated that memories are not exact copies of past events, but rather are reconstructed—like stories.[20] Similar to the game of *Telephone*, every time the story is told and retold, it changes. In fact, completely false memories can be constructed simply by asking leading questions. In what are some of the most influential experiments in human psychology, Elizabeth Loftus demonstrated that if you show adults a video event of a car accident and then ask them leading questions such as, "Did the white car jump the red light?" adults correctly deny that there was a white car in the sequence.[21] However, if several weeks pass and the adults are asked to recall the video, they are more likely to report seeing a white car jump the red light even though it was never in the video. The mere mention of a white car during the initial questioning has now become incorporated into their memories. The neural networks that encoded the memory have become contaminated with neural activations of networks designed to scrutinize the memory for the presence of white cars and red lights. Likewise, when children are told they were once lost in a shopping mall, they can give vivid recollections about the event even though this event never actually happened.[22]

Confabulations of memory are not restricted to the young and naïve. Piaget used to describe the time when an attempt was made to abduct him as a young child.[23] Years later, he had vivid memories of how his nanny fought off the would-be abductors. However, eventually racked by guilt, the nanny confessed that she had made the whole abduction story up so that Piaget's parents would be indebted to her. Half the adults shown a doctored photograph of themselves as children taking a hot-air balloon ride recall the fictitious event and can describe it in detail.[24] Even Elizabeth Loftus, the world's greatest authority on false memories, is not immune to them.[25] When she was only 14 years old, Loftus' mother drowned in a swimming pool. Thirty years later, at a birthday party, Loftus' uncle reminded her that she had found her mother's body. Over the next couple of days, the lucid memories of that terrible moment came flooding back to haunt Loftus—except that these memories were false. Her uncle had made a mistake. Loftus had not discovered her mother's body, but rather it had been her aunt. Later, Loftus said, "The most horrifying idea is that what we believe with all our hearts is not necessarily the truth."

■ Memory as a Compost Heap

We all know that we forget things but to discover that a recollection is completely fabricated is something else. It is shocking because it makes us question our own minds. If we all can vividly remember events that never happened, then this undermines the reliability of memory and ultimately the reality of our self. This is because part of the self illusion is that we know our own minds and recognize our own memories. But we are often mistaken. The reason that we find false memories so shocking is that most people do not understand how memory works. Psychologists Dan Simons and Chris Chabris recently surveyed 1,500 U.S. adults and discovered fundamental misunderstandings held by the general public.[26] Two out of three adults (63%) thought that memory works like a video camera, recording experiences that can be played back later. Half of the respondents believed that once a memory was formed it was unchanged and reliable. These misconceptions have led to comparison with other ways of storing information that evoke some notion of a permanent store. A common metaphor is to liken human memory to a vast library storing volumes of information, which is wrong. Human memory is neither like a computer hard drive nor a preindustrial blank slate upon which experience writes a trace.

If any metaphor is going to capture memory, then is more like a compost heap in a constant state of reorganization.[27] Just like the garden refuse that you put on the compost heap, experiences are laid down with the most recent still retaining much detail and structure. Over time, however, these experiences eventually break down and become mixed in and integrated with the rest of our experiences. Some events stand out and take a long time to decompose, but they are the rare instances. The remainder becomes a mush. When it comes to memory, Dan Simons reminds us that, "People tend to place greater faith in the accuracy, completeness, and vividness of their memories than they probably should."[28]

Our self illusion is so interwoven with personal memories that when we recall an event, we believe we are retrieving a reliable episode from our history like opening a photograph album and examining a snapshot in time. If we then discovery the episode never really happened, then our whole self is called into question. But that's only because we are so committed to the illusion that our self is a reliable story in the first place.

■ Not Total Recall

In Hollywood's adaptation of Philip K. Dick's brilliant story, "We Can Remember It for You Wholesale,"[29] Arnold Schwarzenegger plays the role of Douglas Quaid, a freedom-fighter on a Mars colony who has had the false memories of a construction worker on Earth implanted into his brain. The movie adaptation, *Total Recall*,[30] is a roller coaster ride with a plot full of twists and turns. What makes it relevant to the discussion of self is that Quaid's identity changes as the content of his memory is altered. This is why Elizabeth Loftus was so appalled to discover that she held false memories. It means that we are not necessarily who we think we are. Our identity is the sum of our memories, but it turns out that memories are fluid, modified by context and sometimes simply confabulated. This means we cannot trust them, and our sense of self is compromised. Note how this leaves us with a glaring paradox—without a sense of self, memories have no meaning, and yet the self is a product of our memories.

This may be why there is no memory of the infantile self. As an infant, we did not have the capacity to integrate our experiences into meaningful stories. We did not have the world knowledge. Most importantly, we did not have an idea of who we were. We did not have an initial sense of self to integrate our experiences. That requires world experience and, in particular, learning from those about us who spend so much time in our company. Somewhere around 2 years of age, children start to have conversations with parents about past events. Kids whose parents spent a lot of time talking to them and discussing past events when they were between their second and fourth birthday had much better memories about their lives when they were between 12 and 13 years old. This depends not simply on language, but on the way parents discuss events with their children. By scaffolding their children's early experiences, the kids were able to organize their experiences into a meaningful story. This is because it is easier to remember stories that relate to us when we become a main character. The adults had the experience and the context to organize the events into a coherence that made sense to the child, which led to better encoding and storage in their brains.[31] One thing we know from decades of psychological research is that meaning and context improves memory.

This is why memory researcher Mark Howe argues that babies who fail the Gallup mirror test lack a sense of self, and so their memories are disconnected events—impressions that do not seem to make sense in any meaningful way.[32] In order for memories to possess meaning, they have to be embedded within the self. However, Philippe Rochat, who has made a lifetime study of self development, argues that the mirror test in humans is actually a measure of being self-conscious about how one looks to others.[33] He reasons that, at 18 months, infants are not bothered with what they look like to others and so are not particularly concerned if they have a red smudge on their nose. Somewhere around the second year, children are more concerned with their appearance and how they look to others.

This self-conscious account would explain the surprising finding that mirror self-recognition with the rouge test is not universal. In one study of Kenyan children between 2 and 7 years of age, Rochat found that only two out of 104 children removed a sticker, which previously had been surreptitiously placed on their forehead, when they looked in a mirror. Why? It cannot be that they do not have self-recognition in a mirror. They have seen and groomed themselves plenty of times in front of a mirror. Rather, Rochat argues that, unlike their American counterparts, Kenyan children are not sure what to do in this unusual situation. They don't know whether they should remove a sticker from their forehead that must have been placed there by the strange Western scientist visiting the village.

This is a fascinating twist on Gallup's self-recognition interpretation. It may be that passing the mirror test is not necessarily a measure of self-recognition, but rather a measure of embarrassment in the context of others. The mirror test reveals the point at which you become more concerned by what others must be thinking about you. However, before you can be self-conscious, you must first appreciate that others *are* thinking about you. You need to have a concept of what you are in order to compare that self with the expectation of others. And before you can have that expectation, you need to understand what is on their mind.

■ Theory of Mind

If we are worried about what others think of us, then it stands to reason that we need to understand what's going on other peoples' minds. We need to figure out what they are thinking and, for that, we need to develop a "theory of mind." This term was originally coined by David Premack, who wanted to know if chimpanzees understood that others had thoughts and what those thoughts might be.[34]

Most of us assume that people do things because they want to. In other words, they have thoughts about goals and intentions that motivate their actions. Again, this is something that is so familiar that we take it for granted when it comes to humans, but there is good evidence that this capacity takes time to develop and may not be shared with all members of the animal kingdom.

Animals can pay attention to humans and their actions, but it is not clear that they understand that others possess minds that support those actions. Animals do not engage with their human keepers in social behaviors such as imitation and copying. And yet, we are inclined to attribute sophisticated mental states to animals. Do you remember the female gorilla, Binti, which saved the little boy who fell into her enclosure at a zoo near Chicago, back in 1996? We watched in amazement as this wild animal gently picked up the limp body of the 3-year-old boy and carried him to the door where the paramedics could attend to him. The world's press was quick to attribute empathy and care to Binti, but what they did not know was that she had been trained by her keepers to bring a doll to them in anticipation of her possible pregnancy.[35]

Even our closest primate cousin, the chimpanzee, can be a distant relative when observed in the wild. Jane Goodall, the famous primatologist, observed a chimpanzee named Passion who repeatedly kidnapped the babies of other mothers and, with the help of her own children, consumed them. Despite our inclination to anthropomorphism—the attribution of human qualities to nonhumans—we are unique as a species in our capacity to formulate the complex mental states of others that serve as our bread and butter in daily social interactions.

That capacity starts early. There is ample evidence that human infants are preadapted by evolution to seek out other humans and engage with them.[36] For example, babies pay attention to what others are looking at so they understand the link between gaze and actions—people tend to want what they look at. If an adult stares longer at one of two different toys, but then picks up the toy they were not looking at, babies are surprised.[37] Where we look reveals the focus of our interest and desires, and this is something the baby understands intuitively.

Expressions are also a good indicator of what someone else is thinking. When an 18-month-old infant is offered broccoli or crackers, they usually choose the salty biscuits. Crackers are much tastier than broccoli to a baby. However, if they watch an adult wrinkle her nose at the sight of crackers but make a smiley "num num" face to the vegetable, the baby knows to offer her the broccoli if the adult then asks the baby to pass them something to eat.[38] The baby can figure out what the adult likes.

But none of this people-watching really requires a theory a mind. Likes and dislikes can be easily worked out by simply watching whether people smile or frown. We do this all the time, looking for external markers of behavior that reveal preferences. Even animals can do this.[39] As many pet owners can attest, animals learn when their masters are angry or pleased with them, but this does not require understanding what is on their master's minds. Rather, to prove that we can understand what is really on someone else's mind, we have to appreciate when they hold a mistaken or false belief.[40] A belief is simply an idea that we think is true, but sometimes we may be mistaken. If you can understand that someone holds a false belief, then you can imagine what he is thinking even when what he is thinking is factually wrong. That's a powerful level of insight into someone else's worldview. For example, if you show me a confectionary box and ask me what is inside, then I am likely to say sweets or candy, depending on which continent I am on. However, if you open it up and reveal that it actually contains pencils, then I will realize I was understandably mistaken. My belief was false. Three-year-olds will also make the same mistake.[41] After all, they don't have X-ray vision. But if you now ask me to imagine what my neighbor would reply if he were asked what is inside the box, I know that he too will make the same mistake as I initially did. I can understand that he will not know what is actually in the box. In contrast, a 3-year-old will assume that someone else who comes along will know that there are pencils in the box and answer, "Pencils." They don't appreciate that others will also come to the wrong conclusion about what's in the box and can hold the same false belief. By 4 years of age, most children understand that people will answer, "Candy," when asked what's in the box.

Psychologists think that young children initially lack a theory of mind when it comes to understanding mistaken beliefs.[42] It's as if they cannot take another's perspective. In one classic experiment, children see a doll called "Sally" hide her marble in a cupboard before she goes out. When she is out, another doll, "Anne," comes in and takes Sally's marble and hides it in the kitchen drawer. The critical question is where Sally thinks her marble is. When children watch this scenario, 3-year-olds think that, on her return, Sally will look in the kitchen drawer for her marble, whereas 4-year-olds say that she will look in the cupboard. Clearly, when you understand that people can hold false beliefs, you can lie to them to make them think something that isn't true. When you consider how so much social manipulation involves deceiving others, you can understand why having a theory mind is a valuable tool. You can outwit others by leading them to false assumptions.

An underdeveloped theory of mind in children also explains why they can make such bad liars. Initially, when a child realizes that punishment is imminent—"Did you eat the cake?"—she simply says no, despite the fact that she has chocolate cake smeared across her face. Only later do children get more sophisticated in generating plausible stories for why they might have the tell-tale chocolate on their face—invariably they blame someone else.

Theory of mind is really a form of mental perspective-taking—understanding things from another's point of view—a "he thinks that she thinks" sort of thing. In order to do this, you have to be able to keep track of what developmental psychologist Alison Gopnik[43] calls "counterfactuals—the woulda-coulda-shoulda's of life." *Counterfactuals* are what enable you to imagine different scenarios, including what people may do in the future based on what you know now. It's how we second-guess others and, to do that, we have to possess the mental machinery to generate different possible outcomes and play them out in our heads. This is going to happen mostly in situations of social competition where you have to anticipate what others will do next, which may explain why theory of mind emerges earlier in children who have siblings.[44] The constant battle to keep place in the pecking order means that children have to learn to outwit their brothers and sisters.

■ Mindblindness

Not everyone develops a theory of mind. In his book, *The Empathic Brain*, neuroscientist Christian Keysers[45] describes his encounter with a young graduate student, Jerome, who is finishing his Ph.D. in theoretical physics. His colleague Bruno Wicker introduced Jerome who, on entering the room, spoke with a flat voice and never looked Christian in the eyes.

> Bruno: "We would like to ask you something." (Bruno shows Jerome a box of Danish cookies.) "What do you think is in this box?"
> Jerome: "Cookies."
> Bruno then opened the box to reveal a set of colored pencils instead of the expected cookies.
> Bruno: "What do you think she would think the box contains?" (His research assistant enters the room.)
> Jerome: "Colored pencils."

Here is a man with the mental capacity to think about abstract properties of the universe that would baffle most of us and yet he cannot imagine what someone else might think is inside a cookie box. Jerome has autism—a developmental disorder that affects around one in 500 individuals,[46] although this figure appears to be on the increase and depends largely on how you define it. In general, autism can be thought of as a disorder with three major disabilities: a profound lack of social skills, poor communication, and repetitive behaviors. It is regarded as a spectrum disorder because individuals vary in the extent to which they are affected. Most are intellectually challenged, some are within the normal range, and a few may have rare abilities, such as being able to tell you what day of the week any date in history falls upon. But all individuals with autism spectrum disorder have problems with social interactions.

These individuals have a problem with social interaction because they lack the repertoire of developmental social skills that enable humans to become expert mindreaders. Over the course of early childhood, typical children increasingly become more sophisticated at understanding other people because of their developing theory of mind. By the time they are around 4 years of age, an average child sees other people as being goal-directed, purposeful, and having preferences, desires, beliefs, and even misconceptions.

Not only do typical children become intuitive mindreaders, but they also become councillors as well. They begin to understand other's sadness, joy, disappointment, and jealousy as emotional correlates of the behaviors that make humans do the things they do. Again, by 4 years of age, children have become expert at working the social arena. They will copy, imitate, mimic, and generally empathize with others, thereby signalling that they too are part of the social circles that we all must join in order to become members of the tribe. They share the same socially contagious behaviors of crying, yawning, smiling, laughing, and showing disgust.

However, individuals with autism lack this repertoire of social skills.[47] They are effectively "mindblind."[48] Alison Gopnik captured this notion of mindblindness in her terrifying vision of what it must be like to be at a dinner party if you have autism:

> Around me bags of skin are draped over chairs, and
> stuffed into pieces of cloth, they shift and protrude in
> unexpected ways...Two dark spots near the top of
> them swivel restlessly back and forth. A hole beneath
> the spots fills with food and from it comes a stream of
> noises. Imagine that the noisy skin-bags suddenly
> moved towards you, and their noises grew loud,
> and you had no idea why, no way of explaining
> them or predicting what they would do next.[49]

No wonder individuals with autism find direct social interaction frightening. If you can't figure out other people, social encounters must be intensely baffling. They cannot easily infer what others are thinking and generally withdraw into activities that do not involve people. Maybe this is why many individuals with autism often do not like direct eye contact, do not copy, do not mimic, do not yawn, retch, laugh, or join in with the rich tapestry of social signals we share as a species.[50]

Temple Grandin provides remarkable insight into what it's like to suffer with autism.[51] She has a Ph.D. and is one of the world's authorities on animal husbandry, but she is also a highly intelligent or "high-functioning" individual with autism, able to provide a window into what it is like to be mindblind. Temple was diagnosed with autism from early childhood. She went to progressive schools and eventually college, but always had difficulty interacting with other people. She could not understand or predict their behaviors and so turned her attention toward animals, which seemed less complex. She could get inside the minds of animals better than she could humans, and she eventually went on to study animal welfare and developed techniques to soothe and calm cattle before slaughter. Humans, on the other hand, were unpredictable. Temple taught herself to study people—to pay close attention to their routines and behaviors. In this way, she was able to predict what they would do in familiar situations, so that she could behave appropriately. She described her experience of predicting other people's behaviors to Oliver Sacks as being like "an anthropologist on Mars," a phrase that would go on to become the title of one Sacks' bestsellers.[52]

Although there is no definitive neurological test for Temple's condition, autism must be some form of brain disorder. The incidence of autism is higher in identical compared to nonidentical twins, which suggests a genetic component to the disorder.[53] Autism is also on average four times more likely in boys compared to girls, which again, strongly implicates a biological basis. To date, there is tantalizing evidence based on brain imaging studies that regions in the front part of the brain, most notably the frontoinsular (FI) and the anterior cingulate cortex (ACC) that are activated by social interaction in normal individuals, operate differently in individuals with autistic spectrum disorder.[54] The ACC is like an "alarm center" that monitors goals and conflicts, including social interactions. If these interactions do not go according to plan, if people start to get the wrong idea about us, we get anxious. These regions are part of the mirror neuron system that activates when we imitate others either voluntarily or have our experiences hijacked by watching others.

So far, the brain-imaging studies of the mirror system in individuals with autism are inconclusive and, according to Christian Keysers, indicate that the system is not broken but may be very delayed in development because such individuals are not attending to relevant information during normal social encounters.[55]

Others have targeted specific types of neurons. Neuroscientist John Allman, at the California Institute of Technology, has proposed that the social deficit in autism may be based on a lack of a special class of spindle neurons, called Von Economo neurons (VENs), after their discoverer who located them in 1925.[56] VENs are cortical neurons with highly connective fibers that are thought to branch out to different brain regions that are activated by social learning. This may explain why VENs have only been found in species that are particularly social, including all the great apes, elephants, whales, and dolphins.

Humans have the largest population of VENs found only in the FI and ACC areas—the same regions that may be disrupted in autism. VENs are thought to work by keeping track of social experiences—a strategy that would facilitate a rapid appreciation of similar social situations in the future. They form the neural networks that provide the basis of intuitive social learning when we watch and copy others. VENs may help to create and sculpt the self from copying and reading others.

One intriguing discovery is that the density of VENs in these social regions increases from infancy to reach adult levels somewhere around the fourth birthday in typical children—a time when most child development experts agree that there is noticeable change in social interaction skills and an emerging sense of identity. This may also explain why autistic individuals, who have disrupted VEN regions, have difficulty working out what the rest of us simply know without having to think very much. I recently discussed this with a good friend who is the mother of a high-functioning daughter with autism. Her daughter compensated for her condition by asking those around her to write down a description of who they were and their life stories as a way of understanding them. This was because she was unable spontaneously to integrate information and backgrounds to generate narratives to describe others. Without this capacity to read others and integrate socially, someone with severe autism is going to have a very different sense of self, one that does not include those around them. I can only speculate, as I do not have autism, but I would imagine that individuals with severe autism inhabit a solitary world, very much in isolation from others.

■ The Agony of Adolescence

Perhaps you remember a party you went to when you were 15 and everyone stopped talking and stared at you when you walked into the room. Or, maybe there was a time when the teacher made you stand up in class and everyone was looking at you. Do you remember feeling your face flush bright red and your palms sweating? It was so embarrassing. You felt so self-conscious.

Most of us have had some embarrassing event in our lives that, at the time, was the worst possible thing we could imagine. We felt we could have died and wished the ground would open up and swallow us. Being embarrassed and becoming self-conscious are key components of the looking glass self. If we did not care about what others think, then we would not be embarrassed. Initially, young children are entirely egocentric and the apple of their parents' eye. It is not clear that others would ever be of concern to them. However, with a developing sense of self, the child increasingly starts to care about what others think, aided by her emerging theory of mind that allows her to take another person's perspective. This self-conscious awareness can provide the basis for a moral compass. Even our own reflection can make us acutely aware that we are potentially the focus of other people's attention. For example, in one classic Canadian study of social transgression,[57] children on Halloween night were secretly observed after being told to take only one piece of candy from a bowl while the owner went into another room. If a mirror was placed so that it reflected the child as he or she approached the bowl, the child became self-conscious and did as he or she was told. However, in households where there was no mirror, children took more than one candy. There was no mirror to remind them that they could be seen.

By the time children hit their early teens, they are especially sensitive to the judgment of others. In fact, they often think that an imaginary audience exists to evaluate them.[58] How often do we see children (and quite often adults who think they are unobserved) receiving adulation from this imaginary audience, which has just heard them perform some amazing task or talent? But this imaginary audience is also the agony of adolescence. By the time they reach their teens, adolescents believe that others are constantly judging them even when this is not the case. They think they are the center of attention and are hypersensitive to criticism.

Neuroscientist Sarah-Jayne Blakemore has used brain-imaging techniques to investigate what is going on in the heads of adolescents.[59] She found that regions normally triggered by thoughts about one's self are more active during these adolescent years compared to that of young adults. In particular, the prefrontal cortex (PFC) is activated when individual adolescents are asked to reflect upon just about any task that forces them to consider things from their own perspective. Whether it's thinking about self-reflected actions such as reading,[60] making intentional plans,[61] or simply reflecting on a socially painful memory,[62] the adolescent PFC is hyperactive.

The kids simply feel that, as my teenage daughter says, "Everyone is getting at me." What a hyperactive PFC actually means is not clear, but it does support the idea that this region is specialized for "mentalizing" about others and that much of that mental effort during adolescence is concerned with what others—especially the peer group—think. No wonder adolescents are susceptible to peer pressure, which explains why they are more likely to get into trouble and engage in risky behavior in order to establish their own identities and positions in the pecking order.[63] And who are the worst offenders for risky behavior? Boys, of course. But what are little boys made of? Is it all biology, or does society shape the behavior of little boys more than we have previously thought?

■ Boys Will Be Boys

The first thing anyone asks when hearing the news of a birth is invariably, "Is it a boy or a girl?" So, when Toronto couple, Kathy Witterick, 38, and David Stocker, 39, announced the birth of Storm, on January 1, 2011, but told friends and family that they were not disclosing the sex of their third child, their announcement was met with stony silence. They explained that they did not want their child to be labelled, but rather they wanted Storm to be free to develop *its* own identity. The problem was that no one knew how to treat the New Year's Day baby. Four months later, news of the "genderless" Storm broke, creating a media storm containing a flood of criticism and ridicule of the parents.[64] But Kathy and David have a point. Our identity, based on whether we are a boy or a girl, is greatly influenced by those around us.

We are so preoccupied with the question of sex because it is a core component of how people define themselves, how they should behave, and how others should behave toward them. It is one of the first important distinctions we make growing up as children and, without knowing which sex someone is, we are at a loss to know how to interact with them. Being a boy or a girl is a sexual difference defined in terms of the chromosomes we inherit from our parents. Normally, 23 pairs of chromosomes are inherited from each parent. In each set of chromosomes, one pair is known as the sex chromosomes (X and Y), and the other 22 pairs are known as the autosomes. Human females have two X chromosomes, and males have one X and one Y chromosome. In the absence of the Y chromosome, we would develop into little girls with two X chromosomes.

Gender, on the other hand, is not simply biological but rather is related to the psychological profile of the individual. Gender is not genetic but shaped by the group consensus. It is what it is to think and behave masculine or feminine. By 3 years of age, boys prefer the company of other boys, and girls prefer other little girls;[65] by 5 years, children are already "gender detectives" with a rich set of rules about what is appropriate for boys and girls to do.[66] Some gender stereotypes are universal, such as mothers should be responsible for childcare and preparing food.[67] However, such stereotypes have shifted in recent years as men and women are increasingly able to play a greater role in what were considered traditionally separated activities. This is why "gender-benders" such as Boy George or Marlene Dietrich arouse passions because they challenge stereotypes.

Although not cast in stone, gender stereotypes do tend to be perpetuated across generations. This is what Storm's parents were trying to avoid. Many parents are eager to know the sex of their children before they are born, which sets up gender expectations, such as painting the nursery in either pink or blue.[68] When they eventually arrive, newborn baby girls are described mainly in terms of beauty, whereas boys are described in terms of strength. In one study, adults attributed more anger to a boy than to a girl reacting to a jack-in-the-box toy even though it was always the same infant.[69] Parents also tend to buy gender-appro-priate toys: dolls for girls and guns for boys.[70] In another study, different adults were introduced to the same child wearing either blue or pink clothes and told that it was either Sarah or Nathan. If adults thought it was a baby girl, they praised her beauty. If they thought it was a boy, they never commented on beauty but rather talked about what occupation he would eventually have. When it came to play, they were boisterous with the boy baby, throwing him into the air, but cuddled the baby when they thought it was a girl. In fact, the adults seemed to need to know which sex the baby was in order to play with it appropriately.[71] Of course, it was the same baby, so the only difference was whether it was wearing blue or pink. It is worth bearing in mind that the association of the color blue with boys is only recent—100 years ago it would have been the boys wearing pink and the girls wearing blue.[72]

With all this encouragement from adults during the early months, is it any surprise that, by 2 years of age, most children easily identify with their own gender and the roles and appearances that they believe are appropriate? However, this understanding is still very superficial. For example, up until 4 years of age, children think that long hair and dresses determine whether you are a boy or girl. We know this because if you show 4-year-olds a male Ken Doll and then put a dress on it, they think that Ken is now a girl. By 6 years, children's gender understanding is more sophisticated and goes over and beyond outward appear-ances. They know that changing clothes and hair does not change boys into girls or vice versa. They are already dem-onstrating an understanding of what it means to be essentially a boy or a girl. When they identify gender as a core component of the self, they will tend to see this as unchanging and foundational to who they and others are.[73]

As children develop, they become more fixed in their outlook about what properties are acquired and what seem to be built in. For example, by 6 years, children think that men make better mechanics and women are better secretaries. Even the way parents talk to their children reinforces this generalized view of what is essential to gender.[74] For example, parents tend to make statements such as "Boys play soccer" and "Girls take ballet" rather than qualifying the statements with "Some boys play soccer" or "Some girls take ballet." We can't help but fall into the gender trap. Our interaction with children reinforces these gender divisions. Mothers tend to discuss emotional problems with their daughters more than with their sons.[75] On a visit to a science museum, parents were three times more likely to explain the exhibits to the boys than to the girls.[76]

And it's not just parents. Teachers perpetuate gender stereotypes. In mixed classes, boys are more likely to volunteer answers, receive more attention from teachers, and earn more praise. By the time they are 8 to 10 years old, girls report lower self-esteem than boys, but it's not because they are less able.[77] According to the 2007 U.K. National Office of Statistics, girls outperform boys at all levels of education from preschool right through to university. There may be some often-reported superior abilities in boys when it comes to mathematics but that difference does not appear until adolescence, by which time there has been ample opportunity to strengthen stereotypes.[78] Male brains are different from female brains in many ways that we don't yet understand (for example, the shape of the bundle fibers connecting the two hemispheres known as the corpus callosum is different), but commentators may have overstated the case for biology when it comes to some gender stereotypes that are perpetuated by society.[79]

Stereotypes both support and undermine the self illusion. On the one hand, most of us conform to stereotypes because that is what is expected from those in the categories to which we belong, and not many of us want to be isolated. On the other hand, we may acknowledge the existence of stereotypes but maintain that, as individuals, we are not the same as everyone else. Our self illusion assumes that we could act differently if we wished. Then there are those who maintain that they do not conform to any stereotypes because they are individuals. But who is really individual in a species that requires the presence of others upon which to make a relative judgment of whether they are the same or different? By definition, you need others to conform with or rebel against. For example, consider tattoos as a mark of individuality—an individuality that is increasingly mainstream as evidenced by the rise in popularity for getting inked! Even those who go to the extremes of self-mutilation are inadvertently using others to calibrate the extent of their individuality. The self illusion is a mighty tricky perspective to avoid.

■ The Supermale Myth of Aggression

Consider another universal self stereotype—that of male aggression. Why do men fight so much? Is it simply in their nature? It's an area of psychology that has generated a multitude of explanations. Typical accounts are that males need physically to compete for dominance so that they attract the best females with whom to mate, or that males lack the same negotiation skills as women and have to resolve conflicts through action. These notions have been popularized by the "women are from Venus, men are from Mars" mentality. It is true that men have higher levels of testosterone, and this can facilitate aggressive behavior because this hormone makes you stronger. But these may be predispositions that cultures shape. When we consider the nature of our self from the gender perspective, we are invariably viewing this through a lens, shaped by society, of what males and females should be.

Males may end up more aggressive, but, surprisingly, they may not start out like that. Studies have shown equal levels of physical aggression in 1-year-old males and females, but by time they are 2 years of age, boys are more physically aggressive than girls, and this difference generally continues throughout development.[80] In contrast, girls increasingly rely less on physical violence during conflicts but are more inclined to taunting and excluding individuals as a way of exerting their influence during bullying.[81] Males and females may simply differ in the ways in which they express their aggression.

It seems unquestionable that male biology makes males more physically aggressive, which has led to the "supermale" myth. Some males inherit an extra Y chromosome (XYY), which makes them taller, leaner, and more prone to acne in comparison to other males. About 50 years ago, it was claimed that these supermales are more aggressive, following reports of there being a higher incidence of XYY males in Scottish prisons during the 1960s.[82] The belief was further substantiated in the public's mind by the notorious case of Richard Speck, an American mass murderer who tortured, raped, and murdered nine female student nurses in one night of terror on July 14, 1966, in South Chicago Community Hospital. Speck, who had a history of violence, broke into the nurses' home and held the women hostage. He led them out of the room, one by one, to be strangled or stabbed to death. At the time of his hearing, the defence lawyers claimed that Speck was not responsible for the crime because of diminished responsibility due to the fact that he had the XYY supermale genotype. It later transpired that Richard Speck's defence lawyer knew that Speck did not have an XYY genotype but perpetrated the myth in order to protect his client.

Even if Speck did have the XYY genotype, many of the claims for the link with violence have not stood up to scrutiny. Early studies were poorly conducted using very small samples and, amazingly, if a criminal had acne, this was sometimes taken as sufficient evidence of him possessing the XYY genotype in the absence of any genetic analysis.[83] Speck was tall and had acne. Today, the myth of the XYY supermale persists with many experts still disagreeing about a possible link between the genotype and violence. One extensive Danish study[84] concluded that the prevalence of XYY was about one in 1,000 males and that the only reliable characteristic was that they were of above-average height. This physical difference may have contributed to them exhibiting behavior that is considered more aggressive than normal. It may also explain why nearly half of XYY males are arrested compared with the average of one in ten XY males. Overall, it would appear that XYY males do have behavioral problems, especially during adolescence, which may be compounded by their unusual height. They also tend to have lower IQs and more impulsive behavior that could contribute to the higher incidence of criminality, but these crimes are not typically ones of violence against others but rather property crimes, such as shoplifting.

What makes the supermale myth worth considering in the context of gender stereotyping is that such biological beliefs can have unfortunate consequences. During the 1970s and 1980s, many parents took the decision to abort male fetuses diagnosed with the extra Y chromosome during prenatal examinations because of the supermale myth. The truth is that most males with XYY do not know that they have an extra Y chromosome because most are generally indistinguishable from other XY males.

Even if the XYY genotype was associated with aggression, in all likelihood the environment still plays an important triggering role. In other words, it is a predisposition that requires certain environmental conditions. For example, another gene abnormality linked to aggression affects the production of an enzyme (MAOA) that influences serotonin and dopamine neurotransmitter activity.

This gene has been nicknamed the "warrior" gene because it is disrupts the signalling in the PFC, and this has been linked with impulsivity and increased violence. In 2009, Bradley Waldroup escaped the death penalty in Tennessee after a murderous rampage on the grounds that he had the warrior gene. According to his defence, it was his genes that made him do it. The trouble is that around one in three individuals of European descent possess this gene, but the murder rate in this population is less than one in 100. Why don't the rest of us with the gene go on a bloody rampage?

Researchers studied over 440 New Zealand males with this missing gene from birth to adulthood to look for the biological basis of antisocial behavior.[85] They discovered that over eight out of ten males who had the MAOA gene missing went on to develop antisocial behaviors, but only if they had been raised in an environment in which they were maltreated as children. In contrast, only two out of ten males with the same abnormality developed antisocial adult behavior if they had been raised in an environment with little maltreatment. This explains why not all victims of maltreatment go on to victimize others. It is the environment that appears to play a crucial role in triggering whether these individuals become antisocial.[86] This is why it makes no sense to talk about nature and nurture separately when we consider how individuals develop.

■ Natural Born Killers

If early abuse turns on the effects of the warrior genes, can these negative attributes also be turned off? Neuroscientist Jim Fallon studies what makes psychopaths tick by looking at their brain activity and genes. One day, as he was sorting through lots of scans of psychopathic murderers, he noted that they all seemed to lack inactivity in the orbital cortex, a region of the prefrontal cortex. The orbital cortex is related to social behaviors such as smiling, and is also a region associated with moral decision-making and control of impulsive antisocial behavior. People with low activity in this region tend to be either free-wheeling types or psychopaths. Perhaps these psychopaths had bad brains?

At the time, Jim was also working on Alzheimer's disease and needed control data to compare with patients. He persuaded members of his family to have their brains scanned and provide blood samples to match against the clinical sample. Every one of his relatives' brain scans was normal—except one—his own. Jim discovered that he had the identical lack of activity in the orbital cortex that he had observed in the psychopathic killers. The irony of the neuroscientist discovering that he also had the same abnormal brain pattern as the killers was not lost on Jim.[87]

About a month later, at a family barbecue, he was pointing this irony out to the other family members when his 88-year-old mother, Jenny, suggested that maybe he should do a little research into the family history, as he might be surprised. What Jim discovered was truly shocking. It turned out that his ancestor, Thomas Cornell, was infamous in American history as the killer of his own mother in 1667, the first documented case of matricide. But it didn't stop there. There were another seven murderers in the line of the family from which Jim was directly descended! This was worrying. Jim looked for other evidence. Did he have the genes associated with aggression and violence? He had the blood taken from the Alzheimer study analyzed. Jim's blood was positive for the warrior gene, and he had all the genetic risk factors that could predispose him to become a killer. At the time, geneticists likened the odds of Jim possessing this constellation of genes to walking into a casino and throwing double-six 15 times in a row.

According to the biology, Jim should have been a natural born killer and a menace to society—but he wasn't. Why not? Dr. Jim Fallon used to be the type of scientist who followed a fairly genetic determinist line, believing that your genes pretty much determine your outcome, but his discoveries in brain imaging and genetics forced him to rethink his own rigid view of human nature. He had to accept that, in his case, the role of the environment had protected him, and in particular the nurturing he had received from his own parents had played a major part in the way he turned out. This is because, from the very start, Jim was a special birth for his parents. His mother had four miscarriages in a row before Jim was finally born. It would be a long time before his mother had any more children, and so Jim was treated as a precious child with a lot of attention and affection directed toward him. He believes all this nurturing offset the warrior gene that could have sent him off on a path of destruction.

Jim has avoided a life of crime and violence but recognizes that he still has many of the personality attributes of low orbital cortex activity. However, he recognizes that his own flaws may be residuals of his genetic predisposition. Rather than harming people, Jim simply does not make a strong emotional connection with others. He does not generally care about other people, especially those who are close to him, and he recognizes that he is close to the edge of being a psychopath.[88] I expect that we all know someone like that.

■ Incubated in Terror

How does someone become a psychopath? Bruce Perry is a psychiatrist who believes that the origins of human violence can be traced to the environments in which we rear our children. If an environment is lacking in appropriate role models and examples of how to behave and treat others, then children reared in it fail to develop an appropriate moral dimension to their sense of self. Combine that with the stress of poverty and lack of education necessary to raise one's self out of these conditions, and you have a recipe for disaster. Perry was called as an expert witness in several high-profile cases—the Columbine High School massacre, the Oklahoma City bombing, and the Waco siege. He is a highly acclaimed and respected scientist who argues that human violence is a vicious cycle that begins early in development. To illustrate his case, Perry describes an example of a pointless teenage murder:

> A fifteen year old boy sees some shoes he wants. Another child is wearing them—so he pulls out his gun and demands the shoes. The younger child, at gunpoint, takes off his shoes and gives them up. The fifteen year old puts the gun to the child's head, smiles and pulls the trigger. When he was arrested, the officers are chilled by the apparent lack of remorse. Asked later whether he could turn back the clock and do anything differently, he thinks and replies, "I would have cleaned my shoes." His bloody shoes led to his arrest.[89]

Perry thinks such blindness to the plight of others is a form of retardation results from a lack of appropriate emotional and social interaction as a child. This is an extreme case of Bowlby's social isolation, in which the child has failed to develop a moral dimension to the sense of self. Like Bowlby, Perry argues that such retardation is a consequence of not exposing the child to appropriate experiences in which negative emotions are triggered but are then resolved. Without this experience, vulnerable children fail to lay down the models of appropriate behavior during sensitive periods of social development.

According to Perry, this failure is due to the disruption of the development of neural circuitry that regulates behavior. If you remember back to the organization of the functional structures of the brain, the lower brain systems are the origins for impulsive behavior, including aggression. Perry argues that regulated behavior depends on the relative strength of activation arising from the lower, more primitive portions of the brain and the modulating inhibitory action of higher cortical areas. Factors that increase the activity or reactivity of the brain stem, such as chronic stress and abuse, or decrease the moderating capacity of the limbic or cortical areas, such as isolation and neglect, will increase an individual's aggression, impulsivity, and tendency to be violent. Only by raising children in nurturing environments can we provide the experiences within the right context that enable them to regulate their impulses and drives.

Examples of early violent behavior are not rare. For instance, there has been a much-reported epidemic of fatal stabbings among juveniles in the United Kingdom over the past couple of years. However, the majority of children raised in impoverished backgrounds are not destined to become remorseless killers. According to Perry, they nevertheless carry the emotional scars. They tend to move through life in a series of destructive relationships, often with a profound sense of disconnection and emotional emptiness. This leads to the associated problems of addiction, crime, and social poverty, thus establishing a destructive cycle for the next generation raised in this environment. Life loses its value and effectively becomes cheap, thus providing a fertile ground in which to breed a disregard for others. With over 5 million child victims of domestic violence in the United States alone and, worldwide, vast numbers of children impoverished by war and famine, Perry makes a convincing case that, despite our advances as a civilization, we are still raising children incubated in terror.

■ Learning to Take Control Over Your Life

As every parent knows, young children are impulsive. It's as though they have no way of stopping themselves. They lack self-control. They dash across busy roads, laugh at fat people, and shout out in public.

This inability to control thoughts and actions has been one of my research interests for decades now. I am interested by the fact that we have to develop the capacity for self-control as children in order to be clever and successful as adults. Otherwise, we would always be at the mercy of all the different urges and drives that compete for our attention and action. Young children lack adequate ways of stopping their urges, which manifests as impulsive behavior.

All children go through a phase of impulsivity early in development but, by the time they are ready for preschool, they are beginning to demonstrate the capacity to regulate behavior. They can withhold doing things in order to achieve a greater goal. In medieval Germany, it was thought that, given the choice between an apple or coin, the child who could resist the temptation of the fruit and take the coin was ready for schooling. They were in control of their childish impulses and urges.

In my laboratory, we don't offer children apples, but we do sometimes offer them marshmallows. In what is now a classic set of studies from the late 1960s, Stanford psychologist Walter Mischel offered 4-year-olds a plate holding two marshmallows and told them that they could have one now, but if they waited while he left the room, they could have both on his return.[90] In our lab, to avoid the various ethical problems of using marshmallows, we use a similar test in which we ask the children to turn their backs while we wrap a present that they can have if they wait. They are told not turn around and peek at the present while we leave the room to fetch some tape to finish the wrapping. From behind a one-way mirror in the adjacent room, we record each child's behavior and how long he or she can wait.

Whether it is tempting marshmallows or hidden presents, both of these situations measure what is known as *delay of gratification*. This is the amount of time that children can wait before succumbing to temptation—and it turns out to be a very useful predictor of how children will perform on other tasks that require self-control. What was most remarkable in Mischel's original studies was that he found that delay of gratification measured at 4 years predicted a child's academic performance and how sociable he was at 14 years of age.[91] When these children were followed up as 27-year-old adults, those who had exhibited better self-control as toddlers were more successful, sociable, and less likely to have succumbed to drug taking.[92]

The reason is simple. If you can regulate and control your impulses, then you are more patient at solving tasks, do not get bored so easily, and can resist temptation. When it comes to other people, you are less selfish, which makes you more likeable. Very often, social interactions result in a conflict of interest between different individuals that must somehow be resolved. These coordinating abilities depend on self-control, and without it we can become antisocial.

Regulating our self is one of the major roles of the prefrontal cortex. These brain regions operate to coordinate competing thoughts and behavior by inhibiting the excitatory commands arising from different regions. Without the executive control of our frontal lobes, we would be at the mercy of every whim, distraction, impulse, tic, or urge that could threaten to sabotage any chance of achieving acceptance by the rest of society or fulfilling the goals we have set for our future self.

That's why children with attention deficit hyperactivity disorder (ADHD) are thought to have poor self-control.[93] They find it very hard to sit still. They can be disruptive. They cannot concentrate on a task. They are easily distractible. They are more likely to be shunned by other children, and they find it difficult to make friends. Their hyperactivity and impulsivity can become such a problem that the child becomes uncontrollable. For many decades, such children were labelled naughty and undisciplined. Not surprisingly, ADHD children perform below their classmates on academic tests and many require special schooling. Around half of the children diagnosed with ADHD grow out of it during adulthood, but the remainder still experience problems in later life. Attention deficit hyperactivity disorder emerges in the preschool years and affects around one in 20 children, with about three times as many boys as girls.[94] Since the disorder was recognized in the 1970s, it has remained controversial. However, twin studies support a strong biological predisposition. If one identical twin has ADHD, then, in around three out of every four cases, the other identical twin also has the disorder.

The behavior of children with ADHD is sometimes described as "wired," as if they are on speed. This is ironic because one of the treatments is to give them Ritalin, a stimulant similar to amphetamine drugs. These drugs increase the activity of neurotransmitters that operate in the frontal lobes, which are thought to increase inhibition and the capacity to concentrate. This is why many university students who have no medical problem that requires them to take Ritalin nevertheless use it to improve their academic performance. It helps them concentrate. In contrast, alcohol, which is a depressant drug, reduces the activity of the frontal lobes and our capacity to inhibit drives, which is why people can become hungry, harmful, and horny when they are drunk.

However, there may be another way of controlling your self, other than using drugs. Delay of gratification tasks reveal that children who manage to delay are not just sitting there staring at the marshmallow and using willpower to control their urges. In fact, that would be the wrong thing to do. Rather, the children use different strategies to take their minds off temptation. Very often, they distract themselves by singing a song or doing something with their hands to take their minds off the temptation. In fact, coming up with alternatives might be the secret to resisting temptation. You can even train children how to distract themselves or tell them to imagine that the marshmallow is only a picture and not real. All of these strategies reduce the attention-grabbing properties of the goal, thereby making restraint more possible. It also means that self-control is something that can be practiced, which explains the counterintuitive finding that children raised in very strict households perform worse on delay of gratification. By being too controlling, parents do not allow children to develop their own internalized self-control,[95] which might explain many of the stereotypes of individuals who have led sheltered lives running amok when they are no longer under the control of others.

But who is this person who is out of control, if not the juvenile self? Who is distracting whom? Some colleagues argue that the whole notion of self-control seems to demand that we accept that there is a self in the first place to lose control. Where is the illusion of self here?

One way to think about it is to imagine the self constructed like a spider's web but without the spider. Each strand represents an influence pulling on the overall structure. The self is the resulting pattern of influences pulling together, trying to find a common ground. These are the thoughts and behaviors that compete for our activity. Some strands are stronger than others, and, if they snap, the shape of the web can become distorted. In the same way, our lives are made of different strands holding our self together. The young child without self-control is still constructing his webs of influence and has not yet established ways of offsetting the strong impulses that want to take over. The arrangements of strands are self-organizing by the fact that they are competing. There need not be a self at the center of the web holding it together.

■ The Essential Self

The self can be thought of something at the core of someone's existence. This is sometimes referred to the *essence* of
who someone is. People often refer to a person's essential
properties—what they are really like. In many ways, the
self illusion could become an argument about whether the
essential self really exists. This notion of essence is worth
considering further.

Imagine that I take your wedding ring or any other
object of sentimental value and, using some futuristic
machine, I replace it gradually, atom by atom, until it no
longer contains any original material but it is indistinguishable from the ring that existed before the processing. Would
it still be the same ring at different stages? Most would
accept that a ring with a few atoms replaced was essentially the same ring. A ring with everything replaced was
essentially different. But at what stage would the ring
transform identity, and why would one atom alone make
the difference? Also, if this process was gradual, most people would be inclined to say that it was the same ring
maintaining identity over time even if it contained none of
the original ring. But imagine that we recombine all the
material from the original ring so that we now have two
rings. Which is the original? Does the identity of one object
suddenly cease to exist when another is reconstructed?

Clearly, the identity of material objects is called into
question under these circumstances, but what about the
identity of persons? Imagine we perform the same sort of
replacement using a person. Philosopher Derek Parfit uses
these types of scenario to challenge the reality of the self.[96]
He asks us to imagine replacing a person cell by cell, so
that the original person no longer contains any of the physical material before the process started. In one example, he
asks us to imagine replacing our cells one by one with
those from Greta Garbo. At what point do we become the

famous Swedish actress? When does our self become her self? Using such logic, Parfit dismisses the notion of an essential self in the first place.

These are compelling thought experiments that challenge our intuitions about the nature of reality and identity. Frustratingly, there are no right and wrong answers to these questions, and the academic exchanges between philosophers highlight the disagreements that these scenarios generate among those who have pondered them professionally for years. However, to the man in the street, they reveal a common psychological intuition that there must be some enduring self that exists independently of the physical body—an essential self that defines who we are.

When we think essentially, we believe that an internal property exists that defines the true nature of things, and this way of reasoning emerges somewhere around the third to fourth birthday. In her seminal book, *The Essential Child*, Susan Gelman[97] makes a convincing case that essentialism is a naturally developing way of thinking that children use to chop up the living world into all the different species. When children learn that all dogs are members of the same group, then they do so on the basis of assuming that all dogs must have some form of doggy essence inside them that makes them different from cats, which have catty essence. They understand that if you change the outward appearance of the dog so that it now looks like a cat, it is still essentially a dog and will behave like one.

In truth, this distinction could be made at the biological level when it comes to considering the DNA sequences of both species. But few children are ever told about genetics, and yet they assume there must be an invisible property that differentiates the animals. Essentialism operates initially in young children's reasoning about the biological world but eventually becomes part of categorizing the important things in their world in general. This is especially so when they come to see others as unique individuals with unique minds.

My colleague Paul Bloom argues that essentialism is also at the heart of why we value certain objects or experiences: we believe them to have certain essential truths.[98] For example, we prefer and admire original works of art until we discover they are forgeries. Fakes are never worth as much as the original, even if you could not tell them apart. Most heterosexuals would enjoy sex with a good-looking member of the opposite sex until they discover that the person is a transsexual. For many heterosexuals, the thought of penetration with a member of the same sex is disgusting, even though they may never be aware of the true biological origins of their partner. Although the physical pleasure could be identical, the discovery that things are not what you believe reveals that our enjoyment depends on an assumption of authenticity. This is because we believe that a deception of identity has taken place. The same can be said for our common-sense notions of the self. The true nature of a person is his essential identity and when people are not true to their self, we call them fakes, cheats, and hypocrites, lacking strong core values. All of this language betrays a notion of some internal truth or self that has been violated.

This core self, wandering down the path of development, enduring things that life throws at us is, however, the illusion. Like every other aspect of human development, the emergence of the self is epigenetic—an interaction of the genes in the environment. The self emerges out of that journey through the epigenetic landscape, combining the legacy of our genetic inheritance with the influence of the early environment to produce profound and lasting effects on how we develop socially. These, in turn, can shape the way we interact with others and raise our own children. These thoughts and behaviors may seemingly originate from within us, but they emerge largely in a social context. In a sense, who we are really comes down to those around us. We may all be born with different biological properties and dispositions, but even these emerge in the context of others and in some cases can be triggered or turned off by environmental factors. The extent to which and how this happens is what scientists are trying to discover. We may feel that we are the self treading down the path of life and making our own decisions at the various junctions and forks but that would also assume that we are free to make our choices. However, the freedom to make choices is another aspect of the self illusion.

■ Memory Test

Were the following words present in the list of words you read?

needle
river

4 ■
The Cost of Free Will

We must believe in free will—we have no choice.

Isaac Bashevis Singer

For 96 minutes on a hot summer's day, around noon in 1966, ex-marine Charles Whitman, positioned high up in the tower building of the University of Texas in Austin, fired 150 rounds killing 14 people and injuring another 32 before he was finally shot dead by the police.[1] The University of Texas massacre was one of the first examples of a modern-day phenomenon of mass shootings. Dunblane, Columbine, and Virginia Tech are just a few of the recent atrocities in a growing list of senseless killing sprees that beggar belief. Every time one of these horrors happens, we are left asking the same question—why? In the case of Charles Whitman, we have an answer. He probably wasn't his usual self.

In his prospective suicide note, Whitman wrote about the impulsive violence and the mental turmoil he was experiencing. He had a history of aggressive outbursts and a troubled family life, but in the months leading up to the Austin rampage, Whitman thought things were getting worse. He wrote, "After my death I wish that an autopsy would be performed to see if there is any visible physical disorder." He also asked that after his debts had been paid off, any money left over should go into research to find out if there was some explanation for his actions. He knew that something was not right. And he was unfortunately correct. Deep inside his brain was a sizeable tumor in the region of his amygdala.

The amygdala is part of the brain circuitry responsible for emotional behaviors: damage to this region can cause excessive swings in rage and anger. Overstimulation of the amygdala will cause both animals and humans to lash out violently. Whitman's tumor could have been responsible for his impulsive aggression throughout his life. Together with the fact that his family life was troubled, he abused amphetamines, and he had been under a lot of stress in the summer of 1966, having a tumor of his amygdala would have impaired his ability to remain calm. But now that we know he had a brain tumor, was Whitman responsible for his actions? Did Whitman murder those innocent people or did his tumor?

There is also the strange case of the 40-year-old man who developed an interest in child pornography.[2] He was aware that his pedophilia was wrong because he went to great lengths to conceal his activities, but eventually he was exposed by his stepdaughter and sent to a rehabilitation center for treatment instead of prison. However, he could not avoid soliciting sexual favors from staff and other patients at the center and was eventually expelled. The evening before his prison sentence was due to commence, he was taken into a hospital complaining of severe headaches. There, it was discovered that he had a tumor in his prefrontal cortex—the same region related to suppressing and inhibiting drives and sexual urges. You need your pre-frontal cortex to overcome the impulse to eat the marsh-mallows as a toddler, but as an adult you also need it to curtail the urge to fight, flee, and fornicate.

Was the tumor responsible for the pedophile's behavior? In a way, it was. When his tumor was removed, his sexual urges declined and, after 7 months, he was allowed to go back to his home where his stepdaughter lived. However, a year later, he started collecting pornography again, where-upon another brain scan revealed that his tumor had grown back, again requiring surgery to remove. But how can a lump of cancerous cells have sexual urges toward young children? There is something very wrong in the way that we tend to think about the link between brain, behavior, and mind.

■ My Brain Made Me Do It

Neuroscientist David Eagleman believes that we are enter-ing a new era in which our understanding of how the brain works will force us to confront the difficulty of establishing when others are responsible for their actions.[3] This is the emerging field of *neuroethics*—the brain basis of morality and how we should behave. He makes the point that there are few among us who would attribute blame to Whitman or the pedophile when there is a clear brain abnormality, such as a cancerous tumor. As Eagleman points out, the problem is that, as our understanding of how the brain works improves, we will increasingly encounter arguments that those who commit crimes are not responsible for their actions due to some biological abnormality. As we under-stand more about the microcircuitry of the brain, we are going to discover more about the different imbalances and predispositions that are linked to criminal acts. Where will society eventually draw the line of culpability?

In fact, we have now reached a point at which there does not need to be any evidence of a biological abnormality— you just have to act out of character, in such a way as to not be regarded as your usual self. This is what the Canadian jury decided in the case of Ken Parks who, in 1988, drove 23 kilometers to his in-laws' house in Ontario, where he stabbed his wife's parents, killing the mother-in-law. He then presented himself to the local police station where he said, "I think I have killed some people."

Prior to the attack, Parks was said to have loved his in-laws, who described him as a "gentle giant." His defence team argued that as Parks did not remember the attack, he was sleepwalking; they entered a plea of "homicide during noninsane automatism as part of a presumed episode of somnambulism." He had no prior history of such behavior, but because the attack was so out of character, the jury accepted the defence and acquitted him.[4]

But what does it mean to be acting out of character? This statement assumes a sovereignty of self that is usurped by external forces. Where do these external forces exert their influence if not within us? Does it make any more sense to say that my background or environment is responsible for my actions than to say that my brain made me do it? I once discussed these issues of culpability over dinner with two adults who differed in their political leanings to the Left and to the Right. As you probably expected, the conservative was inclined to see fault in the individual, whereas the liberal saw society to blame. Clearly, these are questions that have no clear-cut answers and may reflect our personal belief systems.

Many legal systems operate on a version of the M'Naghten Rules, a precedent drawn up following the attempted assassination of the British Prime Minister Robert Peel by Daniel M'Naghten in 1843. This is known as the *insanity defence* and is based on the criteria that:

[A]t the time of committing of the act, the party accused was not labouring under such a defect of reason, from disease of the mind, as not to know the nature and quality of the act he was doing, or if he did know it, that he did not know he was doing what was wrong.

The problem is that many of us do things that we do not regard as wrong. We can always find ways of justifying our actions in retrospect to make sense of senseless acts—a point that is important when discussing decision-making. Also, we have all done things when we do not fully take into consideration the consequences of our actions. Are these exceptions, too? If so, how are we to decide what counts as being out of character? Is the one-off act worse than the repeat offender? After all, if someone repeatedly offends, then maybe they are unable to control their actions or do not think what they are doing is wrong. On the other hand, if an act is only done once, does this not mean that the offender should be punished more severely because she should have known better?

These are exactly the sorts of arguments that were raised in 2010, when the world was outraged by an impulsive act of cruelty perpetrated by 45-year-old British bank worker, Mary Bale, from Coventry. She was walking home one August evening when she encountered a cute 4-year-old cat called Lola on a garden wall. She often stopped to stroke the cat on her visits to see her ill father, who she would visit every day in the hospital. On this occasion, she once again stopped to pet the tabby cat, but then glanced around twice before opening the lid of a nearby recycling bin, grabbing the cat by the scruff of its neck, and then neatly dropping it inside before walking off briskly to her home three streets away.

Unfortunately for Mary, her dastardly deed was captured on the home surveillance system of the cat's owners, who posted the video on their Facebook page. The video went global, and soon thousands of people from around the world were calling her "worse than Hitler." When Mary was eventually identified from the video, she was arrested for cruelty but also put under police protection because of all the death threats she had received.

What possessed such a mundane, normal bank worker to commit such a senseless act of cruelty? Bale at first said she "suddenly thought it would be funny" to put the cat in the bin. Later, she claimed her actions were "completely out of character" and that she had no recollection of the event. Surely, this was simply a one-off lapse in morality. When she was tried in October 2010, the court accepted that she had been under stress. She had to leave her job at the bank. Her father had also just died, but the court was less understanding than those who judged Ken Parks. Bale was found guilty of animal cruelty, ordered to pay a large fine, and banned from keeping animals for 5 years. Maybe that says more about the way the British feel about their pets than their willingness to absolve a momentary moment of madness.

■ The Trouble with Free Will

Most of us believe that, unless we are under duress or suffering from some form of mental disorder, we all have the capacity to freely make decisions and choices. This is the common belief that our decisions are not preordained and that we can choose between alternatives. This is what most people mean by having *free will*—the belief that human behavior is an expression of personal choice and is not determined by physical forces, fate, or God. In other words, there is a self in control.

However, neuroscience tells us that we are mistaken and that free will is also part of the self illusion—it is not what it seems. We think we have freedom but, in fact, we do not. As such, we need to start rethinking how we apply the concept of free will or, rather, the lack of it as an excuse for our thoughts and behaviors. For example, I believe that the sentence that I have just typed was my choice. I thought about what I wanted to say and how to say it. Not only did I have the experience of my intention to begin this line of discussion at this point but I had the experience of agency, of actually writing it. I knew I was the one doing it. I felt the authorship of my actions.

It seems absurd to question my free will here but, as much as I hate to admit it, these experiences are not what they seem. This is because any choices that a person makes must be the culmination of the interaction of a multitude of hidden factors ranging from genetic inheritance, life experiences, current circumstances, and planned goals. Some of these influences must also come from external sources, but they all play out as patterns of neuronal activity in the brain. This is the matrix of distributed networks of nerve cells firing across my neuronal architecture. My biases, my memories, my perceptions, and my thoughts are the interacting patterns of excitation and inhibition in my brain, and when the checks and balances are finally done, the resulting sums of all of these complex interactions are the decisions and the choices that I make. We are not aware of these influences because they are unconscious and so we feel that the decision has been arrived at independently—a problem that was recognized by the philosopher Spinoza when he wrote, "Men are mistaken in thinking themselves free; their opinion is made up of consciousness of their own actions, and ignorance of the causes by which they are determined."[5]

Also, logically, there can be no free will. There is no King Solomon in our head weighing up the evidence. We already discussed why the little person inside our head making decisions—the homunculus—can't exist because that solution simply creates the problem of an infinite regress: who is inside his head, and so on, and so on. Nor are we going to allow for a "ghost in the machine," which introduces spiritual influences that scientists have been unable to find into our explanation.

If we remove free will from the equation, some have worried that the alternative is one of *determinism*—that everything is predetermined and that our lives are simply the playing out of a complicated game of set moves in which fate reigns over freedom. Most people find that notion just as scary because it means we have no control in shaping the future. Surely the future is not already preordained?

Faced with such an existential crisis, some have sought a way of introducing randomness into the equation. If there are no spirits or gods, and only physics governs us and the world we live in, then maybe the physics is less predictable than one would think? One seemingly attractive way of escaping the determinist view is to get rid of predictability at the smallest level of the brain. This is where we enter the mysterious and peculiar world of quantum physics, where the rules that govern the physical world we know no longer apply. And if these rules are gone, then so has the predictability of how our brain works, thereby leaving the door ajar for some freedom of choice.

■ Charming Quarks

The world of quantum physics is weird. It doesn't obey the laws of the normal world. Elements can pop in and out of existence, be in two places at the same time, and basically not conform to the sorts of rules of matter that operate in the Newtonian world. Put simply, quantum physics has revealed that the basic building blocks of matter, the elemental subatomic particles, behave in decidedly unpredictable ways. They are known as "indeterminate"—as opposed to determined. They don't behave like objects in the

Newtonian world. These elementary particles of matter are known as *quarks*. Their unpredictability undermines determinism because it indicates that laws of cause and effect do not apply at the quantum level. Advocates of this position argue that if the fabric of the universe is inherently unpredictable, then choices are not determined and multiple potential futures are possible. This is why quantum indeterminacy is reassuring to those of us who want to retain the possibility that we are free to decide our own destiny.

One of the problems of applying quantum indeterminacy to explain free will is that the signaling between neuronal networks in the brain happens at a level much larger in scale than that observed at the subatomic particle level at which indeterminacy happens. It's like saying the individual grains of sand that make up an individual brick could influence the structure of a cathedral made out of millions of bricks, as well as the societies that spawn from such institutions. More importantly, even if randomness at the quantum level somehow translated up to the molecular level of brain activation and the macro level of societies, then that would equally not be a satisfying account of what most of us experience as free will. Decisions would not be choices but rather the outcome of random events, which is not free will either. As I quipped in my last book, *SuperSense*, even if there were a ghost in the machine exercising free will, then we don't want one flipping a coin when it comes to making a decision!

Our belief in free will not only reflects our personal subjective experience of control over our actions on a daily basis, but also our own ignorance of the mechanisms, both conscious and unconscious, that determine our decisions. Many people find such a conclusion deeply disturbing, as if their life is already predictable. Dan Dennett is quoted as saying, "when we consider whether free will is an illusion or reality, we are looking into an abyss. What *seems* to confront us is a plunge into nihilism and despair."[6]

But why should that be upsetting? Many things in life are not what they seem. Arguably, all of our perceptions are illusions because we don't have any privileged access to reality. Our minds are a matrix simulating reality. Even the physical world is not what it seems. Quantum physics reveals that a solid brick is made up of more space than matter. Does a deeper understanding of the nature of the brick undermine how we should behave when someone throws one at our head? Clearly not.

The pessimistic view of determinism is also unwarranted because we simply wouldn't be able to comprehend the patterns of causality in any meaningful way. Aside from very simple actions that we consider next, the complexity of the underlying processes that make up our mental lives is going to be one that proves impossible to predict with any degree of certainty—it might as well be random and undecided. It's like watching a soccer match. We appreciate that the laws of physics govern the movement of the players and ball, but that does not mean you can predict with any certainty how the moves in the game will play out. At best, we may be able to get close to figuring out what will happen, but to use a term borrowed from engineering, there are simply too many degrees of freedom to make an accurate prediction of what the system will do. The problem of too many degrees of freedom means that, every time you add another factor that can exert an influence on your decision-making, you change the predictability of a system.

Let's consider some numbers again. With just 500 neurons, the number of possible different patterns of connections you could have exceeds the estimated total number of atoms in the observable universe. With billions of neurons, each with up to 10,000 connections, that suggests an almost infinite number of possible brain states. So, figuring out what each pattern of electrical activity does is simply not feasible. The other problem is that no two brains are identical. Even identical clones of a very simple organism, such as the water flea, when raised in the same environment have different patterns of neural connections.[7] So, any mapping of one brain is not going to apply directly to that of another.

A final nail in the coffin of predictable determinism is that thousands of different brain states can produce the same output. This is known in philosophy as *multiple realizability*,[8] although I prefer the more familiar phrase, "There is more than one way to skin a cat!" What this means simply is that many different patterns of brain activity can produce the same thoughts and behaviors. There is no unique one-to-one mapping between the brain's activities and the output of the individual. For example, scientists looked at a much simpler nervous system than the human brain—the gut of a lobster—and carefully recorded as many different patterns of activity of the nerves that control the digestive movements. They found that thousands of different patterns produced the same behavior.[9] For any individual cell, there were multiple patterns of activity with other connecting cells that produced the same output.

Multiple realizability is likely to be true for the human brain as well. In other words, our thoughts and behaviors are realized in multiple pathways of activity, which is a good thing. Remember that the neural networks are massively parallel. This means that the same neurons can be triggered by a variety of spreading activations. This parallel structure explains the speed, the complexity, and, ultimately, the richness of mental life, but it also means that you are never going to be able to map it out precisely—even within the same individual brain.

Despite the complexity of the mathematics of brain activity, many are still deeply unsatisfied with a materialist account of the mind, even if it is not predictable. We want to believe that we are more than fleshy computing devices that have evolved to replicate. We are not simply meat machines. Maybe there is some as yet undiscovered force at work? After all, we are continually reminded that most of the universe is made up of stuff that we know is there but cannot measure. How can scientists rule out the non-material explanation for the mind and free will if they themselves admit that they do not know everything?

The answer is they can't. Science can only investigate and evaluate different models of the world, and those models are only going to be approximations of the true state of the universe—which, frankly, we may never know. But science is continually moving forward and progressing by refining the models to better fit the evidence. And the evidence comes from our observations. However, sometimes observations are wrong. The big trouble with free will is that it just feels so real. All of us think that our thoughts happen in advance of what we do. Time moves forward, and we experience that our thoughts cause actions. It turns out that this is wrong, and we know this from the simple press of a button.

■ Living in the Past

Imagine that I ask you to push a button whenever you feel like it. Just wait until you feel good and ready. In other words, the choice of when you want to do it is entirely up to you. After some time, you make the decision that you are going to push the button, and low and behold you do so. What could be more obvious as an example of free will? Nothing—except that you have just experienced one of the most compelling and bizarre illusions of the human mind.

In the 1980s, Californian physiologist Benjamin Libet was working on the neural impulses that generate movements and motor acts. Prior to most voluntary motor acts, such as pushing a button with a finger, a spike of neural activity occurs in the brain's motor cortex region that is responsible for producing the eventual movement of the finger. This is known as the *readiness potential*, and it is the forerunner to the cascade of brain activation that actually makes the finger move. Of course, in making a decision, we also experience a conscious intention or free will to initiate the act of pushing the button about a fifth of a second before we actually begin to press the button. But here's the spooky thing. Libet demonstrated that there was a mismatch between when the readiness potential began and the point when the individual experienced the conscious intention to push the button.[10]

By having adults watch a clock with a moving dot that made a full rotation every 2.65 seconds, Libet established that adults felt the urge to push the button a full half second *after* the readiness potential had already been triggered. In other words, the brain activity was already preparing to the press the button before the subject was aware of his own conscious decision. This interval was at least twice as long as the time between consciously deciding to push the button and the actual movement of the finger. This means that when we think that we are consciously making a decision, it has already happened unconsciously. In effect, our consciousness is living in the past.

One might argue that half a second is hardly a long time but, more recently, researchers using brain imaging have been able to push this boundary back to 7 seconds.[11] They can predict on the basis of brain activity which of two buttons a subject will eventually press. This is shocking. As you can imagine, these sorts of findings create havoc for most people. How can we be so out of touch with our bodies? Do we have no conscious control? The whole point about voluntary acts is that we feel both the intention to act and the effort of our agency. We feel there is a moment in time when we have decided to do something, which is followed by the execution of the act. Brain science tells us that, in these experiments, the feeling of intention occurs after the fact.

However, Libet's findings do not mean that intention cannot precede actions. We can all plan for the future, and it would be ludicrous to say otherwise. For example, in the morning, I made the decision to check the mailbox, at the end of the drive, in the afternoon, and I did just that—I made a plan of action and then enacted it. There was no readiness potential in my brain to visit the mailbox. Likewise, many other actions happen without conscious deliberation, and thank goodness for that. Imagine if you had to think about jamming on the brakes in a vehicle pile-up: you would be a goner. Whether it is long-term goals or automatic behaviors triggered by external events, in both instances, the experience of intention happens either well in advance or sometimes not all. Our actions don't always follow our intentions, as in the Libet demonstration.

What Libet's findings really show is that in a situation where we are asked to both initiate a willed action and monitor when we think we have initiated the action, the preparation for the movement happens well before we become aware of our intention. Most people find this amazing. However, neuroscientists are less impressed because they know the brain generates both the movement and conscious awareness. This makes impartiality and objective evaluation impossible. Another problem for interpreting the time course of events is that the brain activation that generates conscious awareness is not a single point in time but rather is distributed. In other words, although we can suddenly become aware of an instance when we have made a decision, that process must have been building up for some period. It may feel like it happened spontaneously just before we moved our finger, but it didn't. We just thought so. Spinoza figured this out 350 years ago.

One big misinterpretation of Libet's findings, and of appreciating the true nature of the self in general, is that one cannot passively wait for an urge to occur while at the same time monitoring when one becomes conscious of bringing it about. We cannot step outside of our mind and say, "Yes, that's when I felt the urge to move, and that's when I actually started to do so." You cannot have your mental cake and eat it. As the philosopher Gilbert Ryle[12] pointed out, in searching for the self, one cannot simultaneously be the hunter and the hunted. Such reasoning reflects our inherent dualist belief that our mind is separate from our body.

We may think that our mind controls our body but that is an illusion of free will and control. This illusion arises when our subjective conscious intention precedes the actual execution of the movement with little delay. We know this timing is critical because if you disrupt the link between when you experience the intention to act and the execution of the act, we experience a loss of willed action. This is when we feel that we are not in control of our bodies.

■ Being in Two Minds

Most of the time, we feel we have control over our actions. There are exceptions, such as reflexes that do not involve conscious control and, as discussed, some behaviors are surprisingly infectious, such as laughing and yawning when in a crowd. But, for the most part, our normal daily actions seem under our control. However, brain damage can change all of that. When we damage our brain, we can lose control over our bodies. Paralysis is the most common example. Our limbs may be perfectly fine, but if we damage the brain centers for movement then, irrespective of our strongest will, our paralyzed limbs cannot move. Sometimes, though, parts of our body can move by themselves. For example, *alien hand syndrome* is a condition in which patients are not in control of one of their hands and experience the hand's actions as controlled by someone else or that the hand has a will of its own.[13] This is also known as the "Dr. Strangelove syndrome," a nod to Stanley Kubrick's 1964 movie in which Peter Sellers plays a wheelchair-bound nuclear war expert and former Nazi whose uncontrollable hand makes Nazi salutes and attempts to strangle him. Strange as Dr. Strangelove syndrome might seem, there is a perfectly reasonable explanation based on the discovery that each hand is under relatively independent control from the opposite side of the brain.

For reasons that Mother Nature knows best, much of processing and output in the brain is lateralized to the opposite hemisphere. If you were to draw an imaginary line down the center of the human body, then most of the information coming from the left side of the world goes to the right hemisphere. Likewise, most of the information from the right side is processed in the left hemisphere. The same is true for actions. The left hemisphere controls the right side of the body, and the right hemisphere controls the left. If you severely damage the left hemisphere, then you can be left paralyzed down the right side of the body and vice versa.

Some skills tend to be lateralized. For example, the left hemisphere controls language, whereas the right hemisphere is better at the visual processing of the space around us. That's why brain damage to the left hemisphere disrupts language and patients become aphasic (unable to produce speech), whereas damage to the right hemisphere leaves language intact but often disrupts the patient's awareness of objects, especially if they are in the left side of space.

We are not aware of these divisions of labor as the two hemispheres work together to produce joined up thoughts and behaviors. This is because the two sides of the brain are connected together through a large bundle of fibers—the corpus callosum—that enables the exchange of information. It also enables the abnormal electrical activity of epilepsy, which can originate in one hemisphere, to spread to both sides of the brain causing major seizures. Epilepsy can be extremely debilitating but by severing the corpus callosum fibers that connect the two hemispheres, the electrical brainstorm can be contained and prevented from transferring from the original site to the rest of the brain. This containment alleviates the worst of the symptoms.

The consequence of this operation is to produce a "split-brain" patient. The two halves of the brain continue to work independently of each other, but you would be hard pressed to notice any difference. Split-brain patients look and behave perfectly normally. This begs the question of why we need the two halves of the brain connected in the first place. In fact, it turns out that split-brain patients are not normal. They are just very good at compensating for the loss of the exchange of brain activity that is normally passed backward and forward between the two hemispheres of the intact brain.

Neuroscientist Michael Gazzaniga has shown that these split-brain patients can effectively have each half of the body thinking and acting in a different way. One of his most dramatic observations sounds very similar to the Dr. Strangelove syndrome.[14] He gave one of his split-brain patients a puzzle to solve using only his right hand (controlled by the language-dominate left hemisphere). However, this was a spatial puzzle in which the blocks had to be put in the correct position (something that requires the activity of the right hemisphere). The right hand was hopeless, turning the blocks over and over until, as if frustrated, the left hand, which the patient had been sitting on, jumped in and tried to take the blocks away from the patient's right hand. It was if the hand had a different personality.

Sometimes this lack of control takes over the whole body. French neurologist François Lhermitte reported a bizarre condition that he called "environmental dependency syndrome," in which patients slavishly copied the doctor's behavior.[15] Like the Tourette's patient who had to mimic every other person's behavior, Lhermitte's patients were similarly compelled to copy every action the doctor made. At one point, the French neurologist got down on his knees in his office as if to pray, whereupon the patient copied him with her head bowed and hands clasped in prayer. Other patients exhibited a related behavior known as *utilization*, in which the sight of an object triggered an involuntary associated response.[16] Such patients will pick up cups in their vicinity and start drinking from them, even when the cup is empty or not theirs. They will feel the compulsion to flick light switches and pull handles. In all of these examples, the patients' actions are triggered by external events and not their own voluntary actions, although some may reinterpret their unusual behavior as if it arose of their own free will. They will justify their actions as if they willed them when, in fact, it was something in the environment that had taken control over their actions.

■ "The Great Selfini"

When not bedevilled by strange neurological disorders, most of us feel we are in control because the coupling between the mental state of consciousness and initiated actions in everyday experience confirms our belief that we have willed our actions freely and in advance of their initiation. But if the reality of free will is an illusion, then why do we experience it so strongly? Why do we need the experience of free will? Why did it evolve?

Harvard psychologist Dan Wegner has written one of the best accounts of why we evolved the vivid experience of free will.[17] Wegner argues that we have a brain that interprets actions in terms of a "we think we did it" experience as a very useful way of keeping track of our decisions and actions. This is because the multiple conscious or unconscious influences and processes that lead to these choices are too complicated or hidden to monitor, but we can keep track of the outcome as a feeling that we have made the decision. For example, we may be at a party and want to impress some of the guests. Think of all the reasons why we might feel the need to do this—social anxiety, fear of rejection, the need to be at the center of attention, and so on. What do we do? We rely on our experience of past situations to come up with a strategy: we decide to tell a joke. We monitor the outcome and then store this for reference for future parties. We told a joke, but were we free to do otherwise? Of course, we feel we made the decision but there were a multitude of previous experiences, as well as current social norms and rules, that influenced our choice. When our behaviors go wrong or we make a faux pas, we feel self-conscious and embarrassed and privately ask ourselves, "What was I thinking?"

Having an experience of free will over our thoughts and actions binds us to these as the instigator of these decisions, even when that may not be the case. In this way, a sense of free will could help us keep track of what we have done, what we have not done, and what we may, or may not, do in the future. As long as our conscious intention appears to precede our actions, then it is natural to assume that we willed them.

This authorship of actions requires the illusion of a unified sense of self. After all, it is useful to know who is responsible. Wegner[18] has called this master illusionist "The Great Selfini." As we act on the world, we interpret the consequences of actions from the privileged prospective of our singular self. This has some interesting consequences. For example, we remember our actions much better than we do those belonging to others. Whether the actions are walking, throwing darts, or clapping hands, people are better at recognizing their own movements compared to those of others. In fact, we seem to be biased to remember those that pertain to us simply by acting on the world. In one study,[19] individuals either selected slips of paper from a bowl or had them handed to them by the experimenter. The experimenter then read out the words associated with the code on each slip. In comparison to those individuals who had the slips given to them, those who chose their own slips remembered more of the words, even though they were never aware of the purpose of the study. It was a consequence of inconsequential actions, but because most of us are tripped-wired to pay attention to our self, we tend to give special effort to anything we do.

However, just like false memories, sometimes our authorship of action can be mistaken. For example, when we make a plan to do something, we can forget whether we actually did it or not. If you ask subjects to imagine breaking a toothpick a number of times, and then a week later ask them to recall their actions, they have difficulty deciding whether or not they actually did break a toothpick.[20] It's like trying to remember whether you actually posted a letter or simply imagined that you did—did you or did you not? And the irony is that, by forming a mental picture of the action, we become more confused. Simply watching someone perform an action, such as shaking a bottle, can also lead to the false memory that we were the one who did it.[21] Whether we imagine an action or observe others, we can mistakenly attribute our self as the actor. The reason gets back to the built-in mirroring system in our brain that responds to actual movements, imagined movements, and the movements of others. If there is an author of actions, then sometimes he or she may make stories up or plagiarize the work of others.

Wegner thinks that the authorship of actions is like the mind's compass that helps us navigate through the complexity of our daily lives. Like an autopilot, it steers the ship depending on the heading, conditions, and the direction of magnetic north. There is no captain at the helm reading the compass because that would steer us straight back to the illusory self in control.

■ You Are Feeling Very Sleepy

"If you focus on my watch, you will feel sleepy. You will find that your eyelids are getting heavy. You will want to keep your eyes open but you are unable to do so. The more you try to keep them open, the more you want to sleep." This routine should sound familiar as the commanding instructions of the hypnotist who uses them to make people relinquish control of their actions. Hypnotism is probably one of the best examples where people seem to abdicate their personal sense of free will.

Why is this? Hypnotism seems like some magical power that others have to exert control over us—like some external energy emanating from the eyes or the beckoning fingers of the hypnotist with the piercing stare and goatee beard. It is usually portrayed in popular culture as a paranormal power that the hypnotist possesses to overcome the will of others. However, this is the myth of hypnotism. Hypnotism works because not only do we instinctively mimic others, but we also tend to do what they ask of us in the right situation. If you couple that with induction techniques that place us in a state of relaxation, giving us the sense that we are not in control of our bodies, then it can be fairly easy to hypnotize someone. Even when we know we are being manipulated, some of us readily give in. There's nothing paranormal about it.

Imagine the typical dinner party scene where we have eaten too much, but the host urges us to have a bit more cake, "Go on, just one little piece won't hurt." Most of us have encountered such social coercion and most of us give in, as the pressure to comply is so great. The same coercion would not really work in a restaurant, and we would be mighty suspicious of the waiter who insisted that we eat more. In most restaurants (aside from the very expensive ones where many of us feel intimidated and comply to the authority of the maître d'), we are the ones in charge and do not capitulate to others. The dinner party scenario is different because it is primarily a social event in which we submit to the will of the group or the person in charge. We become susceptible to the influence of others we wish to please. This is because we are naturally inclined to be compliant toward others.

In hypnosis, we are similarly asked to submit to the authority of others to the extent that we end up engaging in behaviors that we would not necessarily think we would freely do. Also, we are willing victims. Many seek out a hypnotist for treatment or to help them stop smoking or lose weight. Others pay good money to go see a stage hypnotism show in which we expect to see normal people doing daft things out of their control. In both of these situations, the expectation exists that hypnosis will work, and therefore we are willing to comply.

Techniques vary, but most hypnotic states are induced by a sequence of progressive compliance. For stage shows, the hypnotist works fairly rapidly to select the most suggestible members of the audience by getting them to engage in some motor act, such as clasping their hands tightly. He then tells them that their hands are stuck together with glue, such that they cannot unclasp them no matter how hard they try. This simple technique will identify those who are willing to accept the suggestion of the hypnotist. Other induction techniques rely on various motor illusions, such as trying to keep one's palms separate when held at arm's length. Our arms will naturally move together in such circumstances as our muscles fatigue, but by simply telling the individual that they have no control and allowing them to witness the involuntary actions of their bodies, it is a simple next step for many to begin to give up their sense of personal control. From then on, the hypnotist can focus on these individuals and manipulate them. Around one in ten of us[22] is highly suggestible, which means that any decent-sized audience will have more than enough suitable volunteers who can be made to bark like dogs or eat onions that taste like apples.

Contrary to common wisdom, hypnotized individuals are not mindless. Most of them report that they are aware of their actions but that they no longer feel as if they have control over them. Some report a dream state. Many say that they "felt hypnotized," which probably says more about their expectations about what they should say. It is worth noting that those who think that they would be easily hypnotizable tend to be the ones who actually are.[23]

There are many different accounts about how hypnotism actually works. Various measures of brain activity indicate that those who are hypnotized are in an altered state of consciousness.[24] However, another school of thought is that hypnosis is simply exaggerated role-playing.[25] Because humans are so obliging, some of us are inclined to adopt roles expected of the group. The academic debates over what is actually going on during hypnosis are still raging, but it is fair to conclude that hypnotism is a real phenomenon in which individuals behave and think that they are no longer in control. Their sense of free will has been temporary hijacked by the hypnotist and the social situation they find themselves in.

■ Superstitious Rituals

Superstitious behavior also makes some of us feel compelled to do things beyond our control.[26] Do you avoid stepping on cracks in the pavement? How about throwing salt over your shoulder if you accidentally spill some? Do you have a lucky charm? These are just some of the superstitious rituals that many of us have. Although we may be aware that these superstitions cannot influence outcomes, many of us feel the need to act them out just in case. Some of these superstitions come from culture, handed down over the years to the extent that we lose the original context in which they first appeared. Most of the important events that punctuate our lives, such as births, religious festivals, marriages, and times of important change, are peppered with old superstitions that have become traditions. In such instances, we act them out because that is what is expected.

There is also a whole host of personal superstitious behaviors that many of us entertain. They can take on a degree of compulsiveness that undermines our ability to rein them in with reason. This is because of two mechanisms that operate in our brains. First, our brains have evolved to seek out patterns in the world and attempt to generate explanations for why things happen. Second, in situations in which outcomes are important, we get stressed by uncertainty and feel the need to do something so that we have the illusion that we can control events.

We naturally see the world in terms of causes and consequences, so when something happens, we assume that some causal event preceded it and start looking around for suitable candidates. The problem is that we often identify causes that are not responsible. This generates a cognitive illusion known as *"post hoc, ergo propter hoc,"* which translates from the Latin as "after this, therefore because of this." It is particularly obvious in superstitious behaviors. In one experiment, participants were presented with a machine that had levers and lights.[27] The most important thing about the machine was that it delivered rewards at random intervals. The people taking part in the experiment thought that the machine could be operated to pay out rewards if the correct sequence was discovered. Very soon, individuals were performing elaborate sequences, believing that their actions determined whether the machine paid out or not. One woman thought that jumping up and down on the spot was what triggered the reward. In fact, there was no causal link between their actions and the outcomes.

In real life, the most common examples of superstitious behaviors come from sports and gambling, two activities associated with a lot of random chance and luck. You might have a particularly successful time at the blackjack table. This leads you to try and work out what was unusual about the events leading up to that success, so that you can repeat the winning formula. Maybe it was a particular shirt you wore or something that you ate. The next time around, you try out the same behavior again and, if successful, you have the beginnings of a superstitious ritual. When David Beckham played for AC Milan, his fellow teammates developed a superstitious ritual of always patting the England striker on his bottom after scoring a goal for good luck.[28] Well, at least that was the reason they gave.

The second reason superstitions form is that they are a means of coping with uncertainty. Superstitions are typically found in situations in which an element of risk exists.[29] Rituals provide the individual with an illusion of control that they are doing something to influence outcomes when in fact they have no control whatsoever. If you remove an individual's perception of control, then he experiences uncertain situations as stressful, thereby generating anxiety that impairs both the immune system and the capacity to think clearly.[30] Enacting superstitious rituals inoculates us from the negative excesses of stress. This is why you often find superstitious behavior in dangerous occupations.[31]

Firemen, pilots, sailors, and soldiers hold just some of the jobs that are associated with risk and superstitious rituals. My favorite is the Russian cosmonauts and their pre-launch ritual. Before Charles Simonyi, the billionaire who oversaw the creation of Microsoft Office, hitched a ride on the Soviet rockets that rendezvous with the orbiting International Space Station, he joined in with his companions' ritual of urinating on the back wheels of the bus that takes them to the launch pad.[32] This superstition originated when Yuri Gagarin was caught short on the first manned space flight and has now become a ritual for all who travel on Russian rockets.

The problem is that, if you consider outcomes as both things that do or do not happen because of some action you did or did not take, then just about everything becomes a candidate for rituals. When these rituals start to rule your life, so that they control your actions, you are entering territory where there is no freedom to choose because your emotions have got the better of your free will.

■ The Cleaning Lady

Obsessive-compulsive disorder (OCD) is a loss of self-control and free will that is more disturbing and debilitating than harmless superstitions. I used to drive past an elderly lady on the daily commute to my office in Bristol from my home in the country. Occasionally, I saw her chatting to neighbors but most of the time she was bent over at an alarming angle with her face as close to the ground as possible. At first, I thought she must have dropped something valuable or spotted an extraordinary insect on the sidewalk. What was she looking for, I wondered? One day, I slowed the car down enough to discover what she was up to. With delicate precision, she was picking minute particles of debris off the pavement and gathering them into her other free hand. She was cleaning the street outside her house. Sometimes she resorted to using a hand brush and pan, but most of the time she seemed to prefer the meticulous and laborious hand technique.

This old lady had an obsession with dirt. I never talked to her or visited her, but I bet my bottom dollar that her house was immaculate. There would not be one thing out of place. Everything would be spotless and in exactly the right place. The towels would be neatly folded, and brand new soap would be at the side of the hand basin. The toilet paper would be folded at the end, and everything would smell of disinfectant. I expect that having achieved a level of unearthly cleanliness within her own domain, she had taken to the street around her house, where the wind and daily passers-by conveniently dropped fragments of debris for her to focus on.

This cleaning lady had the telltale signs of OCD, which affects about one in 50 members of the general public. In many instances, OCD reflects concerns about the consequences of failing to do something—lock doors or turn off power switches. The most common one that most of us experience is the checking and then rechecking that we have taken our passport when traveling. No matter how many times we confirm that we have it, for reassurance, we still feel compelled to check that we still have it.[33] Many of us also have routines that punctuate our daily lives, and we prefer not to deviate from them. It might be the way you read the sections of the morning paper in a specific order or how you typically start off your workday. Sometimes these routines become rituals that control and dominate our lives. In one notable case, a British boy with Tourette's syndrome also had OCD that compelled him to step correctly on a white road marking. On the morning of September 11, 2001, he neglected to fulfil his compulsion and ended up traumatized because he believed that he was personally responsible for the terrorist attacks in the United States.[34]

■ The Obsessive-Compulsive Circuit

The symptoms of OCD are the obsessions (the relentless, intrusive thoughts, usually about something bad happening) and the compulsions (the repetitive, ritualistic behaviors often enacted to alleviate the obsessions).[35] Karen, a 34-year-old mother of four, used to obsess that some harm would befall her children unless she carried out certain counting rituals. For example, when she smoked and drank coffee, she had to smoke four cigarettes in a row and drink four cups of coffee, otherwise something bad would happen to her children. She knew this was irrational, but if she didn't perform her counting ritual, she experienced extreme anxiety.[36] This sets up a feedback loop in behavior whereby performing the ritual alleviates the mental anguish and strengthens the grip OCD has over its sufferer.

What starts this cycle of ritual off in the first place? The obsessions that plague sufferers typically derive from concerns that could pose a real threat, such as contamination fears. What appears to go wrong is the evaluation of the perceived threat and the proportional balance of engaging in behaviors to address those concerns. This must be due to a brain disorder that is as yet not fully understood but may be linked to Tourette's syndrome. There is certainly a heritability factor with OCD running higher in families and more common in identical than nonidentical twins.

One current theory[37] is that there is an imbalance of activity of the prefrontal cortex (PFC), the anterior cingulate cortex (ACC), and the caudate nucleus (CN) of the basal ganglia—the so-called "OCD circuit." Functional imaging reveals that activity within this corticobasal ganglia network is higher in OCD sufferers compared to normal individuals, and increases during provocation of symptoms, but that it is attenuated following successful treatment.

The PFC supports the executive functions for planning and suppressing thoughts and behaviors, while the ACC interconnects the frontal lobes with the limbic system of the midbrain and is related to motivation. Together, the PFC and ACC may signal the perceived importance of stimuli that trigger ritualistic behaviors. The CN is involved with initiating intentional behaviors. For example, disruption of this region can result in the inability to start movements (as in Parkinson's disease) or an inability to stop movements (as in Huntington's disease). Drugs that increase activity of the serotonin neurotransmitter, which decreases the activity of the CN, have been found to alleviate the symptoms of OCD. But that does not mean that the disorder is caused by overactivity of the CN. Rather, it may simply be a consequence of the behavior, which is why therapies that work to limit the compulsions seem to produce a reduction in CN activity as well.

The work on the brain circuitry of compulsions and ritualistic behavior is another clear line of evidence to support the proposition that the self most of us experience is an illusion. This work reveals that we are in constant conflict with competing goals and drives, and, for some unfortunate individuals, pathological behaviors reveal when the competition gets out of balance. This is the web metaphor again. You might argue that these victims have a self that is not in control and would prefer not to have to engage in rituals in the same way that an addict would prefer not to be addicted. However, evoking an idealized notion of what we would want to be does not mean that this individual, the Great Selfini, necessarily exists.

■ Ego Depletion

The young Japanese actress is a quietly spoken, 24-year-old former ballerina with a perfectly symmetrical angular face and long dark hair so typical of Asian beauties. Aoyoma has large almond eyes and an enchanting smile. She is the director's onscreen visualization of vulnerability and innocence. But her performance in the infamous torture scene in Takashi Miike's cult horror, *Audition* (1999), is so shocking and indelible that it instantaneously propelled this movie into cinematic notoriety. Believing that all men lie, the beautiful but psychotic Aoyoma tells her lover that, "Pain never lies," as she proceeds to stick needles into his eyes, chirping sweetly, "Kiri…Kiri…Kiri" ("Deeper…Deeper…Deeper"). She then amputates his left foot with a wire saw, laughing gleefully, like an innocent child, as we watch the bloody gore, hear the sound of serrating bone and the "ping" as the wire recoils through the stump. It is so cinematically graphic that most people in the audience squirm in their seats, cover their eyes, or simply walk out of the cinema.

Most people, that is, except for those taking part in psychologist Matt Field's experiments at Liverpool University. Field was showing them the infamous *Audition* torture scene for a study on self-control. Half of the student volunteers were told not to turn away and that they must not show any emotion. They had to resist the nausea and overwhelming feelings of disgust. They had to watch the violence through gritted teeth. They had to control themselves. The other half of the group simply watched the torture scene but were allowed to respond naturally. They were nauseated. They were disgusted. Many closed their eyes. One student fainted. Their mirroring system had gone into empathetic meltdown.

What kind of sadist is Matt Field? How did this study ever get through the university ethics committee? Actually, he is a very likeable chap who is trying to understand some of modern society's worst scourges—alcoholism and drug addiction. It turns out that after being forced to sit through an extreme Japanese horror movie, those participants who were instructed to control their emotions needed a stiff drink.[38] After filling out some bogus questionnaires, both groups were allowed to have as many beers as they liked as part of the reward for taking part in the study. The group that was forced to suppress their emotions drank half as much again as the group that was allowed to wear their hearts on their sleeves. The effect was massive. And it doesn't have to be extreme horror. Tearjerkers, like *Terms of Endearment*, also compel us to respond emotionally, but if we try to suppress our feelings this makes us vulnerable to temptations.

Field, along with a growing body of addiction experts, believe that self-control or willpower is a key component to understanding why some of us succumb to substance abuse after enduring stress. Whenever we exert self-control, it comes at a cost—a cost that makes us more susceptible to temptation later. This may be one of the reasons why so many of us give into behaviors that are potentially self-defeating. Most of us drink too much, eat too much, or engage in activities that we would prefer to avoid or at best limit.[39] And yet, most of us fail, despite our best intentions to control our behavior.

Roy Baumeister is a psychologist who believes in the concept of willpower and the reality of the self.[40] He does not think it is an illusion. Moreover, he thinks the self has three different components: the self as subjective awareness ("I"), the self as defined by relationships with others ("me"), and the self with the mental muscle power to make decisions and avoid temptation (executive functions). Whenever we succumb to the temptations we would rather avoid, Baumeister calls this "ego-depletion," as if the self has some kind of mental muscle that can become fatigued.[41]

With self-control, there is only so much effort you can allocate, and when this becomes depleted you become vulnerable to behaviors and thoughts that want to take over.

Ego-depletion can be induced in a number of different ways. It doesn't have to be by sitting through movies of extreme emotional or violent content. All sorts of experiences can deplete our ego strength, from enduring bad smells, tackling difficult puzzles, putting up with others in crowded situations, or even being electrocuted with an unpredictable mild shock.[42] The need to control and the possibility that our willpower is limited mean that we find it difficult to resist our urges afterward. We eat more junk food, drink more alcohol, spend more time looking at scantily clad members of the opposite sex[43] (especially if we are in a stable relationship and usually have to resist this temptation), and generally fail to control our self as much as we think we can or would like to.

Even when we do things that we think make us look more acceptable to others in the group, such as presenting oneself as competent and likeable to a hostile audience, we are still draining our egos of willpower.[44] That's why we always feel like a stiff drink after a job interview. When we just act like our selves, we are less stressed by these experiences. Even bosses feel it. Having to reprimand others or ostracize others when it is not in your nature to do so is ego-depleting.[45] In an attempt to fit in with others' expectations by changing how we present our self, we are creating unnecessary distortions of control that will come back to haunt us in moments of temptation. Adopting public personas that are at odds with our true emotional profiles may come at a cost. Individuals engage in behaviors that are the antithesis to their reputation, precisely because they are a rebound against the extreme positions that they are expected to maintain in public. Is this why politicians and judges seem to be routinely arrested for cruising for prostitutes?

Much of this sounds so obvious that one has to question whether you need to argue for some form of special mental muscle. Is it just another metaphor? Actually, Baumeister thinks not. He has shown that the brain needs to work out, to exert willpower, and this requires energy. Glucose is one of the brain's vital fuels, and Baumeister and his colleagues have shown that glucose levels are lowered during ego-depleting tasks.[46] In one experiment, adults had to have a discussion with a Hispanic interviewer about equal opportunities in which they had to avoid displaying any prejudice. Those who score highly on questionnaire-based measures of racism had lower blood sugar levels than did those who had no problem with interracial interactions. The good news is that you can reduce your ego-depletion. After drinking one of those sugary energy drinks, the glucose is absorbed into the bloodstream at a rate of 30 calories per minute and, after about 10 minutes, can be metabolized to feed the brain. Compared to those who had been given an artificially sweetened drink, those who had a sugary drink were much more able to deal with stress. In one of their experiments, adults were asked read words about death. This is usually ego-depleting as it has a negative effect on adults' subsequent ability to solve a later word puzzle task. However, not for those hyped up on a sugary drink. Reading about death did not affect their performance at all. Maybe that's why we should order the extra large sugary Coke at the cinema if we are going to see horror movies like *Audition*.

All of this means that much of our efforts of self-control may be misguided. Most of us want to diet, but what do we do? We resist the temptation of that first chocolate only to find that the craving is even greater. Reducing our caloric intake with the initial chocolate reduces our blood sugar and makes us more susceptible to ego-depletion later. It's a vicious circle. Even if you manage to skip a meal, you may find your self gorging on alcohol or cigarettes or some other vice. Even moderation must be done in moderation.

■ Bladder Control

In an extension of his muscle metaphor, Baumeister believes you can exercise your willpower to improve your self-control. For example, he found that by getting students to monitor and control their posture over 2 weeks, they were much better on experiments that measured self-control compared to those allowed to lounge around. Or, you might consider the power stance. Simply broadening your shoulders and clenching your fists gives you more will-power[47] and increases testosterone levels in both men and women.[48] Like the effects of forcing a smile, merely simulating body postures and actions can elicit the corresponding biological changes and mental states that usually trigger them in the first place.[49]

Another important key to success appears to depend on changing routines. Much of the problem of temptation stems from the habitual behaviors that we develop. It is much easier to give in to a set of behaviors than to create a new set. We are literally creatures of habit, and so we easily fall into cycles of behavior that seem difficult to break. If you really want to change your behavior, then don't try to make your self stop. This strategy will only rebound and make you more vulnerable. Instead, find an alternative to replace the activity. Not only does this provide a different scenario to occupy your activity, but it avoids the curse of ego-depletion.

Otherwise, you could simply practice holding your bladder and not going to the toilet. Mirjam Tuk found that after she drank several cups of coffee to stay awake during a long lecture, toward the end, she was bursting to go but had to wait. She wondered if all the mental effort she recruited to avoid an embarrassing accident could be used to suppress other urges. In one of her studies,[50] participants drank 5 cups of water (about 750 milliliters) and then, after about 40 minutes, the time it takes the water to reach the bladder, gave them an adult delay-of-gratification task. They could choose a cash reward of $16, which would be given to them on the following day, or $30 in 35 days. In comparison to those who had not drunk the water, more of the participants who were bursting to go held out for the larger reward. Tuk even suggests that any type of financial decision-making might benefit from increased bladder control. While these findings seem to go against the ego-depletion account, Tuk thinks the difference might be explained by the fact that bladder control is largely under automatic unconscious processes, whereas ego-depletion is more cognitive. It remains to be seen how this story plays out in children, but I think it is very unlikely that we will be attempting such studies with children in our laboratory—I mean, can you imagine the mess to clean up?

■ A Kid in the Candy Store

Remarkable though the ego-depletion research is, one does not need to evoke a core self at the helm of our decision processes and behaviors. Each of the experiments and findings can equally be described not so much as the ego under pressure but rather as the shift in balance between all the external things that compete for activity. It certainly helps to evoke the self illusion in these situations because it provides us with a protagonist who fails to live up to expectations and ideals. Like a kid in a candy store, we see temptation all around us but maintain that the self is the one being tempted into making the decisions and choices. What if it is the other way around? What if there is a kid who likes different types of candy but each different candy competes for his attention? Each candy that pulls the kid closer is offset by yet another more delicious one that looms into view. Now the decisions and choices are not within the kid but reflect the relative strengths of everything out there that jostles for attention. Certainly, there is a kid being tempted in this candy store metaphor, but we are mistaken in locating decisions within the child. The same goes for free will.

Ego depletion sounds like it involves some form of self, does it not? So does the self-control when avoiding eating the marshmallow. Who is making decisions and avoiding temptation if not the self? In his book, *The Ego Trick*, philosopher Julian Baggini points out that it is impossible to talk about the mental processes and behaviors of a person without invoking the ego approach.[51] We find it difficult to imagine how decisions and behaviors could equally arise without a self. For example, we often hear that addicts cannot control themselves, but is that really true? Are they totally at the mercy of the drugs and behaviors that ruin their lives? No one is denying that addiction is a really difficult problem to overcome, but even the addict can avoid drugs if some immediate consequence looms larger. Few addicts would take that next drink or inject that drug if a gun was placed to their foreheads. Clearly, in these situations, the imminent threat of death trumps so-called uncontrollable urges. They are only uncontrollable in some contexts in which the competing influences do not match up to the allure of intoxication. The problem for addicts, then, is that the negative consequences of their behaviors do not match up to the immediate gratification that their addictions provide.[52] They would prefer to not be addicted but that requires prolonged abstention, which is more difficult. When we talk about choices made by individuals, there are multiple influences and drives that compete for those decisions. Many of these arise from external circumstances.

Even if the self and our ability to exercise free will is an illusion, not all is lost. In fact, beliefs seem to produce consequences in our behavior. The ego-depletion we have just described appears to only work in those individuals who believe that willpower is a limited resource.[53] In other words, if we think that our self-control is limited, then we show ego-depletion. If we don't believe in limited self-control, we don't.

Beliefs about self-control, from wherever they may derive, are powerful motivators of human behavior. For example, consider 10-year-old children who were told that their performance on a test was either due to their natural intelligence or their ability to work hard.[54] Both sets were then given a really difficult second task that was well beyond their capability, which no one could complete. However, in a third test, the children who thought their initial successes on the first task were due to their intelligence also gave up more easily because they attributed their failure on the second task to their limited natural ability, which made them less likely to persevere on the last task. In contrast, children who thought their performance was all down to hard work not only stuck longer on the third task, but also enjoyed it more. So it's better to tell your kids that they are hard workers rather than simply smart.

The same can be said for free will. When we believe that we are the masters of our own destiny, we behave differently than those who deny the existence of free will and believe everything is determined. This has been studied experimentally using priming. *Priming* is a way of changing our mindset by manipulating the sorts of information we are made to focus on. (Again, this is a strong indicator that our self is influenced by what we are exposed to!) Half the adults were primed to think in a determinist way by reading stories that refuted the existence of free will such as, "Ultimately, we are biological computers—designed by evolution, built through genetics, and programmed by the environment." The remaining adults read free will endorsing statements such as, "I am able to override the genetic and environmental factors that sometimes influence my behavior." Adults who were primed to reject free will were much more likely to cheat on an arithmetic exam and overpaid themselves with greater rewards than did adults who read the free will endorsements.[55]

To most of us, the absence of free will is tantamount to a determinism that sounds pretty much like fatalism—no matter what you do, you can't change things. That's a pretty demoralizing outlook on life that is bound to undermine any motivation to do anything. Maybe that's why belief in free will predicts not only better job performance but also expected career success.[56] Workers who believe in free will outperform their colleagues, and this is recognized and rewarded by their supervisors. So, when we believe in free will, we enjoy life more.

The moral of the tale is that, even if free will doesn't exist, then maybe it is best to ignore what the neuroscientists or philosophers say. Sometimes ignorance is bliss. The very act of believing means that you change the way you behave in ways that will benefit you. And the main reason this is true is that not only is it important for our self-motivation, but also for how others view us. We like people who are decisive because we believe they are positive and driven, and that makes most of us feel more comfortable than does someone who can't seem to reach a decision.

Finally, just because something doesn't really exist doesn't mean that believing that it does is pointless. Fantasy doesn't really exist but the world would be a much more impoverished place without storytelling. Also, you cannot readily abandon the belief. As the one who has done the most to identify the Great Selfini, Wegner wrote, "If the illusion could be dispelled by explanation, I should be some kind of robot by now." You cannot escape the self illusion.

5 ■
Why Our Choices Are Not Our Own

The point at which we feel that we are making a decision is often well after the fact, and yet it seems as if we were responsible in advance of making our choice. How we make decisions can also rely more on those around us than we realize, and we might not necessarily be the ones in charge. We may feel like we are making our own personal choices, but in many instances these are actually controlled by external influences of which we may not even be aware.

This is something advertisers have long known. Since the very first advertisements appeared in ancient Babylonia, vendors have realized that it pays to let people know the name of what you are selling.[1] Our choices can be greatly influenced by what we are told, even though we may not be fully aware of this. In the 20th century, it was thought that subtle marketing was the way forward to manipulate peoples' choices. For example, in the 1950s, cinema owners thought they could make the audience buy more drinks and popcorn by splicing single frames of pictures of products—too brief to be detected consciously—into the movie. The idea was that such subliminal images would register in the unconscious, leading the audience to think that they wanted to visit the foyer to purchase a soft drink: the advertisements could activate our minds below conscious awareness, making them even more potent. However, the scientific evidence for subliminal marketing is at best equivocal.[2] Subtle messages do indeed shape our thoughts and behaviors, but when it comes to selling a soda drink, big, in-your-face advertising is best. This is why advertising sponsorship is so lucrative. Companies are prepared to spend large amounts of money just to get their brand in front of you because they know that people prefer a name they have heard over one they have not. Given the choice between different brands, people reliably choose the one they recognize or that seems familiar.[3]

Of course, not every decision comes down to a personal consumer choice, especially when we are asked about things of which we have no knowledge. Sometimes the decision can be so important that we seek out confirmation and support from others, especially those we perceive to be experts, such as medical doctors. We may be offered a choice in treatments, but most of us prefer the doctor to tell us what to do because we think she knows best. Yet, in many instances of our day-to-day experience, we generally assume that, given a simple informed choice, we can apply some internal process of evaluation and then, like a judge, we make our pronouncement.

This is wrong because the processes that weigh our choices are unconscious. It may feel like you have reached your decision in the open courtroom of your mind but, in fact, most of the important stuff has been going on behind closed doors. You may be able consciously to consider choices as potential scenarios and then try to imagine what the choice would mean, but the information that is being supplied has already been processed, evaluated, and weighed up well before you have had time to consider what you will do. It's like when you say, "I've just had a great idea!" It seems instantaneous, but no light bulb suddenly went off in your head. It may have felt like a sudden enlightenment, but the boys in the backroom had been developing the idea all along and simply presented you with their analysis. Like Libet's experiment, no single point in time marks the difference between knowing and not knowing when you are about to act. Even if you deliberate over an idea, turning it over in your conscious mind, you are simply delaying the final decision that has, to all intents and purposes, already been made.

None of this is new. We have known since the days of psychology's early pioneers—von Helmholtz and more famously Freud—that there are unconscious processes controlling our thoughts and behaviors.[4] What is new is the extent to which these processes are there to protect the self illusion—the narrative we create that we are the ones making the decisions. This stems from the need to maintain the appearance that we are in control, even when we are not. We are so concerned with maintaining the illusion of the sovereignty of self that we are prepared to argue that black is white just to prove that we are right.

This is why we effortlessly and sometimes unknowingly reinterpret our behavior to make it seem that we had deliberately made the choices all along. We are constantly telling stories to make sense of our selves. In one study, adults were shown pairs of female faces and asked to choose which was the more attractive of the two women.[5] On some trials, immediately after making their choice, the card with the picture of the chosen woman was held up and the participants were asked to explain why they had chosen her over the other. Was it her hairstyle or color of her eyes? The cunning aspect of the study was that, on some of the trials, the experimenter used sleight of hand to switch the cards deliberately, so that participants were asked to justify a choice they hadn't made—to support the choice of the woman who they had actually just rejected. Not only were most switches undetected, but participants went on to give perfectly lucid explanations for why the woman was so much more attractive than the one they rejected. They were unaware that their choice was not their choice. It works for taste tests as well. When shoppers were asked to sample different jams and teas at a Swedish super-market, again the researchers switched the products after the shoppers had selected the flavors they preferred and were asked to describe why they chose one flavor over another. Whether it was a switch from spicy cinnamon apple to sour grape jam, or from sweet mango to pungent Pernod-flavored tea, the shoppers detected less than a third of the switches.[6] It would seem that, once we have made a preference, we are committed to justifying our decision.

This shows just how easy it is to fool our selves into thinking that our self is in control. As Steven Pinker[7] put it, "The conscious mind—the self or soul—is a spin doctor, not the commander-in-chief." Having been presented with a decision, we then make sense of it as if it were our own. Otherwise, it would suggest that we don't know what we are doing, which is not something that most of us would readily admit.

■ Sour Grapes

That we can so readily justify our choices is at the heart of one of the ancient world's best-known stories about our necessity to spin a story. One day, a hungry fox came across a bunch of grapes that hung high on a vine but, despite repeated leaping attempts to reach them, the fox was unable to dislodge the grapes. Defeated, he left saying that he did not want them anyway because they were sour. He had changed his mind. Whenever we talk disparagingly about something that we initially wanted but did not get, we are said to be displaying "sour grapes." It's very common. How often have we all done this when faced with the prospect of loss? Consider all those job interviews that you failed to get. Remember those dates that went disastrously wrong, or the competition you entered and lost? We console our selves with the excuse that we did not want the job anyway, the other person was a jerk, or that we were not really trying to win. We may even focus on the negative aspects of being offered the job, getting a kiss, or winning the competition. But we are conning our selves. Why do we do this?

Who would have thought that a Greek slave born over 2,500 years ago would have produced some of the most enduring commentaries on the human condition through his storytelling, which preempted recent theories in cognitive science? Remarkably, Aesop's fables about animals behaving like humans endure not only because they are immediately accessible metaphors for the vagaries of human behavior, but they also speak to fundamental truths. In the case of the fox and the sour grapes, Aesop is describing *cognitive dissonance*—one of the major psychological mechanisms discovered and researched over the last 50 years that has generated an estimated 3,000 plus studies.

Cognitive dissonance, a term coined by Leon Festinger in 1957, is the process of self-justification whereby we defend our actions and thoughts when they turn out to be wrong or, as in the case of sour grapes, ineffectual.[8] We interpret our failure to attain a goal as actually turning out to be a good thing because, with hindsight, we reinterpret the goal as not really desirable. Otherwise, we are faced with the prospect that we have wasted a lot of work and effort to no avail. This discrepancy creates the cognitive dissonance. It's a dissonance because, on the one hand, we believe that we are generally pretty successful at attaining our goals. On the other hand, we were unsuccessful at achieving this particular goal. This is the dissonance aspect of our reasoning—the unpleasant mental discomfort we experience. To avoid the conflict this dissonance creates, we reinterpret our failure as a success. We tell our selves that the goal was actually not in our best interests. Job done—no worries.

Freud similarly talked about *defence mechanisms* that we use to protect the self illusion. However, the self illusion sometimes has to reconcile incongruent thoughts and behaviors. For example, I may consider myself to be a good person but then have bad thoughts about someone. That is inconsistent with my good self story so I employ defence mechanisms. I may rationalize my thoughts by saying that the person is actually bad, and I am justified in my negative attitude toward them. Perversely, I may do the opposite and go out of my way to think of them positively as a compensation for my unconscious negativity, in what Freud called *reaction formation*. Or I may project my negative feelings about a person onto their pet dog, and blame the poor mutt for my reasons of dislike, when it is actually his owner I despise. All of these are examples of why we try to reframe the unpleasant feelings that we have toward someone in order to maintain our valued sense of self—a self that is not unduly or unfairly judgmental of others.

It is worth pointing out that not only can justification happen at the level of the self, it can also happen at the level of groups. Probably the best recent example is the justification for the Iraq War on the basis of the alleged threat from weapons of mass destruction (WMDs). The British general public was told that Saddam Hussein had missiles that could reach the mainland within the infamous 45-minute warning. The nation was shocked. Despite repeated assurance by United Nations inspection teams that there was no evidence for such WMDs, we were told that they were there and that we had to invade. After the invasion,

and once it was clear that there were no WMDs, the insti-
gators had to justify their actions. We were told that the
invasion was necessary on the grounds that Saddam
Hussein was an evil dictator who needed to be removed
from power, even though such regime change was in viola-
tion of international law. We were told that if he did not
have WMDs before, then he was planning on making them.
The invasion was justified. We had been saved. It would
appear that modern politicians do not need a thick skin so
much as a carefully crafted capacity for mass cognitive
dissonance.

Cognitive dissonance protects the self from conflicting
stories and is at the heart of why the self illusion is so
important, but it also reveals the dangers that a strong sense
of self can create. We use it to justify faulty reasoning.
Although we do not appreciate it, our decision-making is
actually the constellation of many processes vying for attention and in constant conflict. We fail to consider just how
much of our decision-making is actually out of our control.

■ The Monty Hall Problem

There are essentially two problems with decision-making:
either we ignore external information and focus on our
own perspective, or we fail to realize the extent to which
our own perspective is actually determined by external
influences. In both cases, we are fools to believe that our
self is making decisions independent of the external context. This can lead to some wondrous distortions of human
reason.

Consider an egocentric bias that blinds us to important
changes in the world when it comes to decision-making. If
you have not already heard of it, then let me introduce you
to the Monty Hall problem. The problem is named after the
presenter of the American game show, *Let's Make a Deal*,

where the climax was to choose a prize from behind one of three doors. Try to imagine your self in this situation. You have made it all the way through to the final part of the show and have a chance of winning the jackpot. Behind two doors are booby prizes, but behind one door is a fabulous prize. For the sake of argument, let's say that it is an expensive Ferrari. You hesitate initially and then choose door A. The host of the show, Monty, says, "You chose door A, but let me show you what's behind door C." He then opens door C to reveal one of the booby prizes. Monty says, "You chose door A initially, but do you want to change your decision to door B?" What should you do? Most people who encounter this problem for the very first time think that it makes no difference, because they reason that it is a 50–50 chance to win the Ferrari with only two doors left to chose from. Indeed, people are reluctant to change their minds once they have made a choice. Some may say that we stubbornly stick with our decisions because we have the courage of our conviction. After all, it is important to be decisive.

What do you think you should do—switch or stick? If you don't already know, the correct answer is to switch, but if you don't know why, it is incredibly hard to understand. The Monty Hall problem has become a somewhat famous cognitive illusion appearing both in bestselling books and even in the Hollywood movie 21 (2008), about a bunch of mathematically minded Massachusetts Institute of Technology students who counted cards at the blackjack tables of Las Vegas to beat the casinos. The correct solution to the Monty Hall problem is to switch because you are more likely to win than if you stick with your first choice. It is difficult to see at first and when it initially appeared in the popular magazine, *Parade*, in 1990, the problem created a storm of controversy and disagreement among both the general public and experts. Over 10,000 people (1,000 with doctoral degrees) wrote in complaining that the switch decision was false!

The reason you should switch is that, when you first choose a door, you have a chance of one out of three that you are correct. Now, after Monty has revealed one of the booby prizes, with two doors left, the remaining that you did not select has a two out of three chance, which is better odds than the door that you first chose, which remains as one out of three. Remember, Monty always shows you an empty door. Simple—except that it is not simple for most people.

An easier way to solve the Monty Hall problem is to consider a variation in which there are 100 doors instead of three.[9] Again, you get to pick one door. Now Monty opens 98 out of the remaining 99 doors to show you that they are all empty. There are now only two remaining unopened doors. Would you switch now? Here, we can see that our door is unlikely to be the correct one. What are the odds that I correctly selected the right door on my first chance? Actually, it's odds of 100:1 to be precise. That's why we immediately twig that Monty is up to no good. There is something deeply counterintuitive about the Monty Hall problem, which reflects our limited capacity to think outside of the box—or to be more precise, to think in an unselfish way.

Another reason that people fail to switch in the Monty Hall problem is a general bias not to tempt fate. When it comes to making decisions, inherently we fear loss greater than we value the prospect of a win. Despite the so-called rationality of the modern era, people still think that if they change their decision, then there is more chance that they will regret doing so. It's not so much stubbornness or superstition but rather that we fear loss greater than the potential for gains. For example, the social psychologist Ellen Langer sold $1 lottery tickets to 53 office workers. Each stub of the ticket was put into a box from which one lucky winner would receive the whole $53. Just before the lottery-draw a couple of days later, Ellen approached each worker and asked each person for how much he would sell his ticket. If they had just been handed a ticket by the experimenter so they had exercised no choice, the average price for resale was $2, but if they had chosen the ticket themselves it was $8! Moreover, ten of the choosers and five of the nonchoosers refused to sell their ticket.[10] It turns out that it is the fear of regret that looms large in our minds. How many times have you deliberated over an expensive purchase only to hear the salesperson reassure you, "Go on, you'll not regret it!"

■ Risky Analysis

What the Monty Hall problem illustrates so clearly is the limitations of human reasoning—especially when it comes to probability. Probability is all about external information. Reasoning in terms of probable outcomes is very difficult because most of us think in a very self-centered way. We make decisions from our own perspective and often fail to take into consideration the external information that is most relevant.

In fact, most complex science is based on probabilities and not absolute known truths about the universe. After the age of Newton and the scientific revolution of the 17th century, it was assumed that the universe was one big clockwork mechanism that could be understood by measurement and prediction. It was thought that if we improved the accuracy of our measurements, then we would understand better how the universe worked. The opposite happened. The universe became more complex. With increasing efficiency, we discovered that the universe was much messier than we had previously imagined. There was more noise in the system and less certainty. This noise gave birth to the age of statistical modeling, in which mathematicians tried to discover the workings of the universe using procedures that accounted, as best as possible, for all the variation that was observed. This is why the language of science is mathematics and its truths are based on probabilities.[11]

Unfortunately, statistical analysis is not natural for the average man in the street. Our bodies and brains, for that matter, may operate in statistically predictable ways, but few of us explicitly understand statistical principles. This is why the general audience gets so frustrated when they hear scientists in the media refusing to give a straight "yes" or "no" answer to the questions that concern them. They want to know what to do about global warming, the dangers associated with childhood vaccination, or how to prevent pandemic viruses. When answering, scientists talk in terms of probabilities rather than absolute certainties because they look at the big picture, in which they know there is going to be some variation. That's not what the general public wants to hear. They want to know whether vaccination will harm their children. They are less interested in the group because that is not the way individuals think.

The other problem with probability is that humans have not evolved to consider likelihood based on large amounts of data. Rather, we operate with *heuristics*—fast and dirty rules of thumb that generally serve us well. The German psychologist Gerd Gigerenzer has argued that humans have not evolved to work out probabilities such as those operating in the Monty Hall problem.[12] We focus on the task as relevant to our self, and how it applies on an individual basis rather than on populations of people. We tend to only evaluate our own choices, not what is best for the group. Faced with two doors, my chances seem even. It's only when I am faced with two doors a hundred times, or a hundred different people take the Monty Hall challenge, that the patterns become obvious.

We often do not know the true incidence of an event but rather guess at this figure based on whatever evidence we can accumulate. This is where all sorts of distortions in reasoning start to appear. In weighing up the evidence, we easily overestimate or underestimate risks based on the external information. For example, people's naïve estimates related to dying in airplane crashes are inflated because we tend to judge the occurrence of such events as more common than they truly are. These are called *dread risks*, and they attract more salience because they are so uncommon. It's not surprising considering the dramatic coverage such tragedies generate. We focus on them and imagine what it must be like to die in such a helpless way. We attach more weight to these thoughts than we should because they are novel and draw our attention.

This inaccurate risk assessment can be potentially dangerous because we may be tempted to change our behavior patterns based on faulty reasoning. For example, an analysis of road traffic accidents for cars travelling to New York in the 3 months following 9/11 showed an increase in fatalities over expected numbers for that time of year in the build-up to Christmas.[13] In fact, the excess number was greater than the total number of airline passengers killed on that fateful day. Individuals frightened of flying to New York overestimated their risk and took to their cars instead, which led to heavier than usual traffic and the subsequent increase in road accidents. The most likely reason that people felt it was safer to drive was based on another illusion of the self, the illusion of control. We believe that we are safer when we think we are in control of our fate, such as when driving our own car, but feel unhappy when we are being driven by others or, worse still, flown around in a metal cylinder that can fall out of the sky, irrespective of what we do.

■ Analysis Paralysis

Much of the time, our risk analysis is based on the perception of choice—can we get out of a sticky situation? It is often assumed that choice is good—that decision-making makes us happier if we are allowed to exercise some self-control. Most of us feel safer when we drive. When faced with the prospect of not being able to help our selves out of a situation, we become despondent, depressed, and helpless. Information on this reaction to the lack of control is based on experiments during the 1960s, in which animals were put through stressful situations.[14] In one study, two sets of dogs were given electric shocks. One set of dogs could terminate the pain by learning to press a lever. The other set of dogs were yoked to the first group, but did not have the option to press a lever and so received the same amount of shocks. To them, there was nothing they could do to stop the pain because they had no choice.

After these initial experiences, both sets of dogs were then placed in a shuttle box with two sides separated by a short barrier. Again electric shocks were applied to the floor of the cage, but this time both sets animals could avoid the pain by leaping the barrier to the other safe side of the box. What they discovered was very disturbing. Dogs that had experienced control in the first study with the lever readily learned to avoid the pain, but dogs that had not been able to avoid the electric shocks in the first study failed to jump the barrier to avoid punishment. They simply lay down on the cage floor whimpering and resigned to their torture. According to Martin Seligman, the psychologist who conducted this research, the animals had "learned helplessness."

It is not easy to read about this sort of animal experimentation in a detached way. I am not a great animal lover, but I think I would have found such research difficult to conduct. Nevertheless, these studies on inducing learned helplessness have proved invaluable in understanding factors that contribute to human misery and depression.[15] Depression is probably one of the most common debilitating mental disorders. We have all had some experience of feeling low, but clinical depression is a pervasive illness that prevents people from leading a normal life. It can vary in its intensity, with behavioral and psychological symptoms usually related to feelings of worthlessness and despondency. It is commonly associated with other problems, most notably stressful life events such as bereavement, unemployment, and addiction, although there is much individual variation. Some of us are more predisposed to depression because it is a complex disorder that has genetic, biological, psychological, and social components.

Not all depression is the same in its origins, but it is statistically more common among the poor and deprived in our society.[16] One theory is that it is not so much that poverty is the root cause but rather the circumstances that having no wealth entails—the inability of individuals to do anything about their lives. Like the inescapable shocks to the dogs, people learn helplessness, which leads to the negative fatalism that things can never get better. The obvious solution is to empower people with choices. Some would argue that this is what wealth really brings—the opportunity to make choices and not be shackled to a life you can't escape. If nothing changes no matter what you do, you have the basics for despair. The need for control appears to be fairly important for both physical and mental health.

Simply believing that you have the power to change your life makes it more bearable.[17] This is one reason why Liz Murray's "Homeless to Harvard" story offers such hope. We also saw this with free will when we learned that people develop rituals and routines because these behaviors give the illusion of control when in fact there is none. Giving people choices, or at least the perception of control, empowers them to tolerate more adversity. For example, people will tolerate more pain if they think they can turn it off at any moment even when they have no control over the stimulus. Perceived control attenuates the pain centers of the brain.[18] We even enjoy our meal more if is there is choice on the menu.[19] These sorts of findings support a generally held view that choice is good, and the more choices you have, the better. It's a principle that modern societies exhibit through conspicuous consumerism. However, this is only true up to a point. Sometimes you can have so much choice that it can overwhelm the self.

Once again, Aesop knew this in his fable of the fox and the cat. Faced with the impending pack of savage hunting dogs bearing down on them, the fox and the cat had to escape. For the cat, this was a very easy decision to make as she bolted up a tree. However, the fox, with all his cunning know-how of the many ways he could escape, became paralyzed by indecision and fell prey to the savage hounds. Faced with too many choices, the fox had analysis paralysis.

The same problem confronts us every day. The "paradox of choice," as the psychologist Barry Schwartz calls it, is that the more choices we are given, the less free we become because we procrastinate in trying to make the best decision.[20] The whole modern world has gone choice crazy! For example, in his supermarket, Schwartz counted 285 different varieties of cookies, 75 iced teas, 230 soups, 175 salad dressings, and 40 different toothpastes. Any modern electrical appliance store is packed to the brim with so many different models with different features and functionality that we become swamped by indecision.

How many times have you gone to buy something from a large supplier only to leave empty-handed because you could not make a decision? We are so worried that we may make the wrong choice that we try to compare the different products along dimensions that we have not even considered relevant before we entered the store. Do I need it Bluetooth enabled? What about the RAM? What about wi-fi? The majority of us who are not nerds find this overload of choice too much. Presented with so many options, we are unable to process the decisions efficiently. This leads to the sort of procrastination that makes us put off things that we really should do now.

Every spring, I have students who come to me to make a decision about what to undertake in their final-year research project, and they always say that they will make a start and get the bulk of it done over the summer. Certainly they all believe that they will have it ready by Christmas, before the deadline in March. And yet, not one student has ever achieved this. There is always a catalogue of reasons why they never got round to do the work until the last moment, despite all their best intentions. As the English poet Edward Young (1683–1765) observed, "Procrastination is the thief of time." With all the choices available and other temptations that present themselves, we put off what we should do now until it is too late.

All this work on decision-making should clearly tell you that our self is at the mercy of the choices with which we are presented. Our capacity for decision-making is dependent on the context. If there are too many choices, then the alternatives cancel each other out and we are left with indecision. Even when we do make a decision, we are less happy because we dwell on whether we made the right choice. If we had no choice, then there is no problem and the world is to blame. But then we get depressed. However, if we chose something that does not turn out to be ideal, then that is our fault for not choosing wisely. It's often a no-win situation.

■ Relativity in the Brain

Dan Ariely is a behavioral economist from Duke University who makes the argument that humans are not only poor at risk analysis but they are, in fact, predictably irrational.[21] This occurred to him when he was browsing the web and found an ad for magazine subscriptions to the

Economist, which had three yearly options: one, online-only at $59; two, print-only at $125; and, three, online and print for $125.

Clearly, the best offer was option three, where you get both online and print versions for the same price as just the print version alone. When he tested this offer on his students, he found that 84% said they would choose option three and 16% would choose option one. No one chose option two. You'd have to be crazy to choose only the print version when you could also have the online version for no extra cost. But this was a deliberate strategy by the *Economist* to make option three look more attractive by comparing it with a decoy. When Ariely removed option two and gave them the choice again, this time 68% chose option one and only 32% went with option three. The decoy had distorted the student's sense of value. Notice how easily the decision was swayed by the context.

Ariely points out that this is the problem of relativity—humans do not make judgments in absolute values but rather in relative terms. We are always weighing up the costs and benefits of different choices, and we estimate values accordingly. This also explains why people tend not to choose the cheapest or most expensive option, but the one in the middle. The top price is really a decoy. This strategy is sometimes known as the Goldilocks effect, after the fairy tale of the little girl who discovers that she prefers the porridge that is not too hot and not too cold. The preference for the midrange price is why retailers often have an expensive option to increase the likelihood of customers choosing a product that costs less but is not the cheapest. Relativity in decision-making reveals that we do not have an internal value meter that tells us how much things are worth. Rather, our decisions are shaped by the external context.

Relativity does not just apply in economic decision-making but is, in fact, a fundamental principle of how our brains operate. Everything we experience is a relative process. When something seems hotter, louder, brighter, smellier, or sweeter, that experience is one of relative judgment. Every change in the environment registers as a change in neural activity. At the very basic level of neural connections, this is registered as the relative change in the rate of impulses firing. In the early experiments in which scientists recorded the electrical activity of a single neuron, they inserted an electrode to measure the electrical impulses of the cell and played it through loudspeakers. When inactive, one could hear the occasional click of the background activity of the neuron as the occasional impulse was triggered. However, as soon as some stimulus was presented that excited the neuron, the clicks would register like the rapid fire of a Gatling gun.

This is how our brains interpret the world. When a change in the environment occurs, there is a relative increase or decrease in the rate at which the neurons fire, which is how intensity is coded. Furthermore, relativity operates to calibrate our sensations. For example, if you place one hand in hot water and the other in iced water for some time before immersing them both into lukewarm water, you will experience conflicting sensations of temperature because of the relative change in the receptors registering hot and cold. Although both hands are now in the same water, one feels that it is colder and the other feels warmer because of the relative change from prior experience. This process, called *adaptation*, is one of the organizing principles operating throughout the central nervous system. It explains why you can't see well inside a dark room if you have come in from a sunny day. Your eyes have to become accustomed to the new level of luminance. Adaptation explains why apples taste sour after eating sweet chocolate and why traffic seems louder in the city if you normally live in the country. In short, all of the experiences we have are relative.

In fact, your sense of happiness and achievement is based on how you compare your self to others. Ariely cites the observation by the American satirist H. L. Mencken that a man is satisfied so long as he is earning more than his brother-in-law. I expect this holds true for sisters-in-law as well because relatives are the closest individuals with whom we can compare our fortunes. Relativity also explains why people become discontented when they learn that their colleagues earn a higher salary. Industrial disputes are less about wages and more about what others in the company are earning in comparison. When we discovered what the bankers were earning during the recent financial crisis, the general public was outraged. The bankers could not see the problem with their high salaries and bonuses because they were comparing themselves to other bankers who were prospering.

■ Remembered Selves

If relativity is all that we can ever know, then this means that our self is defined by the values against which it is matched. Even our remembered self—what we were like in the past—is a relative decision. Nobel Prize-winner Daniel Kahneman similarly draws the distinction between two different versions of the self, the *experiencing self* and the *remembered self*.[22] The experiencing self is the subjective experience of conscious awareness living in the present. Kahneman thinks that we all have such moments of the experiencing self that last on average for about 3 seconds. He estimates that we have about 600,000 such moments in a month and 600 million in a lifetime, but once these moments have passed, they are lost forever.

In contrast, the remembered self is our memory of our past experiencing self. These moments are integrated into a story that we keep in memory. However, as discussed, human memory is not etched in stone but rather is actively constructed as a story that is retold. This story is a relative one. For example, in a series of studies looking at the pain associated with colonoscopy, Kahneman and colleagues asked patients to report their experiences every 60 seconds. This was the experiencing self—the moments of self-aware-ness that constitute the conscious moments of everyday experience. Kahneman was interested in how patients would recall unpleasant experiences that either ended abruptly in pain or mild discomfort. In half of the group, the tip of the colonoscope was left in their rectums for 3 minutes, which lengthened the duration of the procedure but meant that the final moments were less painful. After the colonoscopy, patients were asked to rate their experi-ences. The group who had the longer procedure that ended in less pain rated their experiences more positively than the group who had a shorter procedure. The relatively painless ending left a lasting impression of the whole experience.[23]

It would appear that we are more sensitive to the begin-nings and endings of experience, and remember them rather than what goes on in between. This has been shown in hundreds of memory experiments in which individuals are asked to remember long lists of items. It turns out that we are more likely to remember items at the beginning of the list, called the *primacy effect*, and items at the end, called the *recency effect*. It's not that we get bored in between but rather that items at the start have the relative advantage of novelty. Items at the end are less likely to be forgotten because subsequent items do not overwrite them in mem-ory. In short, the beginning and end demarcate the dura-tion of the experience, which is what we note. This is why it is always better to be either the first or the last to be interviewed for a job because the first and the last candi-date benefit from primacy and recency effects. These effects of being at the beginning or the end of an experience show that we are more sensitive to the relative changes in our lives. Kahneman argues that these effects explain why we are so poor at evaluating our selves during periods of stability in our lives. For example, we think that we are happier on vacations, but, in reality, most of us are happier at work. Because everything is relative, we focus on transitions in life rather than on the continuities where there is little change.

■ Hot Heads

External events influence our choices in ways that seem to be somewhat out of our control. But what of the internal conflicts inside our heads? The self is a constructed web of interacting influences competing for control. To live our lives in society, we need to inhibit or suppress disruptive impulses, thoughts, and urges. The drives of fleeing, fighting, feeding, and fornicating are constantly vying for attention in situations when they are not appropriate. What of our reasoning and control when we submit to these urges? It turns out that the self-story we tell our selves can become radically distorted.

In what must be one of the most controversial studies of late, Dan Ariely wanted to investigate how our attitudes change when we are sexually aroused.[24] First, he asked male students to rate their attitudes to a variety of issues related to sex. For example, would they engage in unprotected sex, spanking, group sex, and sex with animals? Would they have sex with someone they did not like or with a woman over 60? He even asked them whether they would consider spiking a woman's drink with drugs so that she would have sex with them.

In the cold light of day, these men answered absolutely no way would they engage in these immoral acts. These were upstanding males who valued women and had standards of behavior. Ariely then gave them $10, a copy of *Playboy* magazine, and a computer laptop protectively wrapped so that they could answer the same questions again with one hand, while they masturbated with the other in the privacy of their dorm rooms. When they were sexually aroused something monstrous happened. These men were turned into animals by their passion. Ariely discovered these student Dr. Jekylls turned into veritable Mr. Hydes when left alone to pleasure themselves. They were twice as likely to say that they would engage in dubious sexual activities when they were sexually aroused. More worrying, there was a fourfold increase in the likelihood that they would drug a woman for sex! Clearly, when males are thinking with their "little brain," they tumble from their moral high ground, which they can usually maintain when they are in a nonaroused state. As Ariely put it, "Prevention, protection, conservatism and morality disappeared completely from their radar screen." It was if they were a different person.

We Are What We Have

It's not just our natural drives that are susceptible to impulsivity. To that list we need to add the modern pastime of shopping. Shopping has no obvious evolutionary imperative and yet, in the West, it is often reported as an addictive behavior. There are even Shopaholics Anonymous groups, similar to the more established Alcoholics Anonymous, to help people overcome their psychological need to buy things. I am not personally a shopaholic but I have occasionally made that impulsive purchase that I would not normally make—very often egged on by others. In my case, these have been esoteric objects or art that I think I should own. But why? What is it about owning possessions that gives us a psychological buzz?

I think that objects are a reflection of our self, or at least a perceived notion of how we would like to be seen by others. William James was one of the first psychologists to understand the importance of objects to humans as a reflection of their notion of self, when he wrote, "A man's Self is the sum total of all that he CAN call his, not only his body and his psychic powers, but his clothes and his house, his wife and children, his ancestors and friends, his reputation and works, his lands and horses, and yacht and bank-account."[25]

Objects serve an important function as ostensive markers for self-identity. When we take possession of objects they become "mine"—my coffee cup, my Nikes, my telephone. This obsession with ownership can be traced to early childhood.[26] In our labs, we found that many preschoolers had formed an emotional attachment to sentimental objects, such as blankets and teddy bears, and would not readily accept an identical replacement.[27] Many of these children would grow up into adults who would become emotionally distressed just at the thought of destroying their beloved ragbag. We know this because we wired adults up to a machine that measures arousal and found that they got anxious when they had to cut up a photograph of the object of their childhood attachment. Myself and colleagues have recently created a series of brain imaging studies in which we show adults videos of their objects being blown up, driven over, axed, chainsawed, and jumped on. A brain scanner reveals the different regions of the brain that are activated during these distressing movies. So far, the results look encouraging. Sometimes, I really love my research![28]

Neuroscientists Neil Macrae and Dave Turk have been looking at what happens in the brain when objects become ours.[29] The change of ownership from any object to *my object* registers in the brain as enhanced activity. In particular, there is a spike of brain activity, called a *P300*, which occurs 300 milliseconds after we register something of importance—it's a wake-up call signal in the brain. When something becomes mine, I pay more attention to it in comparison to an identical object that is not mine. This process is fairly automatic. In one study, participants observed as particular products were divided into two shopping baskets—one for them and the other for the experimenter. Their P300 signals revealed that they paid more attention to things that were theirs. After sorting, participants remembered more of the items placed in their own basket compared to the experimenter's basket, even though they were not instructed that there was going to be a memory test.[30]

This is because, as James said, part of who we are is defined by our material possessions, which is why institutions in the past removed them to eradicate the sense of self. Uniformity both in clothing and personal possessions was regulated to prevent individuals retaining their individual identity. Some of the most harrowing images from the Nazi concentration camps are the piles of personal possessions and luggage that were taken away from the victims in an attempt to remove their identity. These objects are now regarded as sacred. In 2005, Michel Levi-Leleu, a 66-year-old retired engineer, took his daughter to see a Parisian exhibition on the Holocaust, with objects on loan from the Auschwitz-Birkenau Memorial and Museum. There, he spotted his long-lost father's cardboard suitcase with his initials and address. Michel demanded its return, leading to a legal battle with the museum that stated that all objects from the death camp were to be retained for posterity as sacred items. Four years later, a settlement was reached whereby the suitcase has been loaned to the Paris exhibition on a long-term basis.[31] The need for identity is so strong that when prisoners or institutionalized individuals are stripped of their possessions, they will confer value on items that would otherwise be considered as worthless.[32]

In some individuals with obsessive-compulsive disorder (OCD), object possession becomes a pathological condition known as *hoarding*, in which the household can become filled with worthless possessions that are not thrown away. In one unfortunate case, a hoarder was killed by the collapsing mound of rubbish that she had accumulated over the years.[33] Most of us are more restrained and have a few cherished personal possession or household items with which we identify. One of the first things individuals do on moving to a new residence is to bring in personal objects to stamp their identity on their new home. In contrast, sometimes people may destroy personal objects as a way of symbolically cutting ties with the past—especially if they are a jilted lover or cheated spouse.

■ When Losses Loom Large

Clearly, for many people, possessions are an expression of personal preference. People choose to buy certain products that they believe reflect qualities with which they would like to be associated. These are objects aligned with an identity to which we aspire. This link between self and possessions is something that modern advertisers have been exploiting for years. They understand that people identify with brands and that the more that a brand signals success, the more people will want it. Rolex watches, iPods, and Nike shoes are just some of the branded objects that people have lost their lives defending from thieves.

Russell Belk, professor of marketing at York University in Canada, calls this materialist perspective the *extended self*.[34] We are what we own, and when these possessions are violated through theft, loss, or damage, we experience this as a personal tragedy. Only recently, this happened to me. I am not particularly car proud, but when someone deliberately scratched the paintwork on my car a couple of months back, I felt very upset, as if the crime had been deliberately perpetrated against me. It was a random act but I felt enraged. I imagine that if I had confronted the perpetrator, I could have lost it and acted violently.

Even ruthless killers and drug-dealers appreciate the importance of possessions. Vince the hitman from the modern classic movie *Pulp Fiction* (1994) complained to Lance, his dealer, about his Chevy Malibu car that got scratched:

> Vince: I had it in storage for three years. It was out five
> days and some...piece of...,...with it.
> Lance: They should be...killed man. No trial. No jury.
> Straight to execution.

Of course, I would not go as far, but there is something deeply emotive when it comes to someone violating your property.

■ The Endowment Effect

Our attachment to objects may have less to do with personal choice than we imagine. In what is now regarded as a classic study in behavioral economics, Richard Thaler handed out $6 college coffee cups to half a class of Cornell undergraduates and then allowed them to trade with their classmates who made them a financial offer to buy the cup.[35] What Thaler found was very little trading because owners placed much greater value on objects in their possession, relative to what other people are willing to pay for them. Moreover, as soon as an object comes into our possession, we have a bias to overvalue it in comparison to an identical object. This bias, known as the *endowment effect*,[36] has been widely replicated many times with items ranging from bottles of wine to chocolate bars.[37]

Even when the object is not actually in one's physical possession, such as when bidding for an item in an auction, the prospect of eventually owning something produces a bias to value it more.[38] People who bid for the same items in an auction but had been allowed to handle the items for 30 seconds, compared to those bidders who only examined the object for 10 seconds, were willing to bid 50% more for the same objects. However, the contact seems to be the critical factor. If we are just told that we own something, then that does not trigger endowment. The longer we are in personal contact with an object, the more we value it and don't want to part with it. Is it any wonder that we are always being invited by salespersons to go for a spin or try things on? They know that once we have made that first contact, achieving the sale is much easier.

A commonly accepted explanation for the endowment effect is not so much that we value everything we can potentially own, but rather that we fear what we might lose. This bias is called *loss aversion*—a core component of the prospect theory proposed by Daniel Kahneman, the same scientist who left colonoscopes up the backsides of patients for an extra 3 minutes. According to this theory, losses are weighted more substantially than potential gains. Just like switching doors on the Monty Hall problem or selling our lottery ticket, we fear losses greater than we welcome gains. The prospect of regret seems to weigh heavily for us.

■ The Trading Brain

Brian Knutson has been looking at brain activation during buying and selling product scenarios using functional magnetic resonance imaging (fMRI) technology.[39] He found that when we look at products we like, irrespective of whether we are buying or selling, there is increased activation of the nucleus accumbens, a region of the brain's reward circuitry. When we think that we can buy it at a bargain price, the mesial prefrontal cortex, another region of the reward system, is also activated, but not if the price is too high—after all, most of us like a bargain. However, if people were presented with an offer to sell the desired product at a lower price than expected, then the insula in the right hemisphere became active. This region signals discrepancy between anticipated goals and outcomes and could be regarded as the neural correlate of disappointment. Moreover, the insular activity was predictive of the size of endowment effect for each participant. These imaging findings are consistent with the loss aversion account, whereby a discrepancy of perceived value and the offered sale price produces a negative emotional response. It's not that we simply have a bias, but rather we *feel* bad about selling a possession for a price below what we believe it is worth.

This aversion to loss sounds remarkably similar to insecure attachment—when individuals cannot bear to be separated from loved ones. Individuals who were rated anxious in their personal relationship attachment style showed a much stronger endowment effect in that they demand a higher price for personal possessions.[40] They weren't just clingy to people but also clingy to objects! Moreover, if they were primed to think about past relationships that made them feel anxious and insecure, the endowment effect was further increased. Clearly, emotions linked with our past social relationships are registered in our brain and can spill over into reasoning systems when it comes to how we value possessions.

■ The Extended Self

Despite 30 years of research on the endowment effect, only recently have researchers started to look at the phenomenon in populations other than North American students. This is an important limitation as other cultures have different attitudes toward object ownership. For example, in comparison to Westerners, Nigerians are reported to value gifts from others more and exhibit less of an endowment effect for personal possessions.[41] A recent study of the Hadza hunter-gatherers of Northern Tanzania also found no evidence of endowment for possessions.[42] This difference is believed to reflect the cultural difference between Western societies, in which the self is thought about mainly as one of independence, compared to non-Western societies, especially those in East Asia, in which the self is thought of in terms of its relationship to others or interdependence. For example, there is a self-characterization task[43] called the "Twenty Statements Test" in which participants have to write 20 statements in response to the question at the top of the page, "Who Am I?" It is a fairly simple measure of their self-concept reflecting various attributes, such as physical characteristics ("I am tall"), social roles ("I am a father"), or personal characteristics ("I am impulsive"). After completing the 20 statements, these are categorized as being internal (traits and intrinsic qualities) versus external (social roles in relationship to others). In comparison to individuals from interdependent societies, Westerners typically make more internal statements compared to external references.

How do these differing self-concepts manifest when it comes to ownership? One suggestion, following from Belk's extended self idea, is that the endowment effect is at least partly a function of the tendency to value the self. But not every personal attribute is fixed. Psychologist William Maddux and his colleagues[44] first established that the endowment effect was not as strong in East Asian compared to Western students attending Northwestern University. However, in a clever twist, Maddux asked the students to either write about themselves or their relationships with other people. This task can shift the self-perspective from being focused on one's self to one's relationships with others. When East Asians focused on themselves, they endowed things they owned with greater value, whereas Westerners instructed to write about others showed the opposite—a reduced endowment effect.

Not only do we overvalue our own possessions but we also covet that to which others seem to pay attention. It turns out that when we watch other people looking and smiling at objects we automatically prefer them to objects that have not been looked at.[45] These sorts of studies show that, when we come to value things, make choices, and exhibit preferences, we can easily be manipulated simply by considering context and our role among others. Being a member of a group generates our self-concept in ways that seem to defy the notion that societies are a collection of individual selves. Rather, our self is a reflection of our extension not only to our possessions, but also to everyone around us.

6 ∎

How the Tribe Made Me

Did you know that one of the most terrifying experiences people can imagine is speaking in front of other people? When this fear becomes so extreme that it begins to affect how people live their lives, it is known as *social anxiety disorder*. According to the American Psychiatric Association, it is the number one most common anxiety problem and the third most common mental disorder in the United States. More than one in ten of us have social anxiety disorder, which is surprisingly high given that we are such a sociable species.[1] Why is this?

The mind that generates our sense of self is a product of a brain that has evolved to become social. But in being social, the self is radically altered by the presence of others and our need to fit in with them. This is such an imperative that being in a group can be one of the most life-affirming experiences but also one of the greatest anxiety-inducing challenges.

One theory is that other people trigger our emotions reflexively.[2] As soon as we are in a crowd we become aroused. The limbic system that controls our behavior responds automatically to the presence of others. Arguably, this is the basic function of emotions—to motivate social behavior to either join or avoid others. When people simply look at us we become aroused by the focus of their attention. In one of our studies,[3] we showed that direct attention from staring eyes triggered increased pupil dilation, which is controlled by the limbic system. This system controls how we interact with others—whether we fight them, flee from them, or fornicate with them.

Sometimes, arousal can improve performance. We run faster, cycle faster, and basically up our game when others are about. However, this energy can also impair performance when we are not that skilled in the first place. When others look at us, our mouths dry up, our voices tremble, and our hands shake—all signs of limbic arousal. These are the butterflies that we get in our stomach, and it explains why opening night nerves are a common experience for actors who are not yet comfortable in their roles. It's only when we become expert that we can rise to the occasion.[4]

However, not all group behavior leads to increased performance. In a tug of war, teammates expend about half as much less energy than when they pull as individuals, in a phenomenon known as *social loafing*.[5] As soon as we blend into the crowd, we no longer feel the need to put in as much effort if it is not recognized. It is only if the group appreciates our efforts that we try harder. This need for recognition also explains why groups can become more polarized on issues that would normally generate only moderate views.[6] In an effort to gain group approval, individuals adopt increasingly extreme positions that they feel represent the group, which in turn drags the group further toward that position. If you couple that dynamic force with "groupthink,"[7] the tendency to suspend critical thinking when we are one of many decision-makers so as to try and galvanize the gathering, then it is easy to see how we behave so differently in groups than we would as individuals. It explains why the rise of political extremism requires not only the determination of the few but also the complacency of the many. When we are in large groups, whatever self we believe we have is swamped by others. The illusion is to assume you are more autonomous than you really are.

■ Suicide Baiting

In January 2010, a distressed woman on a bridge over the M60 motorway in the United Kingdom brought traffic to a 4-hour standstill while the police attempted to talk her down. A radio DJ, Steve Penk, thought it would be a funny prank to play Van Halen's hit track, "Jump," for the frustrated drivers caught up in the drama.[8] Moments later, the woman jumped, allegedly after hearing the song on a radio turned up by one of the waiting motorists. Luckily, the woman survived her suicide attempt but Penk was unrepentant.

Left to his own devices, the DJ would not have taunted the potential suicide victim unless he thought his clowning would please the listeners. The drivers trapped on the motorway would probably not have normally wished this woman harm either. They were sufficiently removed from the incident that they did not feel any consequences of their actions. This kind of crowd behavior is known as *suicide baiting*. Fortunately, it is very rare, probably because most suicides are not public spectacles. However, there are well-documented cases where crowds have urged individuals to kill themselves. How can we understand such behavior? Conceivably, this is not the sort of thing that individual members of a crowd would normally encourage on their own.

One explanation is that groups create *deindividuation*, a loss of the individual self. An analysis of 166 failed and successful suicide attempts across the United States between 1966 and 1979 found that crowds were present in about 20 of them and, of those, half were found to bait or jeer the victim.[9] The factors that seemed to link to baiting were larger crowds, the distance between the crowd and the victim, and the cover of night—arguably all factors that lead to greater anonymity.

Anonymity to outsiders appears to be the crucial factor when individuals feel that they are not accountable, which leads to greater antisocial behavior. Riots, lynching, and hooliganism are all believed to be examples of mob mentality that are thought to thrive through the process of deindividuation.[10] In contrast, the more that we lose anonymity, the more we conform and behave. In one simple study, researchers placed a picture of a pair of eyes on the wall above a collection tin in the coffee room where staff members paid for their beverages.[11] For the next 10 weeks, they alternated posting pictures of flowers or watchful eyes above the coffee pot. People were more honest in paying for their beverages when the eyes were posted. Just like the self-conscious Halloween children, we are more honest when a mirror is present to reflect our behavior. When we are made self-conscious, we become more accountable. For example, students consider working on an exam paper after time is up as cheating, and yet 71% of them continue to do so if left alone. However, only 7% do so if they are made self-aware by a mirror hanging in the exam room.[12] Anything that exposes the self to the scrutiny of others makes us more prosocial. Groups can bring out both the good and bad sides of our self.

Does one really lose his individual identity in a crowd, as deindividuation suggests? As psychologist Vaughan Bell[13] points out, anyone who has ever found themselves in a situation in which they are suddenly under threat as a group does not necessarily lose identity—they just see themselves as part of a different, larger collective. For example, imagine you get on a crowded late-night bus home where there are group of drunken students, an elderly couple, and maybe a teenager playing his music too loudly through his personal stereo. You do not feel anything in common with them and might even resent your fellow travellers. However, if looters, aliens, or zombies suddenly attack the bus, you spontaneously feel like a group and formulate plans to fend off the threat. You do not lose your identity but form a new one to address the group concern, of which you are now a member. It's the storyline of many movie scripts in which individuals discover themselves in threatening situations and, of course, this is where the heroes and villains emerge. So, groups do not cause deindividuation but rather trump individualism, depending on the context.[14]

■ Monkey in the Middle

Do you remember the childhood game, "Monkey in the Middle'?" It's a wicked teasing game. Usually, two players are supposed to pass a ball backward and forward to each other, and the "monkey" is the person in the middle who has to intercept it. Sounds harmless, doesn't it? Except that whenever I was the monkey, I used to get very upset because it seemed as if I was being excluded.

Caring about what others think may be one of the strongest preoccupations we have as an animal. Indeed, as Philippe Rochat[15] has pointed out, "To be human is indeed to care about reputation." To be ostracized from the group is the worst fate, which he calls "psychological death." Being ignored and rejected by our peers is painful. Most of us can remember being very upset when we were teased as children or not picked to play on teams. At the time, these events seemed like personal tragedies.

This is why bullying is not simply physically abusive but psychologically traumatizing. According to a 2001 survey by the U.S. National Institute of Child Health, one in three teenage children was involved in bullying.[16] It is more prevalent in boys than girls, and the patterns of abuse are different.[17] For males, both physical and verbal bullying is common, whereas for females verbal bullying through taunting and rumor-mongering is typically more common. However, even though girls use less physical violence, neuroscience indicates they might as well punch their victims, as the pain of social rejection is just as real.

This is something that psychologist Kip Williams from Purdue University knows from experience. He was out in the park walking his dog one day when he was hit in the back with a Frisbee. He threw it back to one of the two guys who were playing with it, who then began tossing it back to Kip. This was fun but, after about a minute, they stopped throwing the Frisbee to Kip and returned their attention to each other. At first Kip thought it was amusing, but then it became clear that they were not going to include Kip in their game again. The psychology professor was surprised at how upset he was by this exclusion, given that he had only been included in their game for a minute and that these were complete strangers. He realized how sensitive we are to ostracism.

Kip took his experiences from the park and developed a computer simulation known as "Cyberball," in which adult participants had their brains scanned as they played a game in which they had to toss a ball back and forth between two other playmates.[18] Just like the Frisbee event, Cyberball was going along fine, until the two others started to only pass the ball back between themselves and ignore the adult in the brain scanner. When this exclusion became obvious, the anterior cingulate cortex (ACC) regions of the brain, which are activated by social cognition, started to light up with activity. This is because the pain of rejection also triggers the ACC—a result of its importance as a mechanism for conflict resolution. The social exclusion of the game had initially caused consternation and then distress, as it activated areas associated with emotional pain. Just like ego-depletion, those who were rejected by colleagues were more likely to eat fattening cookies, which is probably where comfort food gets its potency.[19] When we say that our feelings are hurt, it may not simply be a metaphor we are using. We really feel as much pain as from a punch in the stomach.

What is remarkable is how sensitive we are to being rejected. Even when participants played Cyberball for only a couple of minutes and were told that it was only a computer simulation, they still felt the pain of rejection.[20] And this pain had nothing to do with the personality of the players either. They were not overly sensitive. Rather, there is something very fundamental and automatic about ostracism.[21] Williams argues that this reaction must be hardwired and points out that, in many other social species, ostracism often leads to death. That's why humans are so sensitive. As soon as it looks as though we are in danger of being ostracized, we become hypervigilant to those around us, looking for clues in the way people are interacting and opportunities to reengage with the group.[22] Excluded individuals engage in behaviors that increase their likelihood of being reconciled back into the group. We are more likely to mimic, comply with requests, obey orders, and cooperate with others who don't deserve it. We become obsequious to the extent that we will agree with others who are clearly in the wrong.

If these ingratiating strategies fail, then ostracized individuals switch tack and turn from being likeable to being angry and aggressive: "Look at me, I'm worthy of attention. I am not invisible, damn you." Individuals no longer care about being liked but rather want to exert their influence on others to take notice. People who have been ostracized are less helpful and more aggressive to others, whether or not the others are the perpetrators of the ostracism. For example, in one study, ostracized individuals sought revenge by giving an innocent bystander five times the amount of hot chili sauce as a punishment even when they knew the victim hated the sauce.[23] Many of the tragic cases of school shootings and murderous rampages involve individuals who feel they have been socially rejected. An analysis of the diaries of school-shooters found that in 13 of the 15 cases examined, the perpetrators had been targets of ostracism.[24] Clearly, not everyone who has been ostracized goes on a shooting rampage, but if the ostracism persists, then excluded individuals eventually experience alienation and worthlessness. They often withdraw from society and become profoundly depressed and contemplate suicide. As humans, we all need to belong.

■ Do You Want to Be in My Gang?

In his resignation telegram to an elite Beverly Hills social club, Groucho Marx wrote, "Please accept my resignation, I don't want to belong to any club that will accept people like me as a member."[25]

Whether we like it or not, we are all members of clubs. As a social animal, we cannot help but hang out with others. Even those of us not in a family can identify significant others in our lives—friends, Romans, and even countrymen. Ultimately, we are all members of one very big club: the human species. No man or woman is an island. Of course, there are some among us who reject being with others and seek out the isolated life of a hermit, but that is not the norm. They are the weirdoes amongst us. Most of us just want to belong. There is a drive, deep inside us, that compels us to be accepted by others.

Some group membership is relatively fixed and independent of what we want—age, sex, race, height, and nationality, for example—although sometimes we try to change even these: lie about our age, cross-dress, have surgery, wear elevator shoes, and become a nationalized citizen. Other groups we aspire to join throughout our lifetime—the in-crowd, the jet-set, the highfliers, the intelligentsia, or the seriously wealthy. Some of us are assigned to groups we would rather not join—the poor, the uneducated, the criminal classes, or the drug addicts. People do not normally choose to be any of these, but we are all members of groups whether we like it or not. Furthermore, it is in our human nature to categorize each other into groups. Even those who don't want to be characterized are a group unto themselves—they are the dropouts and the outsiders.

We categorize others because it makes it much easier to deal with strangers when we know where they are coming from. We do not have to do as much mental work trying to figure out how to respond and can react much quicker when we categorize. This is a general principle of our brains—we tend to summarize previous experiences to be prepared for future encounters. It's likely to be an evolutionary adaptation to optimize processing loads and streamline responses. When we identify someone as belonging to a group, this triggers all the stereotypes we possess for that group, which, in turn, influences how we behave toward the person. The problem is, of course, that stereotypes can be very wide of the mark when it comes down to the characteristics of the individual.

Those stereotypes can also be manipulated by others, as well as by prejudice, which means we can all be biased to be biased. In one study, participants had to inflict painful punishment on fellow students in a learning experiment, and they were allowed to choose the level of pain to administer.[26] If they "accidentally" overheard an experimenter describe the students as "animals" before start of the experiment, the participants chose more severe punishments. They were influenced by others' opinions. Most of us say we hate to be pigeonholed, but the truth is that it is in our nature to label others and be labeled our selves, and that process is highly dependent on what other people think. We are less self-assured than we believe in making our minds up. It is the group consensus, not the individual opinion, that determines how most of us evaluate others.

The groups we belong to define us, but we are constantly entering, leaving, expanding, and swapping our groups. People obviously benefit from the collective power of groups, as well as from the resources and companionship that can be shared, but membership is also necessary for generating a sense of self-identity. Just belonging to a group shapes our self because we automatically identify with other members. We know this from the work of social psychologists like Henri Tajfel, who used to be the head of my department. Before he came to Bristol in the 1960s, Tajfel witnessed the power of groups when he was a French prisoner-of-war, having been captured by the Germans during the Second World War. (In fact, he was a Polish Jew, but he kept this aspect of his identity secret from his German prison guards.) After the war, Tajfel dedicated his life to understanding group psychology. In what is now regarded as a classic study, he showed that arbitrarily assigning Bristol schoolboys into two groups by the toss of a coin produced changes in the way that they treated each other.[27] Those in the same group or "in group" members were more positive to each other and shared resources, but hostile to "out group" members, even though they were all from the same class.

■ What's In Your Eye, Brother?

In fact, Tajfel's study had been preempted a couple of years earlier in the United States by Jane Elliot, an Iowa third-grade teacher from Middle America.[28] The class had just been studying Dr. Martin Luther King, Jr. as American of the Month when news came that the civil rights leader had been assassinated on April 4, 1968. The children had little experience of discrimination and could not understand why anyone would want to kill their man of the month. The following day, Elliot planned an audacious class project to teach them about discrimination. She told her class that there was very good evidence that children with blue eyes were superior to students with brown eyes.

Following this revelation, Elliot afforded the blue-eyed students privileges such as extra long breaks and being first in the lunch queue. However, the next day she said that she had been wrong, and that in fact the evidence proved that it was the brown-eyed children who were superior. This role-reversal produced the same pattern. On both days, children who were designated as inferior took on the look and behavior of genuinely inferior students, performing poorly on tests, whereas the superior group became more hostile to the inferior group, thinking them less worthy. Simply by belonging to a group influences how you feel about your self and how you feel about others not in your group. In fact, it is the favorable comparisons that we draw against others not in our group that help to define who we are. This is how we formulate our identity—by focusing on what we are not. The trouble is that by focusing on others, we miss our own imperfections. As Matthew (7:3) in the Bible reminds us when talking about small grains (motes) of imperfection, "And why beholdest thou the mote that is in thy brother's eye, but considerest not the beam that is in thine own eye?"

Social identity theory has been refined and elaborated over the decades with research demonstrating that people see themselves within a hierarchy of different groups that can shift periodically over the lifespan. Clearly, some changes in circumstances change our group affiliation. If we marry, have children, or become crippled, the groups to which we belong change by default. Because we occupy so many different positions throughout our lifetime—child, adolescent, worker, parent, etc.—most of us see our selves occupying multiple groups. In most instances, we perceive group membership as bolstering self-esteem; by being part of a larger affiliation, we gain a sense of who we think we are as individuals. This is a delicate balance we strive to achieve between our desire to be an individual and the need to belong alongside others,[29] although not every culture sees the need to strike this balance. Most of us believe that we know our own minds and whether we decide to identify with a group, or not, is really up to us to decide. However, if anything has emerged in the field of social psychology, it is the revelation that such a belief is naïve as we are all susceptible to the power of the group—whether we like it or not.

■ Conformity

How good is your vision? Take a good look at the lines in Figure 6.1 and decide which one matches the line on the left—A, B, or C? This is pretty much a no-brainer and

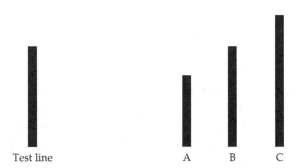

FIGURE 6-1   Asch test of compliance. Which line (A, B, or C) matches the test line?

unless someone has serious visual problems, you would predict that everyone would answer B. However, it depends on what others around you say.

In what is considered one of the most important studies of the power of groups,[30] Solomon Asch had eight participants take the line test. He held up cards with the lines on them and went round the room asking the participants which line matched the test line. In fact, there was only one real subject as the other seven participants were actually confederates of the experiment. At first, everything seemed above board. Everyone agreed on the length of the test line on the first two trials. However, on the third trial, the confederates gave the wrong answer by saying that it was line C that matched. The real participant stared in disbelief at his fellow students. Were they blind? What would the participant say when it came to his turn? On average, three out of every four participants went along with his fellow participants and also gave the wrong answer. Each did not suddenly become blind, but rather conformed in accordance with the group so as not to be the outsider. Each participant was fully aware of the correct answer, but each did not want to appear different. They did not want to be ostracized, so they conformed to the group consensus.

What about situations that are not so clear-cut, as in the case of a jury evaluating evidence? In Sidney Lumet's classic portrayal of the power of group psychology, *Twelve Angry Men* (1957), Henry Fonda stands alone as the one dissenting member of a jury. In the movie, a Spanish-American youth is accused of murdering his father, but Fonda gradually convinces the other jury members that the eyewitness testimony is not only unreliable, but false. This movie was made long before the experiments on false memories were conducted. As the movie unfolds, we see the dynamics of allegiances shift as Fonda tries to win the jury over man by man. It is a dramatic portrayal of the power of compliance and group consensus.

When we conform, it is not so much the power of the group or peer pressure that shapes our behavior, but rather our desire to be accepted. Our need to conform is a powerful force that shapes us and literally changes the way we think. In other words, it is not just public compliance when we conform to the group but true private acceptance of group norms. For example, when asked to rate the attractiveness of music or faces,[31] if there is a discrepancy between an individual's liking and the group consensus, this triggers activation in brain regions associated with social cognition and reward evaluation. However, as soon as we have an ally, we become more self-opinionated. In Asch's line test, it only required the presence of one other dissenter to give the right answer for the effect to reduce significantly. When we are accompanied by another dissenter, we are no longer an individual but part of a new group. The same thing unfolded in *Twelve Angry Men*. That's why we seek out others who share our opinion, because there is strength in numbers. It's also one of the reasons that oppressive regimes quash any resistance as soon as it starts to appear. If we feel isolated and powerless, then we submit more readily to authority and are less likely to resist. History teaches that authoritarian regimes have managed to control people by terrorizing them into submission with acts of human cruelty and atrocity, but to suppress dissent you need others to do your bidding unquestioningly. This is where the power of the group can be manipulated to change the nature of the individual. This is where normal, good-natured people become monsters.

■ The Lucifer Effect

Do you consider your self evil? Could you inflict pain and suffering on another human being or a defenceless animal for that matter? Consider how likely it is that you would do any of the following:

Electrocute a fellow human until they were dead
Torture a puppy
Administer a lethal dose
Strip search a coworker and make them perform a sex act on another worker

Most readers are appalled by such suggestions. However, Stanford psychologist Phil Zimbardo forces us to think again in his recent book, *The Lucifer Effect*,[32] about how to make good people become evil by putting them in toxic situations that generate a downward spiral into degradation. Zimbardo convincingly argues that all of us are capable of doing the despicable deeds in this list, even though none of us thinks we ever would. This is because we believe that we are essentially good and that only bad people do bad things. Our whole legal system is based on this assumption that individuals are responsible for their own moral choices. But Zimbardo argues that the situations we can find our selves in and the influence of those around us determine how we behave and treat others. If we believe our self illusion has a core morality, then it is one that is at the mercy of those around us.

Zimbardo, who rather resembles a popular portrayal of Lucifer with his goatee, is known for his infamous 1971 Stanford Prison Experiment, in which he investigated the consequences of simulating an incarceration scenario using ordinary students playing cops and robbers. It was to be a 2-week study of the effects of role-playing in the basement of the Stanford psychology department, which had been turned into a makeshift prison. Like Tajfels's Bristol schoolboy study, on the flip of a coin, the volunteers were divided. Half of the student volunteers were to be the guards and the other half were to be their prisoners, each earning $15 a day for 14 days. Most thought it would be easy money to loaf around for a couple of weeks. However, what happened next shocked everyone involved and has left a legacy in the literature on the psychology of evil that now explains many unbelievable examples of human cruelty.

To simulate authenticity, the prisoners were arrested on a Sunday by real policemen, handcuffed, blindfolded, and taken to the prison where they were stripped and put in smocks without underwear. This was only the beginning of the humiliation. Then the "guards"—uniformed fellow students wearing mirror shades—met them. When they wanted to go to the toilet down the hall, the inmates were led out with bags on their heads. Their guards gave them a long list of rules that they had to memorize, and failure to do so led to punishment. Within a very short time, things began to deteriorate. Even though they had never been instructed to harm the inmates, the guards began to spontaneously torment and torture the inmates. In this authoritarian atmosphere, the inmates became psychologically distressed while their guards were getting increasingly out of control.

From a scientific perspective, this was exhilarating. Even though everyone involved knew the set-up was not real, the situation was creating real cruelty and suffering. Thrilled by the speed and ease at which morality seemed to be deteriorating, Zimbardo pushed on largely as the scientist overseeing the project but also as his role as the Superintendent in charge of the prison. He was becoming a player immersed in his own fantasy story.

His girlfriend at the time, another psychology professor, Christina Maslach, visited to see how the experiment was progressing and was shocked by what she observed. She told Zimbardo, "What you're doing to those boys is a terrible thing!" A heated row between the lovers ensued, and she would later recall, "Phil seemed so different from the man I thought I knew. He was not the same man that I had come to love." Zimbardo had lost the plot. He seemed unable to see what cruelty he had created. After 6 days, largely at the bequest of Christina, he terminated the experiment. He married her the following year.

For the next 40 years, the Stanford Prison Experiment has remained a controversial study both in terms of the ethics of putting people in this situation, as well as in its interpretation.[33] Zimbardo thinks that the devil is in the deindividuation, whereas others claim that all that was demonstrated was overenthusiastic role-playing. That may be true to some extent. Maybe some of the students had watched too many prison movies like *Cool Hand Luke*, in which the guards also wore the same mirrored sunglasses and behaved sadistically.[34] One of the student guards even adopted a Southern American accent indicating a well-formulated stereotype of the typical correctional officer. They behaved as they thought the officers and prisoners should. But even if it was all acting, one is still left wondering: what is the difference between role-playing and reality? What does it mean to say that I may act in a terrible way but that's not the way I really am? Who is the real me, or self?

■ The Man in the White Coat

Some questioned the authenticity of the Stanford Prison Experiment. What would happen in a real situation of authority? This is where the work of Stanley Milgram is so relevant. Milgram was one of Solomon Asch's research assistants, and in early1960s, he wanted to take his mentor's work further. In what has become one of the most notorious psychology studies, Milgram demonstrated the power of authority when compliance becomes blind obedience.[35]

It began with a simple advertisement in which participants were asked to volunteer and would be paid $4 an hour to take part in an experiment on learning and punishment to be conducted at prestigious Yale University. When each of the volunteers arrived at the laboratory, he or she met with the experimenter, wearing a white lab coat, and another middle-aged man, who was introduced as another participant but who was actually a trained actor. After a supposedly random decision, the experimenter explained that the volunteer would play the role of teacher and the actor would play the role of learner. The learner was led off to another room and it was explained that the teacher would read words to the learner over an intercom. The learner would then repeat the words back to the teacher. If the learner made a mistake, the teacher would press a button that delivered an electric shock to the learner in the other room. There were 30 levels of shock rising in 15-volt increments from an initial 15 volts to 450 volts. Each switch had the level and a description of the shock, ranging from "mild" at the start, through the 10th level (150 volts), "strong"; 13th level (195 volts), "very strong"; 17th level (255 volts), "intense"; 21st level (315 volts), "extremely intense"; 25th level (375 volts), "danger, severe shock." The final two levels of 435 and 450 volts had no label other than an ominous "XXX." To give them an idea of what it felt like, the participant teacher was given a taste of the third level (45 volts), which induced a very real, tingly pain.

Initially, the experiment began fairly well as the learner repeated back the correct answers. However, when the learner began to make errors, the teacher was instructed by the man in the white coat to administer punishment shocks. Of course, the actor in the next room was not really receiving any shocks but duly gave a more and more distressing performance as the intensity of the punishment shocks increased. At first, he started to complain that the shocks hurt. Then they were painful. As the punishment voltages increased, so did the intensity of the screams. Soon, the learner was pleading with the teacher and telling him that he had a heart condition. Many of the participants protested that they could not go on but the man in the white coat replied impassively, "Please continue." At this point, the teachers were clearly stressed, shaking, and sweating, and yet they went on. Even after the intercom went silent and they reached the 20th level of 300 volts, they were told that the learner's failure to answer the question was an error and that the teacher must proceed with the punishment.

What do you think you would do in such a situation? Before Milgram had started his study, he consulted a panel of 40 psychiatrists and asked what they predicted that members of the public would do. As experts on human psychology, they agreed that less than one in 100 participants would go all the way to the end. How wrong could they be? It turned out that two out of every three of the participants in Milgram's shocking study went all the way to the end at 450 volts. They were prepared to kill another human being at the request of the man in the white coat.

Maybe the participants knew that this was all a trick and that no one was being hurt. I doubt it. I have watched the early recordings of this study, and it is fairly disturbing viewing as the teachers are clearly distressed as they become resigned to administering the lethal shocks. In a later study that would never get ethical approval today, researchers conducted the almost identical experiment using puppies punished with real electric shocks.[36] This time there was no charade. The animals were clearly suffering (although they were not receiving lethal shocks and the voltages were way below the descriptions the teachers thought they were administering). Half of the male teachers went all the way to the maximum punishment and, surprisingly, all of the female teacher participants obeyed the order to give the maximum shocks.

The authority figure does not even have to be in the room. In another study with real nurses in a hospital,[37] the participants received a telephone call from an unknown doctor who asked them to administer a 20 milliliter dose of a drug, "Astrogen," to a patient that he was on his way to visit. The label on the drug indicated that 5 milliliters was a normal dose, and it should not exceed 10 milliliters. All but one of 22 nurses knowingly gave the dose that was double the safety limit. This is a very old study and guidelines have changed over the years to prevent exactly this sort of blind obedience operating, but Zimbardo documents more recent examples in which people working in hierarchical organizations succumb to the pressure of their superiors even when they know that what is requested is wrong.

Outside of the workplace, the power of authority is most evident in law enforcement. Whenever we have been pulled over by men in uniforms, most of us become obedient. I know I do. In an incredible account of blind obedience, Zimbardo describes how he served as an expert witness in one case of a spate of 60 sexual assaults that had taken place in fast-food chains across the United States during the late 1990s and early 2000s. In a typical scam, the caller asked to speak to the assistant manager and then informed him that he was a police officer and that one of the recent employees had been stealing money and concealing drugs. The assistant manager was asked to cooperate by restraining the suspect employee and performing a strip search while the police made their way to the restaurant. Of course, this was not a real police request but a pervert who wanted the manager to describe the intimate search in detail into the phone. In the case with which Zimbardo was involved, a terrified 18-year-old female employee was stripped naked and then commanded to perform oral sex with another male coworker, simply because they were told to so by an anonymous phone caller who they believed was "the law."[38]

■ The Banality of Evil

Much of the research on compliance and obedience was conducted in a period of history still recovering from the atrocities of the Nazi concentration camps. Asch, Milgram, and Zimbardo were Americans of Jewish descent who wanted to know how the Holocaust could ever have taken place. It was a question to which the world wanted the answer as well. Even today, we still ask the same questions. How can ordinary people perform such extraordinarily cruel acts on other people?

Perhaps the Milgram experiments were products of the era—when authoritarianism ruled the day. We are much more liberated today and wary of the corrupting power of authority in the post-Watergate years. However, in 2007, the ABC News *Primetime* TV show in the United States decided to recreate the Milgram study to see whether a sample of 40 men and women would go as far as to administer the highest level of shock.[39] Again, two-thirds of them obeyed a man in the white coat and went all the way to the end of the dial. We are fooling our selves if we believe we can resist the influence of others. We can all become the instruments of torture.

We still question how people can be so evil whenever we hear of another example of human atrocity inflicted on fellow human beings around the globe. One example that was so surprising was the treatment of Iraqi prisoners at Abu Ghraib by U.S. professional soldiers. In 2004, images of naked male Iraqi detainees piled high on top of each other in a human pyramid were circulated through the world's press. Alongside their victims, grinning American guards posed, with smiling faces and thumbs-up gestures, for trophy photographs. The images also showed the psychological torture of hooded detainees balanced on boxes with outstretched arms, who were told that, if they fell, they would be electrocuted by the dummy wires attached to their fingers. The pictures bore a shocking resemblance to those of hooded prisoners in Zimbardo's prison experiment. Others detainees were forced to wear women's clothing or simulate fellatio with other male prisoners. All of these images showed that Abu Ghraib prison, originally used by Saddam Hussein to torture his opponents, continued the tradition of sadistic human behavior under the occupation of the coalition's liberating Army.

At first, U.S. Army generals dismissed the scandal as the work of a few "bad apples"—disturbed sadists who had managed to infiltrate the honorable corps. In particular, the most upsetting images were of a young female guard, Private Lynndie England, who was photographed grinning as she led a naked male prisoner around in a dog-collar. There was nothing out of the ordinary about Lynndie England's upbringing to suggest that she was a sadist. One of her ex-teachers described her as "invisible." If anything, it appears that Lynndie England was just a simple woman who followed others and was under the influence of her lover, Charles Garner, who instigated the abuse and took many of the photographs. But it is the cherub-like smiling face of 21-year-old England, and not Garner's, that will forever be associated with the atrocities.[40]

This is probably the most disturbing thing about evil. When the philosopher Hannah Arendt was commissioned by the *New Yorker* to cover the war crimes trial of Adolf Eichmann in the early 1960s, she reported that the trouble with Eichmann and his ilk was that they were neither perverted nor sadistic, but simply "terribly and terrifyingly normal." Seemingly ordinary people had committed extraordinary crimes. It was as if, as she called it, the "banality of evil" was proof that the self had capitulated to the cruelty that war and conflicts engender and that people were generally incapable of resisting the will of others.[41]

■ The Human Chameleon

When you consider the power of groups in these studies, it seems unlikely that anyone was totally unaware of their behavior in the conformity and obedience experiments of the 1960s and 1970s. People were also probably aware of their actions in the real-life examples of blind obedience described by Zimbardo. They simply don't feel responsible for their actions. They may still believe in their self illusion, that they could do otherwise should they wish, but rather, they prefer to suspend their decision-making in order to fit in with others or obey authority figures. It's not a pleasant realization, but then we can always justify it later by weighing up what is in our best interests in the long term. It is our old friend cognitive dissonance, again.

Sometimes, our behavior can also be hijacked unknowingly by the influence of those around us. This is when the self is covertly manipulated. In these situations, we are not even aware that we are being shaped by social influences. For example, Dutch psychologist Ap Dijksterhuis recalls the time when he and a few members of the Nijmegen Psychology Department went to watch a soccer match.[42] On their walk to the stadium, the academics, behaving calmly and orderly, were soon surrounded by hundreds of yelling and shouting soccer fans and hooligans. At that point, something odd happened. One of academics saw an empty beer can and, in what seemed to be an impulsive act, he kicked it violently as far away as possible. For a moment, he stood there, transfixed and aghast at what he had just done. He was no longer an individual—he had become like the crowd around him.

This change in behavior to match others around us is known as the *chameleon effect*[43] after the exotic lizard that can change its skin color to blend in with its surroundings. It is not a deliberate effort to change but rather reflects the automatic way that we mimic others around us. This can be anything from simple postures, expressions, and gestures to more complicated patterns of behavior, such as speech or moods. Simply the way we move about can be influenced by others without us even being really aware. The brain's mirroring system that is activated during our own movements can also be triggered by the goal-directed actions of another when we observe him or her performing the same goal. These mirror neurons provide a convenient way of mapping the behavior of others directly into our own brains through a process much like resonance. It's like when you are in a guitar salesroom. If you strike the "G" string loudly enough on one guitar, all the other "G" strings on all the other guitars will eventually vibrate in synchrony.

Human mirroring works in the same way. Most of us have a repertoire of behaviors that can be triggered by others without us being aware that we are mirroring someone else's movements. We may cross our legs, yawn, stroke our nose, play with our hair, and change the way we speak or sit simply because we are unwittingly copying another person.[44] This unconscious imitation, known as *mimicry*, is a powerful mechanism for binding the self to others.[45] It is not entirely automatic as we only mimic those we like in a virtuous self-fulfilling circle—we copy others who we like, who in turn like us more, thereby increasing the likelihood that they will copy us in a synchronized sycophantic symphony of mutual appreciation.[46]

Not only do we like people who mimic us more, but we are willing to help them out if they request favors from us.[47] We even feel like a better human being after we have been copied, and it can last long after the encounter. In one study, after being mimicked, participants donated twice as much money to a charity box as they left the experiment compared to those who had not been copied, even though the donations were anonymous.[48] We even tip waitresses more when they mimic us.[49]

However, we are not simply puppets at the mercy of others tugging on our strings to control how we feel about them.

Even though we may not be consciously aware of the mimicry, riding on top of this mirroring system of social interaction is an appraisal veto that seems to be double-checking for interlopers. We tend to mimic only those people from our own social circles and those with whom we want to be affiliated. We don't mimic those outside our social groups. In fact, we dislike individuals from outside of our social group more if they mimic us. In one study, white Dutch adults who scored highly on tests that measure prejudice disliked a computer-generated avatar that mimicked them if it appeared to have a Moroccan face rather than a white European one.[50]

■ The Rhythm of Life

This process of liking others who copy us appears early in development. The young infant's facial imitation could be an early example of mimicry, in which the motor system of the brain is automatically triggered by watching the movements of others. This might explain why the repertoire of behaviors is very limited at first—this is not too surprising given what movements newborns can actually make by themselves. Over the next 12 months, the opportunity to copy others increases and the Machiavellian babies look out for those who copy them. Five-month-old babies placed in a baby walker that enables them to scoot about the floor prefer to approach a stranger who has mimicked them and acted in a synchronized manner than one who did not respond to the babies' behavior in a contingent way.[51] Sometimes, it is not only the lack of mimicking that puts babies off, but the timing and amount of effort. Mothers with postnatal depression can have either very flat, emotionless interactions with their babies or go over the top with an exuberant flurry of attempted interactions. Either way, 2-month-old babies prefer the more measured and synchronized interactions.[52]

Synchrony seems to be an important characteristic of social interaction. Turn-taking is essential during conversations, as anyone listening to a radio interview knows that not everyone can be heard at once. We have to take turns during communication. Again, these patterns are established early in development. As mothers breastfeed their infants, they instinctively know how to synchronize their movements and baby talk to fit with their child's sucking patterns, which come in bursts and pauses.[53]

Synchrony of movements and timing continue to influence the nature of social interactions throughout our lives. Children must learn to take turns and control their impulses and urges. Routines are learned that emphasize the importance of coordination with others. Those who fail to develop control of their selves in the presence of others are said to be "out of control." All the institutions that make up our societies—schools, churches, and armies—thrive on synchrony to solidify ties between their members. Dancing and singing are synchronized activities that depend on timing to be pleasurable. In today's modern army, where the combat troop member is more of technician than a field grunt, soldiers are still taught to march in unison as a means of establishing group harmony. This is why we say that individuals failing to conform to the group are "getting out of step" or "falling out of line."

Regimentation is not just a way of gaining control over large numbers of individuals. Rather, it actually promotes prosocial behavior. In one study, participants were walked around a college campus either in step or out of step with their colleagues.[54] Both groups then played a trade-off game in which the goal was to optimize winnings by members choosing the same but riskier option than a safer option that paid out less. In short, if members thought there was less group cohesion they tended to go for the safer bet. What researchers found was that those who walked in unison before the test did much better by selecting the responses that indicated a sense of group cohesion even though they were completely unaware of the purpose of going for a walk. Even Americans who sang along with the Canadian national anthem "O Canada," rather than simply listening to it or reading the lyrics, were more likely to succeed in trade-off games that tested how much we trust others.

■ Walk This Way

Yale psychologist John Bargh has shown that these chameleon effects can operate simply by reading about the attributes of others. This is priming, which reflects the way that the circuits of the brain that store related information can be influenced by external events. For example, when students were asked to unscramble sentences that contained words related to being elderly such as, "forgetful, retired, wrinkle, rigid, traditional bitter, obedient, conservative, knits, dependent, ancient, helpless, gullible," they left the experimental room walking like an old person. They were slower and frailer. If they read sentences that contained words related to being rude such as, "bold, bother, disturb, intrude, annoyingly, audaciously, brazen, impolitely, infringe, obnoxious," they were more likely to interrupt a conversation than were students who had read polite words.[55]

These influences of external events work because the mere exposure to words triggers thoughts that for a moment can influence our behaviors. It is not only actions— even our general knowledge can be primed to be better or worse. If you are asked to imagine what it must be like to be a professor for 5 minutes, then you will perform better on "Trivial Pursuit" questions than if you imagine being a soccer hooligan.[56] Claude Steele, one of the most prominent African American psychologists, has been looking at how stereotypes distort behaviors.[57] White students primed to think about being black African Americans responded with hostility when asked to repeat a task they had just completed, indicating that negative stereotypes can be triggered in the same manner. Just listing your race can influence the way you perform on a task. When asked to list their race before taking an IQ test, African Americans did significantly worse than if they had not been asked.

These priming effects can even be triggered unconsciously through mimicry by others. For example, in mathematics tests there is a racial stereotype that Asian Americans do better than Caucasian Americans who do better than African Americans.[58] To see if this stereotype could be triggered by mimicry, Asian American, African American, and white Caucasian students were asked to take a mathematics test.[59] Before they took the test, each one sat in a waiting room where there was another student of the same ethnic background, who was also taking the test. The other student was, in fact, a confederate of the experimenters and had been instructed to either mimic or not mimic the real subject. When there was no mimicking, all three groups performed equally well, showing that the stereotype was not activated. However, if they had been mimicked by the confederate, Asian Americans performed significantly better than the white Caucasians, whereas the African Americans tended to show poorer performance. The same mimicry effect was found with the sex stereotype that women are not as good at mathematics as are men.

Despite it being in our best interests to perform as well as we can, we are nevertheless at the mercy of stereotypes and those around us who can trigger them unconsciously.

■ When East and West Collide

Perhaps one of the most surprising lines of research in recent years has shown that cultural stereotypes operate at a much more basic level in the brain than has previously ever been considered. This is true even in the way we perceive the world around us. For example, it is often assumed that while people around the world may have different preferences and tastes, when it comes to music and art we all have essentially the same brain. When someone in Beijing hears Mozart, they hear the same music as someone from Boston. When someone from Tokyo looks at a painting by Magritte, they see the same image as someone from Tennessee. They may not agree about whether they like the work, but they have the same perceptual experience. But is that really true? Psychologist Richard Nisbett thinks not. He has accumulated a vast body of evidence to show that cultures can shape the way we literally perceive the world and, ultimately, the way we think about our self.

In his book, *The Geography of Thought*[60] Nisbett argues that cultures influence not only the way we process the world, but also the way we interpret it. He draws a sweeping dividing line between Eastern and Western cultures and argues that peoples from the East tend to see and interpret the world in a holistic or collectivist manner, noticing connections and patterns between everything. Peoples from the West, on the other hand, tend to be more focused on the individual objects in the world. Admittedly, we must bear in mind that here "West" usually means U.S. students whereas East typically means Japanese and Chinese students.

In spite of these caveats, according to Nisbett, the collectivist–individualistic divide can explain a multitude of complex behaviors and traditions that vary from one culture to the next. For example, one characteristic of Eastern holism accounts for a philosophical leaning toward notions of order, resonance, and harmony. Such leanings are exemplified in the Eastern notion of *feng shui*, a need to achieve balance for happier home and work environments. In contrast, studies of Westerners reveal the comparatively more individualistic attitude of an independent self.[61]

Nisbett thinks that the origin of this cultural divide can be traced back thousands of years to the times of ancient Greece and China. However, the recent modern history of the United States is sufficient to explain why, as a whole, this nation is individualistic. In a comparatively short space of time, the United States was rapidly forged out of the struggle of groups who had immigrated in order to establish a better life. Other nations tend to evolve over much longer periods as one invading army conquered another, but the United States experienced sudden rapid growth primarily from immigration. Initially, some of these early immigrants sought religious freedom, which again, strengthened their sense of independence. The early settlers formed self-sufficient communities, struggling to adapt to their new environment and compete against the indigenous peoples. There was little room for social loafing or slackers in these early communities and so to survive you had to rely on your own efforts.

In many ways, the notions of individualism and independence have been branded into the American psyche. For example, when asked to come up with 20 statements that we think define our self, Westerners typically respond with traits centered from their own perspective (e.g., "I am tall"), whereas those from collectivist cultures typically provide relational statements, such as "I am taller than my sister." Maybe this focus on relationships to others explains why social loafing is not as strong in these societies, where one is inclined to consider one's self in social contexts.[62]

What is most remarkable about the work coming out of this field of cultural psychology is that individuals from the East and West not only describe themselves differently but may in fact see the world differently. For example, study the diagram in Figure 6.2 and concentrate on the figure on the far left. You have one of two tasks: either draw

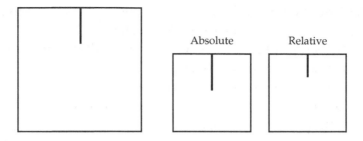

FIGURE 6-2 The Frame Test: The task is either to draw the length of the vertical line either exactly (absolute) or proportionately (relative).

an identical line of the same length independently of the frame (absolute), or draw a line of the same relative length to the frame dimension (relative). The correct solutions are on the right.

The absolute task requires focusing on the line and ignoring the frame, whereas the relative task requires estimating the relationship of the line to the frame. Remarkably, Japanese students are significantly better at the relative task than the absolute task while U.S. students show the opposite profile by being significantly better at the absolute task compared to the relative task.[63] This finding is interpreted to mean that the Easterners focus more on the relative rather than the absolute. But this difference does not exist in the youngest children who have been tested. Below 6 years of age, both Eastern and Western children show the same pattern of finding the relative task much easier than the absolute task. It's only after schooling begins that the typical switch in thinking styles between East and West starts to appear.[64]

Our cultural upbringing can even influence how we watch a movie. In one study, Japanese and U.S. students watched an underwater scene with various fish and plants.[65] Students from the United States could recall information about the large fish, whereas Japanese students recalled more detail about the background and the relationship between objects. When presented with a recognition task in which individual fish were presented alone, against the original background or different background, U.S. students recognized the fish irrespective of the background, whereas the Japanese students were thrown by the absence of background or the presence of a different background. In another study using a different Eastern population, U.S. and Chinese participants watched movies of a shoal of fish with one fish swimming out front that could be interpreted as either leading the shoal or ostracized by the other fish.[66] U.S. students thought the lone fish was more likely to be leading the shoal, whereas Chinese students interpreted the movie as the lone fish being rejected by the group.

It's not only what you see that is influenced by culture, but also what you don't see. We may think that we have a good grasp of events that take place around us, but unless we pay special attention, we often miss conspicuous events. This happens in "spot-the-difference" puzzles. Take a good look at the two pictures in Figure 6.3. Something is different between them (answer at the end of the chapter).

Our inability to notice changes between the images is called *change blindness*, and we vary in the extent to which

FIGURE 6-3 Change blindness: Individuals from Eastern cultures tend to notice changes faster.

we can spot the difference. If you are someone who can rapidly process the whole picture, then you are more likely to notice differences. Those who focus on individual elements are going to take longer because they cover less territory during inspection. They can't see the woods for the trees. It turns out that Westerners are much slower on measures of change blindness than Easterners, who are quicker to spot the difference. The Easterners are considering more of the picture rather than focusing on individual elements. In fact, measurements of eye movements indicate that Easterners make more eye movements and spend less time dwelling on individual targets when inspecting scenes compared to Western participants.[67] That's pretty low-level stuff. We are generally not even aware of how we control our eye movements, so how could culture shape these?

■ How Does Development Shape the Way
   We See the World?

How could people from the East and West see the world so differently? One possibility is that brain plasticity enables the developing brain to encode relevant experiences to shape the way we see faces and hear languages. Nisbett believes that the same developmental process shapes the way we pay attention to things in the world. The world is full of complexity, ambiguity, and missing information, "a blooming, buzzing confusion," as William James once wrote.[68] We make sense of it by organizing the information into meaningful patterns. Much of this happens automatically, as part of the package we inherit through our genes as the organizing brain processes that generate our perceptions. Sitting atop these built-in perceptual processes is cognition—the higher-order operations that guide perception.

Cognition organizes our thinking and gets better at this as we become more expert at noticing the regularities of the world and remembering them. This leads us to form expectations, so that we can predict events. For example, if we know what to expect next from previous encounters, we can look out for familiar patterns. That's why foreign games of sport can seem so disorganized to those unfamiliar with the rules.

In addition to our built-in rules for learning about the world, the most important source of expertise is other people. We have previously described how babies are tuned into other people from the very beginning. Nisbett believes that our early interactions with adults also shape the way we view the world. For example, Western and Eastern mothers interact and talk to their infants in different ways. U.S. mothers are much more likely to engage in play that involves naming individual toys. Japanese mothers are more likely to engage their children in social games. In one study, U.S. and Japanese mothers were observed interacting with their children with the same toys.[69] U.S. mothers were twice as likely to label toys and focus the child's attention on the attributes of each item. In contrast, Japanese mothers did label the object, but they were much more likely to then engage the child with exchange games such as "I give it to you, now you give it to me." Even the languages in these different cultures emphasize differently the individual from the relational properties of items.[70] This may explain why Eastern children are delayed in learning to sort objects into different categories compared to Western children, who are comparatively more skilled at considering the properties of individual objects as opposed to grouping them together.

These differing ways of categorizing the world reflect the way that children can learn to adopt the prevalent social norms. But this learning is not set for life, as are other critical period phenomena. These ways of processing the world do not satisfy the biological imperatives that require hardwiring. It seems unlikely that there are going to be significant permanent differences between individuals who view the world from collectivist or individualistic perspectives. More importantly, these differing perspectives are easily reversible, suggesting that they are not cast in stone. For example, European and American students were asked to circle either independent pronouns ("I" or "mine") or interdependent pronouns ("we" or "ours"). Those primed with independent pronouns gave higher endorsements to individualistic statements, whereas those primed with interdependence gave higher endorsement to collectivistic values.[71] Clearly, such manipulations reveal that we are much more malleable to conforming to group norms rather than holding deep-seated notions about group and self-identity.

Also, if you prime Hong Kong residents who have grown up under the influence of both Western and Eastern cultural perspectives, you can shift their attitudes toward collectivist perspective if you show them an image of the Chinese dragon, or shift them toward individualism with a picture of the U.S. flag. In one study, groups of bicultural Hong Kong Chinese were primed with either Eastern or Western attitudes and then told about an overweight boy who cannot resist the temptation to gorge on food.[72] They were then asked to rate how much of his weight problem was due to his own disposition and how much was due to his social circumstances. Both groups were equal on rating the boy's obesity as due to his own problems of self-control, but those primed with the Chinese icons rated his situational circumstances significantly higher than those primed with the U.S. flag.

■ Who Am I?

These studies reveal that the vast body of evidence undermines the notion of a core self, but rather supports the self illusion. If we are so susceptible to group pressure, subtle priming cues, stereotyping, and cultural cuing, then the notion of a true, unyielding ego self cannot be sustained. If it is a self that flinches and bends with tiny changes in circumstances, then it might as well be nonexistent. Most humans entertain some form of a self illusion, but it is one that is shaped by context. For many in the West, their self illusion is characterized by the individual fighting against the odds, whereas in the East, the most common form of the self illusion will be the team player. If these different types of selves were intrinsic, then they should not be so easily modified by context. Note that both ways of seeing the world, and more importantly one's self illusion, require some form of public validation. Both require the presence of others.

It is worth pointing out a lesson to be learned. In this day and age, when we increasingly need to share our limited living space on the planet, most people entertain a belief that they are considerate, reasonable, and fair. Not many would readily accept that they are prejudiced, unreasonable, and racist. However, we can easily harbor many stereotypes and distortions that shape the way that we behave and think. We are certainly more pliable through the influence of others than we ever thought. If we wish to be fair and just individuals, I think a good starting alternative is to accept that prejudice may be the norm and not the exception, and is inherent in group psychology, as Tajfel and others claimed. The first step to fixing a problem is acknowledging that you have one to begin with, and so long as we entertain a self illusion, we are not going to accept just how much external circumstances have shaped us in the past and continue to exert an influence throughout our lives. We don't see this because our cognitive dissonance is constantly shielding us from our failings by trying to maintain an integrated self belief—an idealized story of who we think we are.

(Answer Figure 6.3: There is a gorilla next to the pencils)

7 ■

The Stories We Live By

I looked around, it was like a horror movie, people
were mounted on each other, the smell of burnt skin
and people's insides was gagging. I kept thinking about
my fiancé, about our wedding, I wanted to wear that
white dress and swear my love for him. Something
gave me the strength to get up. I believe today that
it was my fiancé on his way to heaven.

Tania Head[1]

Who can forget the day they saw the attack on the Twin
Towers? You didn't even have to be there. It was the first
live televised terrorist atrocity witnessed by the world. I
was at work in Bristol, England, and recently had a television mounted on my office wall, which I used to review
research videos, but that afternoon I had it turned on to
watch the horror unfold on that crisp, sunny September
morning in New York. It was surreal—it couldn't be happening. I remember trying to be disconnected from it—as

if it was just another piece of news. I did not want to think too hard about what I was seeing. And yet I will not forget that day. It is seared into the memories of all who witnessed the events that have simply become known as 9/11.

As discussed, memories are not recordings but stories we retrieve from the compost heap that is our long-term memory; we construct these stories to make sense of the events we have experienced. They change over time as they become distorted, merged, turned over, mixed in, and mangled with other experiences that eventually fade. But some memories remain as vivid as the day they happened—or at least they seem so, those episodes that refuse to decompose. These are the events that we can't forget. When we witness something that is truly terrifying, then a memory can be branded into our brain, like a hot searing iron that marks our minds forever. This is because emotionally charged memories are fuel-injected by the electrical activity of the limbic system.[2] Arousal, triggered in the amygdala, produces heightened sensitivity and increased attention. The dilation of our pupils reveals that our vigilance systems have been put on high alert to look out for danger. The world suddenly becomes very clear and enriched as we notice all manner of trivial details that we would not normally care about. It's like the scene has suddenly been illuminated by bright light—as if some paparazzi photographer has lit up the world in a brilliant blaze of light during our moments of terror—which is why these recollections are called "flashbulb" memories.[3] And we experience the emotion—we feel the past. It is the heightened arousal and emotional significance that seems to lay down the life-track in the brain that becomes a flashbulb memory.

We usually lament our loss of memory as we age but sometimes it is better to forget. Although many flashbulb memories are associated with the more joyous events in life, such as births and weddings, most are generated by the horrors. Victims and survivors typically experience traumatic memories that they can't erase—a common symptom of post-traumatic stress disorder (PTSD). Following 9/11, one in five New Yorkers living in vicinity of the Twin Towers developed PTSD.[4] They were haunted by nightmares and constantly ruminated on the events of that terrible day. Our emotional systems seem compelled to never let us forget the worst things that can happen to us. In truth, details of flashbulb memories can be as false as any other memory, but they just seem so accurate. For example, many people (including George Bush) remember seeing the plane hit the first tower on 9/11 even though video footage did not emerge until much later. Maybe flashbulb memories serve some form of evolutionary value to always remember the worst case scenario. When it comes to surviving, it would seem that Mother Nature has decided that it is more important to remember how we felt when endangered, rather than when involved in the pleasures of life.

One way to combat PTSD is to administer a beta-blocker such as propranolol immediately after the event.[5] Beta-blockers dampen the arousal of the limbic system, so that events are not encoded with the same degree of emotional kick. People still remember what happened but feel less upset. Currently, research is under way at Yale Medical School by Deane Aikins to determine whether propranolol alleviates PTSD in combat troops, and some have even suggested that the drug should be given to all soldiers. This raises concerns. Do we really want to have a moral "morning-after pill" that shuts down a system that usually prevents us from doing things that might lead to remorse and regret?[6] Some have even suggested giving propranolol to soldiers before they go into battle as a prophylaxis. If you have no pangs of guilt, then you could become immune to suffering. But do we really want blind obedience without a moral compass in our solders? Remember the lessons of

Milgram and Abu Ghraib. There is a big difference between inoculating against PTSD and helping those to overcome events out of their control and no fault of their own. This future of the psychopharmacological treatment of PTSD is a moral minefield.

In any event, the scale of the emotional devastation created by 9/11 was unlikely to be solved so easily with a pill, and certainly not for those who had managed to escape the collapsing towers. The survivors of 9/11 were left traumatized and tormented by their flashbulb memories. Initially, the nation joined them in their grief as everyone tried to comprehend the sheer horror of 9/11 but, eventually, things started to return to normal. Memories started to fade, and people wanted to move on, but not those who had been there. Two years after the event, survivors sought each other out and gathered in small meetings to share their experiences, nightmares, and pain. There was a lot of guilt that they had survived, and they needed to talk. Gerry Bogacz, who cofounded the Survivors' Network, explained, "After a while, you can't talk about this anymore with your family. You've worn them out. Your need to talk is greater than their ability to listen." The Survivors' Network began to expand their meetings across Manhattan. More and more sought the solace and comfort of fellow survivors because only those who had undergone the same ordeal themselves could relate to the legacy left by 9/11. At these meetings, they would exchange stories and, with each retelling, it seemed to help unleash or ease the feelings and emotions that had been bottled up.

Very soon, one particular story started to spread among the groups. It was the story of Tania Head, who had survived the attack on the South Tower. She had been on the 78th floor, waiting for an elevator, when United Airlines flight 175 slammed into her tower. Tania had been badly burned by aviation fuel but managed to crawl through the rubble and even encountered a dying man who handed her his wedding ring, which she later returned to his widow. She would be only one of 19 above the impact point who would survive that day. Tania recalled how she was rescued by 24-year-old volunteer firefighter, Welles Crowther, who always wore a red bandanna. Witnesses say he was later killed making his fourth return to the collapsing tower to save more victims trapped in the debris. But Tania was not entirely without loss. Although she was saved, she later discovered that her fiancé, Dave, who had been in the North Tower, had been killed. The wedding, for which she had bought her dress only weeks earlier, was never to be.

Like other survivors, Tania needed to do something to deal with the emotional aftermath. She started an Internet group for survivors, and eventually news of her efforts reached Gerry Bogacz, who invited her to join the Survivors' Network. Tania's story was noteworthy. She had lost more than most others but somehow she had found the courage and conviction to overcome adversity. Tania's tale was a story of triumph. She offered hope to those who had been lost in the pits of despair. How could anyone wallow in self-pity when Tania had managed to overcome her own loss?

Soon Tania was campaigning for the survivors. Their voice had to be heard. She championed the group's right to visit Ground Zero, the site of the collapsed towers, which up to that point had been off-limits to all. She became the spokesperson for the Survivors' Network and then their president. She gave the inaugural guided tour of the Tribute W.T.C. Visitor Center in 2005, when she showed New York City Mayor Bloomberg, former Mayor Giuliani, former New York Governor Pataki, and other important dignitaries around the facility, regaling them with her experiences during that fateful day.

Tania Head had become the figurehead of 9/11 survivors. Except...Tania had never been there. She did not have a false memory. She was a fraud. Like me, Tania had watched the events on television back in her native Spain. She had not been in the South Tower. She did not work for Merrill Lynch. She had not been on the 78th floor of the World Trade Center. She had not crawled through rubble to retrieve a dying man's wedding ring. She had not been saved by a real hero, Welles Crowther. And she did not lose her fiancé, Dave, in the collapsed North Tower. Tania was really Alicia Esteve Head who only arrived in United States in 2003—2 years after 9/11. She had made everything up.[7] However, the authorities could not arrest Tania because she had not broken any law. In 2007, she disappeared and, in February 2008, a telegram was sent from a Spanish account to the Survivors' Network informing them that Alicia Esteve Head had committed suicide. Not surprisingly, very few believe this.

Alicia Head came from a wealthy Spanish background, but something must have been missing in her life that money could not buy. She needed attention and sympathy from others, and saw herself as the victim in a romantic tragedy set against the backdrop of the world's worst terrorist attack. As Tania, Alicia would have lived out this lie if she had not been exposed. We will probably never know exactly why she created this charade, but we must assume that this was the story she wanted to live. She may have come to even believe her own false memories, locked in her own fantasy world where she recast herself as a survivor against the odds.

■ We Are Our Memories

What is a memory? Can you hold one? Can you make one? Can you copy a memory? If we are our memories, can we be re-created? Memory is information stored as a pattern of electrical activity that "re-presents" the original pattern at the time it was formed. This representation is what memories are—although human memories are not rigid but dynamic and continually changing as new information is encountered. If we are our brains and our brains are a network of physical cells connected together in a pattern of weighted electrical activity, then it really should be possible to copy a memory in the same way we can copy any information. We should be able to copy our selves.

The possibility of copying memory is at the heart of what it is to be unique. Imagine a machine that can copy any physical object right down to its basic atomic structure. It can perfectly duplicate any material thing, irrespective of what it is made of or how complicated it is. Remarkably, engineers are working on precisely this type of machine, known as a *3D printer*. They typically work using a laser to scan a target object to calculate its dimensions and then relay that information to a jet-molding device where liquid plastic is squirted in to gradually build up a reproduction of the object. It's the sort of technology that would make constructing colonies on distant planets more feasible without having physically to transport every object. At the moment, the technology is fairly crude and solving how to build the internal structures of complicated objects made of different substances presents considerable challenges. However, just as the wooden block printing press of Johannes Gutenberg was considered a technological marvel of the 15th century and yet seems so primitive by today's standards, it may simply be a matter of time before we can reliably manipulate matter to create accurate duplicates.

Whatever way we achieve it, let us assume that we have the technology to reliably duplicate anything. Imagine now that you step into the machine and an identical physical copy of you is created. What would this new you be like? Let's also assume that you accept that there is no immaterial spirit or soul that cannot be reproduced. Would this identical copy be you? It's the sort of question that has entertained philosophers and writers[8] in one form or another for centuries, although in recent years it has enjoyed a resurgence of interest because of rapid developments in technology, such as gene sequencing and 3D printers. In all of these different scenarios, the same fundamental question of identity is raised: what makes us unique?

John Locke thought about this issue in the context of reincarnation[9]—something that was of interest in the 17th century when it came to the notion of the immortal soul. Locke was of the opinion that conscious awareness of one's own history was important when it came to unique personal identity. In short, he was thinking about the role of autobiographical memories in defining the self. Even if one does not believe in the immortal soul, modern adults also regard personal memory as the most important thing that defines who we are. In one study, adults were told about the unfortunate Jim, who was in a serious accident in which his body was irreparably damaged so that he needed a transplant.[10] Only this was a science fiction story in which the transplantation was very advanced. In one version of the story, Jim had lost all his memories but they could transplant his amnesic brain into either a robot or genetically engineered biological body. In another version of the story, doctors had managed to download all of Jim's life memories before his brain died and could transfer them to the replacement body. After the transplantation, Jim's original body was cremated. Adults were then asked if each operation was a success—was the patient still Jim?

The most important thing that determined whether adults considered the patient to be Jim was whether his memories had been saved, irrespective of whether they were now stored in a mechanical body or a biologically engineered one. In fact, the biologically engineered body that contained Jim's original brain was considered less Jim than the robot with his memories. In the absence of his memories, Jim was gone.

The relationship between memory and identity is an intuition that starts to emerge in children from around 4 to 5 years of age. We used duplication machine studies[11] to see if children would think that a live hamster could be copied exactly and whether its doppelganger would have the same memories.[12] To achieve the illusion of duplication we used two identical-looking Russian hamsters that were indistinguishable to the untrained eye. Once children had been convinced by the power of the machine to faithfully duplicate any toy, we introduced our pet hamster and proceeded to tell children about some of the unique physical properties the hamster had that could not be directly seen. We said it had swallowed a marble in its tummy, had a broken back tooth, and had a blue heart. We then created some memories that were unique to the hamster. Of course, memories are also invisible but they are not physical, like marbles and blue hearts. We showed the hamster a drawing by each child, whispered the child's name into the hamster's ear, and got the child to tickle the hamster. These are all episodes that can be stored in memory. We then placed the hamster in the duplicating machine and after the buzzer sounded, we opened both boxes to reveal that there were now two identical hamsters. What would the children think? Would the invisible physical properties and the memories be the same or different for each animal? So, we asked the child whether each hamster had a blue heart, a broken tooth, and a marble in its tummy. We also asked about the memories. Did each hamster know the child's name and what picture the child drew, and remember being tickled?

What's your intuition? If you walked into the machine, would the duplicate of you have the same memories? We conducted a straw poll online with 60 adults to get a sense of their intuition about duplicating hamsters and themselves in our machine. We asked whether the identical copy created by the machine would have the same body and memory. Around four out of five adults agreed that both the copied animal (84%) and human (80%) would have the same body. About half (46%) thought the hamster would have the same memories, compared to just over a third when it came to the human (35%). So, overall, adults thought that bodies were more likely to be copied compared to memories, and this belief was stronger when related to humans compared to hamsters.

Back in the lab, we repeated the hamster study a number of times with variations to check the results and found the same basic pattern. About one-third of children from 4 to 6 years of age thought that the second hamster was completely different on both mental and physical properties. Maybe they did not believe that the machine could copy something alive. Another third thought that the second hamster was identical on all properties. However, the interesting group was the remaining third of children who thought that the physical properties but not the memories were copied. In other words, they believed that the machine worked but could not copy the mind, just as the adults did.

In another version, we found this uniqueness effect of memories was stronger when we gave our first hamster a name, suggesting that it really does have something to do with identity. It's remarkable how naming an animal confers a new sense of identity, which is why you should not name your livestock if you intend to eat your animals. The uniqueness and identity conferred by names also may explain why young children are often affronted when they first learn that they share their name with another child.

We think our findings show that children begin to appreciate how minds and memories, in particular, create the unique individual. Earlier, we saw that there is an increasing awareness of other people's mental states from 4 years of age, as shown by the theory of mind research.

Initially, young children appreciate that other people have minds. As they develop, children come to increasingly appreciate the importance of their mind and the contents of their mind as being different to others and unique.

By the time we are adults, most of us think that our autobiographical memories are crucial to our sense of self. Our bodies could be copied but not our memories. Our memories are what make us who we are. Aside from the science fiction movies we have already discussed, anyone unfortunate enough in real life to witness the decline of a loved one with rapidly progressing dementia, which destroys memory, knows how the person's identity and sense of self can unravel. That loss of identity is one of the reasons why memory failure is considered such a trauma-tizing symptom for relatives, because the sufferer no lon-ger recognizes those around him.

Once again, neurologist Oliver Sacks reminds us of how we rely on others to create our sense of self-identity. One of his patients, a former grocer called William Thompson, had Korsakoff's syndrome, which produced a profound amnesia so that he was unable to remember any-thing for more than a second or two—just like Clive Wearing, whom we encountered earlier. He lived in the eternal present and was unable to generate a stable sense of self. In one exchange, Sacks walked onto the ward in a white coat to see William, who greeted him:

> "What'll it be today?" he says, rubbing his hands.
> "Half a pound of Virginia, a nice piece of Nova?"
>   (Evidently he saw me as a customer—he often
> would pick up the phone on the ward, and say
> "Thompson's Delicatessen.")
>   "Oh Mr. Thompson!" I exclaim. "And who do
> you think I am?"
>   "Good heavens, the light's bad—I took you for
> a customer. As if it isn't my

old friend Tom Pitkins...Me and Tom" (he whispers in an aside to the nurse) "was always going to the races together."

"Mr. Thompson, you are mistaken again."

"So I am," he rejoins, not put out for one moment. "Why would you be wearing a white coat if you were Tom? You're Hymie, the kosher butcher next door. No bloodstains on your coat though. Business bad today? You'll look like a slaughterhouse by the end of the week."[13]

It was as if William reeled effortlessly from one self-reflected identity to the next depending on who he thought Sacks was. He was oblivious to his circumstances. He had no awareness that he was a Korsakoff's patient in a psychiatric hospital but rather, as Sacks put it, had to "literally make himself (and his world) up every moment." Unlike the woman with Tourette's syndrome who could not stop incorporating the mannerisms of others, William used the identity of those around him to create his own identity.

■ Being in Two Minds

Constructing a plausible story is known as *confabulation* and is found in various forms of dementia as the patient attempts to make sense of his or her circumstances. Remember TH, who could not recognize himself in the mirror and thought his reflection belonged to his neighbor who had snuck into the house? However, we can all confabulate to some extent even though we are not aware we are doing this. These produce the biases, selective interpretations, reframing, and cognitive dissonance processes in which we are less objective than usual. We are all naturally inclined to interpret the world in terms of meaningful stories, and this probably reflects the activity of a system known as the "interpreter," which appears to be localized to the left hemisphere.[14]

We are not aware of this system normally as our brain processes are effortlessly and invisibly integrated below our levels of awareness. We simply experience the output of the interpreter as our conscious appraisal of our situations, our thoughts, and our behaviors. After all, we are our minds, and if that is largely constructed by unconscious processes, why should we ever become aware of the so-called interpreter? However, the activity of the interpreter was revealed by neuroscientist Michael Gazzaniga in his research on split-brain patients.

The normal brain is really a tale of two cities on the left and the right. Gazzaniga demonstrated that you could reveal the autonomy of the two hemispheres by selectively feeding different information to each. To do this, he presented words and images on the left and right side of a computer screen while the patient stared at a spot in the middle. This ensured that each hemisphere processed stimuli on the opposite side, and because they were no longer connected to each other through the corpus callosum, there was no exchange of information. For example, if the words "Key" and "Ring" were briefly flashed in the left and right halves of the screen respectively, the patient reported seeing the word "Ring" because this was processed by the opposite left hemisphere that controls language. However, if the patient was asked to choose the corresponding object from a selection on the table, he would pick up a key with the left hand that was controlled by the right hemisphere. Experiment after experiment revealed that the two hemispheres were functioning independently of each other. In one study, a naked man was flashed into the right hemisphere, causing the female patient to laugh but not be able to say what it was she was finding amusing. Her left hemisphere was unaware of the naked man and so could not explain what was amusing.

Sometimes, however, the patients make up a story to make sense of their unconscious activity. In one classic example told by Gazzaniga, one of his split-brain patients, Paul, was shown a snow scene in this left visual field and a picture of a chicken foot in his right visual field, and asked to choose the correct image from a selection on the table. He picked out a picture of a shovel with his left hand and a picture of the chicken foot with his right. When his attention was drawn to the discrepancy, and he was asked why he had chosen two different images, Paul replied, "Oh that's simple, the chicken claw goes with the chicken, and you need the shovel to clean out the chicken shit!"

Gazzaniga has proposed that there are not two separate minds or selves in these split-brain patients. Rather, the mind is a product of the mental processes of the brain that are shared across the two hemispheres. Language has the advantage of providing the narrative output, so the interpreter in the left hemisphere is able to articulate a coherent account to integrate the different pieces of information. Normally, theses processes are a collaborative effort, with information streaming in from all the different processing regions. But in the split-brain patient, no shared communication is possible. Presented with the choices of the right hemisphere that are inconsistent with the information in the left, the interpreter reconciles the difference with a plausible story.

What the split-brain studies reveal is that the self illusion is really the culmination of a multitude of processes. These usually work together in synchrony to produce a unified self; but, when inconsistencies arise, the system, strongly influenced by language, works to reestablish coherence. Probably one of the most compelling examples of this process comes from a personal anecdote that Gazzaniga[15] tells that comes from the late Mark Rayport, a neurosurgeon from Ohio. During one operation on a patient, in which Rayport was stimulating the olfactory bulb, the brain region associated with smell, the patient reported experiencing different aromas depending on the context. When the patient was asked to reminisce about a happy time in his life, stimulation of the region produced the sensation of roses. Rayport then asked the patient to think about a bad time in his life. This time stimulation of the same cluster of neurons produced the sensation of rotten eggs! This anecdote suggests that the neural networks of the brain store associations that fit together into a coherent story. In many ways, confabulation in the patient unaware of the true nature of his surroundings or disrupted brain processes is the same storytelling we all use to make sense of the inconsistencies that punctuate our lives when we deviate from the normal storyline of what we believe we are our selves.

■ Know Thy Self

Psychologist Dan McAdams proposes that when it comes to making sense of our lives, we create narrative or personal myths to explain where we have come from, what we do, and where we are going.[16] This is the narrative arc of our lives—the background, the struggle, the climax, and resolution that people readily attribute to the story of their lives. For example, some may see themselves as victims of circumstances beyond their control, reinterpreting events to fit with this perspective. Another could take the same set of circumstances and cast herself as the resilient heroine, triumphing over adversity to get where she is today. Presumably, these myths reflect the influences of culture and those close to us when it comes to providing a meaning to our lives. These accounts are myths because they are not grounded in reality but rather follow a well-worn narrative path of a protagonist character (our self) and what the world throws at them. In some individuals, the reality is complete fantasy, as in the case of Tania Head.

Our self-centered way of constructing the story means that we only pay attention to those events as we see them being related to us. This personal myth is constantly being revised and updated throughout our life by both conscious and unconscious processes, and it reemerges at times either through deliberate retelling to others to explain who we are, or at times of insight, when something from our past seems to become surprisingly poignant or relevant. Even cultures continually recycle the same old stories in the form of myths.[17] For example, *Star Wars* may have been set in the future but it is just as much a Greek myth as Homer and *The Iliad*. We like stories that are about journeys and conflicts, with goodies and baddies. The same is true for our own personal stories.

The problem with self-narratives is that we are the ones writing the story, which means our myths are open to all manner of distortions of what we think we should be like. This has been called the "totalitarian ego," in which we repress, distort, and ignore negative aspects of our lives that do not fit with our idealized self-narrative.[18] For example, we tend to remember information that fits with our idealized self and conveniently ignore that which does not. If we believe that we have a particular trait of personality, then we selectively interpret events that are consistent with that belief. In fact, we can easily interpret general statements to make them seem particularly relevant to us. For example, how accurate is this description of your personality?

> You have a great need for other people to like and admire you. You have a tendency to be critical of yourself. You have a great deal of unused capacity which you have not turned to your advantage. While you have some personality weaknesses, you are generally able to compensate for them. Disciplined and self-controlled outside, you tend to be worrisome and insecure inside. At times you have serious doubts as to

whether you have made the right decision or done the right thing. You prefer a certain amount of change and variety and become dissatisfied when hemmed in by restrictions and limitations. You pride yourself as an independent thinker and do not accept others' statements without satisfactory proof. You have found it unwise to be too frank in revealing yourself to others. At times you are extroverted, affable, sociable, while at other times you are introverted, wary, reserved. Some of your aspirations tend to be pretty unrealistic. Security is one of your major goals in life.

Spookily accurate isn't it? In 1948, psychologist Bertram Forer gave a personality test to his students and then provided them with an individual analysis based on their performance.[19] In fact, every student got the description above as their "unique" analysis. Just about everyone thought the analysis was an accurate description but Forer had, in fact, assembled the analysis from various different horoscopes to prove that the descriptions were sufficiently general as to apply to most people. This effect, known as the "Barnum effect" after the showman who famously quipped, "We've got something for everyone," shows that our self-stories are probably more similar than we imagine. Also the Barnum effect is particularly strong when the analysis contains many positive traits that support the inherent bias most of us hold.[20] Most of us think that we are funnier, smarter, better looking, and kinder than the average person, which, of course, is statistically impossible. Some of us have to be less funny, less clever, less beautiful, and crueller to balance up the sums.

The Barnum effect reveals that we all entertain illusions of a unique self, which turns out to be remarkably consistent and familiar between different people. Our uniqueness is closer to the average than we think. Also, if you look at the sort of generic statements in Forer's description, most are all to do with how we think others perceive us, social anxieties, and concerns that we are more complicated than others realize. Again, this is more damning evidence that most of us are preoccupied with what others think and less independent than we imagine!

■ Swimming in the OCEAN

Although the Barnum effect reveals that we share many beliefs and attitudes, we are clearly not clones of each other, like aphids or other simple organisms. When we describe different people, we come up with varied accounts that emphasize those characteristics that we think are the most notable. Even babies are not identical. We are born with different temperaments and form varying patterns of social attachment that appear to be strongly influenced by continual interaction with the environment. In short, we believe in the concept of personality—a stable set of characteristic styles of behaving, thinking, and feeling that define us as individuals.

Assessing personality is a major industry backed up by decades of research showing that some people are better suited to particular occupations. The science of personality can be traced back as far as the Greek scholar Theophrastus (c. 371–c. 287 BCE), who described his fellow Athenians in terms of a limited number of characters.[21] More recently, psychologists have argued that personality is the culmination of a combination of five distinct traits or the "Big-Five" model of Openness (the willingness to try new and imaginative experiences), Conscientiousness (the extent of self-disciplined organization), Extraversion (the extent of social gregariousness), Agreeableness (the willingness to help others) and Neuroticism (the extent of insecure self-centered worry): OCEAN for short.[22] The Big-Five approach is one of the most commonly used measures of personality assessment to predict how happy people are with their lives, the quality of social relationships, life expectancy, and even job success and satisfaction.[23]

With such high praise for the Big-Five, one might be tempted to conclude that personality psychologists have dispelled the self illusion—that there is indeed a core personality that defines each of us. However, in seeking to find stable measures of the Big-Five, personality theorists have ignored the variation in the OCEAN scores that can come about by changes in the different situations and roles we adopt.[24] For example, students were asked to consider themselves in five roles that that they typically occupy at that time in their life: as a student at college, as a temporary employee working to put themselves through college, as a friend of other students, as a child of their parents, and as a romantic partner. They were then assessed on the OCEAN measures, which revealed both inconsistency and consistency in their personality. The inconsistency was that individuals varied on their self-assessment of OCEAN measures over the different roles they imagined themselves in, but, as a group, they were consistent on which personality factors were most prominent in each role. On the Big-Five measures, respondents were consistently most Open to experience when they were in the role of the romantic partner, most Conscientious in the employee role, most Extraverted when they were in the friend role, least Agreeable in the student role, and most Neurotic in the student role.

These findings indicate that although the Big-Five factors of personality might be reliable within an individual in one role, they can completely change in another, just as the looking glass self predicts. In other words, people are not necessarily consistent in all aspects of their lives. This is why you can live with someone who is fastidious at work when it comes to detail but hopelessly disorganized when it comes to the domestic situation. This influence of context on the self has been shown over and over again. In one classic study, Princeton theology students were asked to present a sermon on the "Good Samaritan" in a building across campus.[25] If they were told that they were running late, only one in ten stopped to help a sickly man in a doorway on their way to the meeting, compared to six out of ten who were not in a hurry. What were they thinking? Clearly, nothing about the message of the sermon. How do they deal with such inconsistencies?

The answer is that we easily use our cognitive dissonance to reframe the events to justify our actions. Alicia Esteve Head may not have been a true victim of 9/11 but what Tania initially did was good for the survivors: Alicia could not have achieved this without becoming Tania. The theology students were aware of the ill man, but it was more important for their calling to deliver a sermon that would have greater impact on more people. It's all too easy to reframe a story to protect the self-narrative from disentangling when presented with inconsistency.

Why do we create these distortions? Isn't it better to be honest with oneself, so that we do not only end up fooling our selves? For one thing, positive illusions (that we are better than most others) may actually be beneficial to our mental well-being.[26] These positive illusions ensure that our self-esteem is protected by downgrading our failings ("Everybody cheats on their tax returns") to overegging our positive attributes as being special ("Unlike most people, I have a really creative mind"). Armed with these positive illusions, we feel that we have more control over situations when, in fact, we have little or none. Remember how the illusion of control inoculates us from the stress of uncertainty?[27] Positive illusions mean that we tend to see positive outcomes as a direct consequence of our actions, whereas negative outcomes are someone else's fault.[28] This makes us unrealistically optimistic, given the trials and tribulations that life can throw at us. Positive illusions make us more resilient and willing to carry on.

Maybe this resilience gave us a selective advantage as we evolved. Somewhere back in the mists of time, this way of thinking may have been the difference between the hunter on the Serengeti who was willing to keep trying that bit harder and the hunter who gave up the chase too early and failed to make it back to camp to mate. It is speculation, of course, but believing you will succeed means that sometimes you will, whereas believing that you will fail means that you inevitably do.

■ Listen With Mother

When we describe our self to others, we refer to our past experiences by way of an explanation of who we are and how we have arrived at this point in our life. This seems such an objective exercise that we never really question the truthfulness of our storytelling. However, culture plays an influential role in how we interpret the world around us. It turns out the individualism that is so characteristic of Western thinking and the collectivism of the East shape our autobiographical memories as well.

Qi Wang, a developmental psychologist at Cornell University, has shown that childhood memories differ between Eastern and Western cultures, with a greater focus on the individual in the West when it comes to recounting past experiences.[29] The self-obsessed Western perspective ("I remember the time I won the class test") drives our thought processes to focus on an elaborate encoding of moment-to-moment personal events. This is why Western children recall more specific details compared to their Eastern counterparts.[30] Those Eastern children who also had demonstrated greater detail for personal memories also scored higher on measures of individualism, thus proving that it was not the culture or language that determined autobiographical memory but rather the way they viewed the world.[31]

The way children remember is partly aided by parents reminiscing with their children. As we learned earlier, we know that if parents talk over events with their young children, then the amnesia barrier that is typically reported in 2- to 3-year-olds can be pushed back much earlier. This indicates that the framework of interpretation provided by the adults helps the child to make sense of his experiences and form better memories.[32] However, studies have also shown that parents from the East and the West differ in the way they reminisce with adults and show the typical individualistic or collective frameworks when talking to their children about their memories.[33]

What's more surprising is that the full content of memories is not always lost either. If you prime individuals from either the East or the West to think more individualistically or collectively, then they recall more personal or group-oriented memories accordingly. This means that the memories are still available: it is just that they are not usually retrieved. The context in which we find our selves even defines how we retrieve memories to describe our inner self—memories that we know are selectively processed. As Sir Frederick Bartlett said, "Social organization gives a persistent framework into which all detailed recall must fit, and it very powerfully influences both the manner and the matter of recall."[34] Even the memories we recall to define our self-story are defined by the groups to which we belong.

■ A Flight From Reality

For some individuals, their self-story is unacceptable—it's too much to cope with so they seek to create a new self or at least lose the one they had. Take the case of Gene

Saunders, who had been experiencing considerable difficulties in his home life and had a huge argument with his 18-year-old son who called him a failure. Gene simply packed his bags and ended up 200 miles away in another town where he became "Burt"—a short-order cook who had no memory of his past existence. This kind of memory loss is known as a dissociative *fugue state*, from the Latin for "flight."

Fugue states typically emerge in early adulthood and not very often after 50 years of age. They usually occur rapidly but also end abruptly and are thought to be a reaction to stress, in which the individual ceases to acknowledge who he or she is.

For example, Jeffrey Alan Ingram turned up at a television news conference in Denver in 2006 looking for his identity. All that he knew was that his name was "Al." He asked the viewing audience, "If anybody recognizes me, knows who I am, please let somebody know." It turns out that he had been on his way to visit a friend dying of cancer but on arrival in Denver had gone into a fugue state. Eventually, his fiancée's brother, who had watched the news, recognized Jeffrey, who lived over a 1,000 miles away in Olympia, Washington. His own mother explained that this was not the first time Jeffrey had entered a fugue state, as a similar disappearance occurred in 1995 on trip to the grocery. Then, he turned up 9 months later with no knowledge of who he was.

Fugue states are just one of a number of conditions known as *dissociative identity disorders* (DIDs), formerly called *multiple personalities*, in which alternative selves or "alter egos" are present. The first popular fictionalized account of DID was *The Strange Case of Dr Jekyll and Mr Hyde* (1886) by Robert Louis Stevenson, but the idea than an individual can split into different personalities is a recurrent theme in modern culture. A notable recent example is Ed Norton's alter ego, Tyler Durden, played by Brad

Pitt in *Fight Club* (1999). Just like Jekyll and Hyde, we watch as the anarchic character of Tyler Durden increasingly drags Norton's upstanding character into criminality only to discover at the end of the movie that Durden is in fact his own alter ego.

The notion that we all have a good and bad side has become accepted wisdom, although few of us would regard the different characterizations as different individuals. And yet this is exactly the claim with DID, to the extent that it has been used in criminal cases as a defence plea. The first such case was in 1978, when 23-year-old Billy Milligan was arrested following an anonymous tip-off for the rape of four college women on Ohio State campus the previous year. At first, he seemed like the typical drifter: troubled childhood, abused by his stepfather, constantly in trouble. That changed after a psychological examination indicated he had at least ten different personalities, two of whom were women. In fact, it was one of the women, Adelena, a 19-year-old lesbian, who claimed responsibility for the rapes. Another of Milligan's personalities was the fearful and abused child, David, 9, who it was claimed made the telephone call turning in Billy. According to *Time*, investigators found the police telephone number on a pad next to Milligan's phone.[35] Milligan ended up being sentenced to 10 years in secure psychiatric hospitals and was released in 1988.

Another famous case in which DID was used as defence was that of the Hillside Strangler, Ken Bianchi, who claimed that an alter ego, Steven Walker, had been responsible. However, this defence fell apart when a dubious psychiatrist suggested that most cases of DID had at least two alter egos. In the following hypnosis session, Bianchi conveniently manifested another alter ego, Billy. When police investigated further, they found out that Steven Walker had been a real psychology student whose identity Bianchi had tried to steal in order to commit fraud. Bianchi is currently serving a life sentence.

Although DIDs are recognized in the major psychiatric manuals, they are still considered highly controversial. The first cases, reported in the 19th century, are linked to the psychoanalytic movement. Not much was heard of DID again until 1957, with the release of a popular movie, *The Three Faces of Eve*, about a woman with DID, followed by a similar movie, *Sybil*, in 1976. Prior to the 1970s, there had been very few cases of DID but suddenly the incidence exploded, which led many to question whether it was a real medical disorder or a fashionable fad. Also, DID was primarily a North American problem, with few cases reported in other countries. Those that were reported in North America also tended to come from the same specialists, which cast doubt on the source of the disorder.

Just like hypnosis and the actions of student prison guards, DID has been dismissed as an extremely elaborate example of role-playing, in which a belief about dissociated states is promoted by society and supported by a few influential experts, namely the psychiatrists who are experts in the field. That is not to say that individuals with DID are deliberating faking their symptoms. Support for this comes from studies that reveal that different brain states can be manifest when the individual is in one of his or her alternative personalities. For example, brain imaging studies have shown that patients with DID can manifest different patterns of brain activity when in different characters.[36] In one patient, the memory region seemed to shut down during the transition between one personality to another, as if a different set of memories was being retrieved.

The evidence from brain imaging studies is less convincing if one considers that we can alter our brain activity by simply thinking about different things. If I think about a time when I was upset or angry, my brain activity will change. However, one dramatic case in which brain science backs up the claim of true, separated selves comes from a recent German DID patient who, after 15 years of being diagnosed as blind, gradually regained sight after undergoing psychotherapy.[37] At first, only a few of the personalities regained vision, whereas others remained blind. Was the patient faking? Not according to the electrical measurements recorded from her visual cortex—one of the early sensory processing areas in the brain. When her personality was sighted, electrical activity was normal over this region but absent when the patient was experiencing a blind personality. Somehow, the parts of her brain that were generating the multiple personalities were also shutting on and off the activity of the visual part of the brain. This finding is beyond belief—literally. To believe that you are blind is one thing, but to switch off parts of the lower-level, functioning sensory processing areas of your own brain is astounding. Somehow, the network of connections that operates further upstream in the brain to deal with complex concepts, such as the self and personality, can control earlier basic processing input relay stations downstream in the brain.

■ How the Mighty Have Fallen

If we are not brain damaged or suffering from DID, to what extent can we experience a different self? In modern Westernized cultures, some people appear to lead complicated, multifaceted lives by juggling private and public personas, whereas others lead a more simple existence, such as subsistence farming in rural villages. The selves we present to the world must be a reflection of the different circles we inhabit. Sometimes those worlds can clash, which occurs when we discover a different side to individuals whom we thought we knew so well—the unfaithful spouse, the pedophile priest, the sadistic nurse, or the corrupt politician. These are the contradictions in the self that we see so often in others. Public figures seem to constantly fall from grace by engaging in activities that seem so out of character. Is there anything that the science of the self illusion can do to cast some light on these transgressions?

The first question to ask is why people put their public self image unnecessarily at risk. For example, why do upstanding members of society with supposedly impeccable moral standards often seem to get caught with their pants down? Why did Sir Allan Green, the former Director of Public Prosecutions in the United Kingdom, go cruising around London's King's Cross station—at the time, a notorious hangout for prostitutes—when he must have known there was a good chance he could be arrested? Likewise, few could understand why Hollywood heartthrob Hugh Grant would pay Divine Brown for sex in a car on Sunset Boulevard, a notorious nightspot where the vice squad regularly operated. He must have known how risky were his actions. But maybe that is the whole point. There might be something thrilling and exciting about taking risks, and it is only a risk when you have something to lose. When called to account, many are at a loss to explain their actions and say they were not their usual self.

Another fascinating facet of this type of behavior is sexual role-playing, in which people act out a very different sort of self from what they exhibit in their daily lives. For the most part, members of repressed societies have to maintain dignity and decorum, no more so than our leaders. For example, they have to be dominant and yet how often do we hear about captains of industry or politicians engaging in submissive sexual fantasies where they pay to be dominated and subjected to humiliation? In 2010, three Long Island lawyers teamed up with a New York dominatrix to run a $50 million mortgage scam. Their victims were the many willing and wealthy clients who attended the dominatrix's private dungeon in Manhattan. Paying for bondage, discipline, sadism, and masochism (BDSM) appears to be fairly common in the corridors of power. But why?

For obvious reasons, getting people to talk about their sexual behavior is very difficult. Luckily, there are some who ask the sort of questions about sexual behaviors that the rest of us would shy away from. Katherine Morris, a psychologist from the United States, interviewed 460 heterosexual men who regularly engaged in BDSM. The majority of the men she interviewed were high-level professionals, including a fair number of corporate executives, including several chief executives of corporations. Her interviewees also included psychiatrists, attorneys, engineers, scientists, and other professionals who spend a great deal of time in high-pressure intellectual pursuits on a daily basis.[38]

Morris detected a pattern in which their emotions during these private BDSM sessions were ones that they did not feel they could express as part of their daily public lives. It was as if something was missing in their lives that needed addressing for total satisfaction. These men felt forced to reintegrate the missing components in privacy as part of a sexual ritual. Morris described how many of the high-level corporate executives felt that they were frauds and that in her view, "humans seek balance" between their public and private lives.

It is not only due to inadequate fulfilment that people seek out such role-playing. The practice of BDSM also allows the individual to lose his or her identity and adopt a role that he or she finds sexually gratifying by being someone else.[39] For the most part, our sexual activities are private compared to our public behavior. It is almost as if we are allowed to become a different person in the bedroom. The cliché is the shy and demure wallflower in public who transforms into a sexual demon behind closed doors. It's as if the persona we portray in public is just a front for the real person in private. Certainly, we are all

expected to control our sexual behaviors in public—
something that we are taught from a very early age. Those
who cannot are regarded as perverts or mentally ill. In
some societies, there are very strict codes of conduct, very
often based on religion, but all societies have some rules
about what sexual behaviors are permitted in public.
Members of these societies must conform to these rules,
but, ultimately, one consequence is to suppress thoughts
and behaviors that do not go away but may eventually
need to be vented, like those patients with Tourette's syndrome who lack the ability to suppress screaming profani-
ties. The more they try to stop themselves, the stronger the
compulsion becomes. This is the ego-depletion effect again.
The illusion is that we have the self-control to decide
whether we give in to our urges or not. The problem is that
abstinence may lead to pent-up frustration to do exactly
the things we are trying to avoid. That's when the mighty
fall down in such a spectacular way.

Technology may provide us with a way out. One place
where we may be able to play out these fantasies and urges
without exposure is on the Internet. The next chapter considers how the Internet is changing how we interact and
share stories and, ultimately, how the web is going to play
a major role in the self illusion we construct. This is because
storytelling on the Internet flows in two directions, with
everyone having the capability to contribute to receiving,
generating, and sending information to others. If our looking glass self is a reflection of those with whom we sur-
round our selves, then there are inevitably going to be
implications for our self illusion in the way new media
change, open up, or restrict the others with whom we come
into contact.

8 ■

Caught in the Web

It started with a man shouting in the crowd. Why was he shouting? Did someone say, "Bomb?" No one was certain, but no one stuck around to check. Within seconds, there was a mass stampede. It was the Second World War remembrance ceremony in Amsterdam, in May 2010. One witness reported,

> Just after the moment of silence, a very loud shriek could be heard not that far away from where I was standing. Immediately, a huge amount of people started to move away from where the sound had come from. It was scary when this mass of people attempted to run away from the shout.[1]

This is an example of stampeding—a common phenomenon found among animals that live in groups. It occurs whenever something triggers a sudden movement of a small number that causes the whole to respond en masse. This is the herd mentality, the hive mind. When someone in a crowd starts to run, we instinctively follow. In the same way, we tend automatically to copy and mimic others. This makes a lot of sense. Like meerkats, we can benefit from the collective wisdom and awareness of others when some threat arises. Because we instinctively respond to other humans, a simple action in one individual can rapidly spread and escalate to complex group activity. The problems occur when large numbers gather in limited spaces and the threat is disproportionate to the danger of the moving crowd. Over 60 people were injured in the Amsterdam stampede, but they were lucky. Every year, hundreds of people are killed when large crowds gather in confined spaces and panic breaks out.

It is in our nature to assemble in groups. Many of us seek out crowds and groups to satisfy a deep need to belong. In doing so, we cluster with like-minded individuals who share common interests (this is why most stampedes occur at religious festivals and sporting events). This is because we substantiate our self in the crowd. Sometimes others feel their individual self is lost in the crowd as they become one with the others around. Whether we feel lost or found, our self is ultimately influenced by the collective properties of the groups we join. As soon as we join others, our self is reflected in the crowd.

This relationship between the individual and the crowd is a key interest in the field of social networking, in which scientists try to understand the nature of groups in terms of how they form, how they operate, how they change, and how they influence the individual. Some of the most dramatic examples are the riots that periodically erupt in otherwise civilized societies. In 2011, the police shooting of a black man set a London mob burning and smashing their way through the capital. Although the killing was in London, copycat rioting broke out in other English cities. Commentators were quick to look for culprit causes—social class, education, ethnic group, poor parenting, unemployment, boredom, and so on. When they started to look at the profiles of those arrested in the London disturbances, however, it soon became apparent that there was not just one type of rioter but a variety from different backgrounds, ages, and opportunities. Many were disaffected youths from deprived backgrounds, but there was an Oxford law graduate, a primary school teacher, an organic chef, children of a pastor, and other unlikely "criminals." In attempting to categorize the typical looter, the authorities had failed to understand that coherent groups emerge out of very different individuals.

It doesn't even have to be a perceived miscarriage of justice that triggers riots, as witnessed in London, or the 1992 Los Angeles riots after the police beating of Rodney King. In 2011, another riot exploded in Vancouver in response to the outcome of the Stanley Cup ice hockey final. When the Canucks lost to the Boston Bruins, it sparked a flurry of rioting and looting. Canadians take their ice hockey very seriously!

Harvard's Nicholas Christakis says that when you take a bird's eye view of humans through the prism of social networks, the picture of both the individual and the group changes.[2] He draws the analogy with graphite and diamonds. Both materials are made of carbon atoms but it is the way these individual atoms are connected that determines why one material is soft and dark and the other is hard and clear. The layered lattice arrangement of graphite carbon atoms means that it shears easily, whereas the highly interconnected arrangement of diamond carbon atoms means that it is as hard as—well, diamonds, of course. Therefore, when it comes to carbon atoms, the whole is greater than the sum of its parts. Similarly, understanding the individual self only really makes sense in terms of the groups to which they are connected. To extend the carbon metaphor, when we are well connected, we are more resilient because there is safety and strength in numbers. Alone, we are more vulnerable and weaker.

The mechanisms for joining groups are not completely random. We all possess individual differences that mean we join some groups and not others. There are strong historical, geographic, and physical factors at play. We tend to form friendships and associate with others who represent our culture, live close by, resemble us, and with whom we can easily connect.[3] We also form friendships with those who share the same interests and worldviews. We tend to like those who resemble us physically. For example, obese people are more likely to hang out with other obese people and the friends of obese people.[4] If one friend is overweight, there is a 45% increased likelihood above chance that the other friend will also be overweight. If you are the friend of a friend who has another overweight buddy, then your likelihood is going to be 25% above chance. This is known as *homophily*—the tendency for bird's of a feather to flock together, for like to be attracted to like. Only by the time the relationship is a friend of a friend of a friend of a friend has the link to obesity disappeared.

Homophily can arise for various reasons, such as shared external environments or interests. Groups formed on the basis of national identity, religious beliefs, team allegiances, or musical tastes are examples of homophilic groups resulting from external factors. There is nothing genetic about being a British, Christian, Manchester United supporter who likes Dolly Parton. More surprising, however, is the recent discovery of genetic factors in homophily in social groupings. It has long been known that good-looking people tend to hang out with each other and that looks are partly genetic, but a recent study by Christakis and colleagues has shown that genes associated with behavioral traits are also related to friendship formation.[5] For example, one gene, *DRD2*, associated with the disposition to alcoholism, was found to predict homophily in clusters of friends, whereas another, *CYP2A6*, linked with openness, surprisingly produced the opposite effect of *heterophily*—the tendency to associate with others where there are no shared interests ("opposites attract"). The causal mechanisms by which genes might exert this influence on behavior is unclear, and investigation of the genetic factors implicated in social networking is in its early days, but the discovery that genes operate in social environments means that we have to rethink the extent to which our biology influences our behavior.

■ The Technology Savannah

Technology is changing the way we communicate, and this is going to have an impact on the way we behave socially. Specifically, social networking may have very significant consequences for the way we develop. Our human mind, which was forged and selected for group interaction on the Serengeti, is now expected to operate in an alien environment of instant communication with distant, often anonymous individuals. Our face-to-face interaction that was so finely tuned by natural selection is largely disappearing as we spend more time staring at terminal screens that were only invented a generation ago. The subtle nuance of an intonation of voice or a facial micro-expression[6] is lost in this new form of communication. The physicality of interaction is disappearing, which may be something to which we will need to adapt. But ultimately, it will change the way we assemble our sense of self because of the influence of groups. Even if this turns out not to be correct, we would be wise to give these new technologies some careful consideration as they have the potential to have profound effects on the way we live.

For some time now, man has had the capability to shape his own future. With our capacity to communicate and our ability to form societies, we hand down knowledge from one generation to the next. We have used this communication to develop technologies, such as writing. With the advent of science, most of us in modern societies have been freed from the shackles of hostile environments and hard times. Civilization has enabled humans to take control of processes that used to whittle out the weak. In the distant past, natural selection ensured that the old, the sick, and the infertile lost out in the mating game. This has been changed by technological innovation. Modern medicine, with its fertility treatments and health care, has shifted the goal posts. Of course, natural selection will always be with us, but we can use our science to outwit its relentless cull of the least suited. Human development is increasingly shifting away from natural selection to *Lamarckian inheritance*—the idea, named after the French biologist Jean-Baptiste Lamarck, that we can change our selves while we are still alive and pass on the benefits of that change to our children by tailoring their environments. It's not clear how we will continue to evolve, but science and technology seem unlimited in their ingenuity to bend the rules. Similarly, our technologies and advances in communication through the Web will forever shape the future of humankind in ways that are not yet clear. One thing that is certain is that the Web will influence our sense of self as we increasingly live our lives online, as members of virtual groups.

I remember when the Web first emerged. I had just arrived at the Massachusetts Institute of Technology (MIT)'s Department of Brain and Cognitive Science in the autumn of 1994 as a visiting scientist. I was checking e-mail in the computer room where Zoubin Ghahramani and Daniel Wolpert, two brilliant young scientists, were getting excited about Netscape, one of the first Web browsers that had just sent through some image files to Zoubin's terminal. The Internet had already been in existence for years to allow academics and the military to exchange e-mails, but the invention of hypertext markup language (HTML; the Web programming language) provided the first opportunity to share more than just text. This was my first encounter with the Web. In the past, people could e-mail you files directly, but now anyone with the right address could visit and view material on a remote website. It was like creating something permanent in the electronic landscape that others could come and visit well after you were gone—almost like the virtual immortality of scratching a mark on an electronic wall for others to find. As nerdy scientists, that afternoon, we all recognized the importance of this capacity to share remote information, but I doubt any of us fully understood its potential power.

The subsequent rise and spread of the Web into everyone's lives has been astonishing for those of us who remember the pre-Web days, but my daughters seem oblivious because they have grown up with today's rapid change of pace and assume it has always existed. I tell my own children that they are living during one of the major transitions in human civilization, that humankind is currently in the midst of the next great evolutionary leap. This sort of statement may sound sensationalist. It may sound nostalgic as some of us hanker for simpler times. It may even sound like the curmudgeonly grumblings of a middle-aged dad who laments that, "Things were different in my day." Indeed, every generation probably says this, but I cannot overstate this transition too much. I think that most of us are sleepwalking into uncharted territory. We need not fear it. It is one of most exciting times to be alive in the history of humankind.

◼ Who Hath Not Googled Thyself?

Have you ever searched for your self on the Web, entering your name into the Google search engine to see if you come up? Go on. Be honest. Only the very few cannot be curious to know what's been said about them, if anything at all. And where better to find your self than on the Web? It's the electronic version of looking first for your self in the group photograph or hearing your name mentioned in a crowded cocktail party and then straining to listen to what is being said about you. The advent of the Web has made our preoccupation with what others think about us a part of human nature. For better or worse, most of us in industrialized countries are now on the Web whether we like it or not.

Many of us enjoy being on the Web and actively use it socially to interact with others. Social networking sites such as MySpace, Facebook, and Bebo have attracted millions of users, many of whom have integrated these sites into their daily lives. The mightiest at the moment is Facebook, which currently has over 750 million active users. There are several core features of the different social networking sites. First, they enable users to construct public and semi-public profiles on a website. Second, the website enables users to view other users who subscribe to the service and, most importantly, enables them to communicate with each other by messaging and facilities for sharing files. It's like a 24/7 virtual cocktail party where you mix with friends but sometimes meet new acquaintances, swap stories and opinions, share a joke, maybe look at each other's family photographs, and flirt (or sometimes even more). Or, perhaps you sign a petition or start a cause to change things. As the new media expert Jenny Sundén succinctly put it, social networking sites enable users to "type oneself into being."[7]

Not surprisingly, an analysis of personal profiles posted on social networks reflects a great deal of narcissism[8]—the tendency to be interested in one's self and what others think about us. After all, why wouldn't we want others to know about how successful our lives were? However, this obsession with our self on the Web will depend mostly on who you are. Being online is not for everyone. For example, my wife refuses to join social networks—but then she also does not want to appear in the public light. Like my wife, many of the pre-Web generation cannot understand what is going on and frankly do not feel the need to surrender precious time, effort, and especially privacy to join online communities. They don't get YouTube, they don't get Facebook, and they certainly don't get Twitter, which seems to be the ultimate in broadcasting trivial information about one's self. However, even stalwarts against the onslaught of social networks are being dragged, kicking and screaming, into a new era. The social networking sites that have sprung up in this last decade are changing communication between people and will play an important role in self-identity. If the self illusion is correct, social networking sites will continue to expand in popularity and will increasingly shape the sense of who we are for the next generation and those that follow. As long as we remain a social animal, social networks in one form or another are here to stay.

This is because most of us want to be noticed. Surveys consistently show that the West has embraced the celebrity culture. When 3,000 British parents were asked what their preteen children wanted to be when they grow up, one in three said they wanted to be a sports figure, actor, or pop star. Compare that to the professions that topped the aspiration list 25 years ago: teachers, bankers, and doctors.[9] Children now want to be famous for the sake of being famous because they equate fame with success. A recent survey of the U.K. Association of Teachers and Lecturers revealed that the majority of students would prefer to be famous than academically gifted.[10] The Web facilitates this obsession with fame and popularity by providing a readily accessible and updatable medium in which individuals can indulge their interest in the famous but also begin to make an impact of their own. Anyone can gather a following on the Web. It has leveled the popularity playing field so we can all be noticed.

Also, for most people, the Web is first and foremost a social medium. According to the Neilson Company, which specializes in analyzing consumer behavior, the majority of time spent online is engaged in social networking sites, and that is increasing each year.[11] By August 2011, we were spending over 700 billion minutes per month on Facebook alone. One in five U.S. adults publishes a blog, and over half of the American population have one or more social networking profiles. Even when we are at work, we are social networking: on average, a U.S. worker spends 5.5 hours each month engaged in this activity on company time.[12]

It is even more pervasive in adolescents and young adults. At the moment, if you grow up in the West and are between 16 and 24 years of age, being online is essential. This age group spends over half of their online time engaged in social networks, in comparison to older age groups. Many Western teenagers feel they do not exist unless they have an online presence. Life online has taken over from the school playground and the shopping mall where the kids used to hang out.[13] It has extended the window of opportunity to socialize at anytime and anywhere. We used to tell our kids to get off the phone. Now they use their own phones and can be chatting online whenever they want. According to the most recent report by Ofcom, the industry regulator of communications, half of all U.K. teenagers, compared to a fifth of adults, possess a smartphone.[14] The most common use of the phone is not for making calls but for visiting social networking sites. Two-thirds of teenagers use their smartphones while socializing with others; a third of teenagers use them during mealtimes, and nearly half of teenagers use their phones to social network in the bathroom or on the toilet. No wonder that six out of ten teenage users consider themselves addicted to their smartphones. They get to continue socializing well after the school is shut, the mall is closed, or their families have moved them to another town.

How is this online activity going to affect their development, if at all? A child's social development progresses from being the focus of their parent's attention as an infant and preschooler to stepping out and competing with other children in the playground and class. Initially, children's role models are their parents but as they move through childhood and develop into adolescents, they seek to distance themselves from the family so that they can establish an independent identity among their peers. As a parent, I have come to accept that what peers think can easily trump whatever a parent wants for his or her child. This may not be such a bad thing. I am not a therapist, but I can easily believe that overbearing parenting creates later problems if children are not allowed to establish their identity among their peers. These are the popularity contests that preoccupy most adolescents in Western culture. It is through this chaotic period of self-construction that the adolescent hopefully emerges out the other side as a young adult with the confidence to face the world.

As every parent in the West knows, adolescence is typically a time of rebellion, bravado, showing-off, risk-taking, pushing boundaries, arguments, tears, strategic allegiances, and Machiavellian negotiation. Some blame immature brains, which has perpetuated the "teen brain" hypothesis—that the disruptive behavior of this age group is the inevitable consequence of lacking of inhibitory control in the frontal lobes, which are some of the last neurological structures to reach adult levels of maturity. Teenagers are hypersensitive to social evaluation, but does that explain the increase in risky behavior? Psychologist Robert Epstein believes the teen brain account of delinquency is a myth—that adolescent turmoil is more to do with culture and the way we treat our children.[15] He points out, for instance, that teenage misbehavior is absent in most preindustrialized societies. He argues that teenage delinquency is an invention of modern societies and media stereotypes, and describes how, before the arrival of Western media and schooling, the Inuit of Canada did not have the problems of teenage rebellion. For him, the problems we see in Western teenagers are more to do with the way we isolate this age group and effectively let them establish their own social groups and hierarchies. These are the pecking orders of popularity achieved through the processes of affiliation, competition, and establishing one's self esteem in the eyes of one's peers. In this situation, teenagers think that in order to gain a reputation among their peers, they have to be outsiders to the rest of society.

Others argue that the data on teenage risk-taking is incontrovertible. It may be somewhat culturally influenced, but far from being erratic, teenagers are just as good as adults at reasoning about risk. They simply consider some risks to be worth taking to prove themselves. Developmental psychologist Lawrence Steinberg has shown that teenagers perform just as well as adults on simulated driving tasks when they are alone, but run more risks when friends are watching them. [16] When friends were present, risk-taking by speeding and running red lights increased by 50% in teenagers whereas there was no increase in adults. One neural account is that the reward centers in the teenage brain are highly active during this period of development. Rewards are thus supercharged when individuals succeed in front of their friends, which makes success all that more sweet and the risks to achieve them worth taking. But it is not enough to succeed. One has to be seen to succeed.

In the West, adolescents are faced with the paradox of wanting to be accepted by their peers but at the same time needing to be different. Music, fashion, movies and, of course, sex are the things adolescents care about the most because these are the very things that help to create the unique identities they seek. It is no coincidence that these are the main topics of "likes" and "dislikes" in online social networks. Whenever you put something up on a social network, you are inviting a response from your peers. It is not for your own private viewing; rather, you are broadcasting your presence to the world. The number of comments and hits your activities generate tell you and, more importantly, others, that you matter. Most of us want to be noticed, and social networking sites make this universal yearning the core of its activity. Having others validate your presence is the currency of popularity that individuals seek.

■ What a Twit I Am

One day earlier this year, the famous British actress, Dame Helen Mirren, started to follow me. I wasn't walking down the road in London or Los Angeles, where the Oscar-winner probably spends most of her time. Rather, I was seated at the kitchen table in my Somerset barn, taking a break to look at my Twitter account, when I saw that @HelenMirrenDBE was following me. Or at least I thought she was. My heart skipped a beat.

For the uninitiated, Twitter is a site where you can post any message so long as it is less than 140 characters long. It's like open-access texting to the world where anyone who follows you can read your messages or link to images and other websites that you might put up. I currently have over 5,000 Twitter followers. I don't personally know that many people and if you sat me down, I would be hard-pressed to name a couple of hundred individuals. Even though my following may sound impressive, I am way down on the Twitter hierarchy. Individuals whom you would never imagine being icons of interest are huge on Twitter. Lance Armstrong, the top cyclist, has well over a million followers. So does the actor Brent Spiner. Who was

Brent Spiner, I wondered? None other than the actor who played the android, "Data," on *Star Trek*. There are a lot of Trekkies out there!

What is it about Twitter that makes it so appealing? Why do we follow and want to be followed? It probably comes down to a number of related issues to do with the self. First, the human brain is a gossiping brain—we are nosey and want to know what others are up to even if that includes what they ate for breakfast that day. Second, we like our opinions to be validated by others. When someone responds positively to an opinion or shares it with others, we feel vindicated. Of course, if our opinion is rejected or ridiculed then our self-esteem is deflated. Having the option to follow or unfollow others means that individuals within a social network tend to share the same values and attitudes.

We also like to be the first to know something or spread the word. This is something we did as children. Remember how important it was to be the first to spread the word in a playground? If you were the last to find out something then that was a reflection of how important you were in the pecking order. By being the first to know something, we cement our self-importance with others. However, one of the most powerful draws of social networking sites like Twitter is that they make you feel important if you have a large number of friends or followers. Your self-worth is validated, and the more followers and friends you have, the more you value your self.

Another reason why Twitter has taken off (it is the fastest growing social network) is that celebrities happily post their thoughts and updates on a regular basis. These used to be off-limits to the general public. Suddenly, we have access to the famous in a way that was never possible before. The public's appetite for celebrity trivia has long been insatiable. There is a whole industry of paparazzi and tabloid press that has evolved out of the primeval slime to provide the gossip to feed the masses, but Twitter is far superior because it comes directly from the celebrities. Of course, celebrities need their followers because without the fans, they are out of the public eye, which usually also means out of work. So, most now have Twitter presences. In fact, many employ writers to compose their tweets so that the illusion of accessibility and visibility is sustained.

The biggest boost to your self-esteem is if a celebrity such as Helen Mirren follows you. Whenever someone of a perceived higher status befriends us, then we are raised in our standing by association. This is known as *basking in reflected glory*. Many of us take vicarious pleasure by associating with the success of others. This is why fans are so passionate about the individuals and the teams they support. Sports fans are probably the most common example. I have heard many a pub argument in which fans lament the team manager's decisions as if it were a family feud. Fans even talk as if they are a member of the team by using the pronoun, "we."[17] Twitter facilitates these distortions of reality by generating the illusion of easy accessibility to the famous. Anyone can follow a celebrity who is on Twitter, thus creating an interesting social phenomenon in which we feel an intimacy with others whom we would never have the opportunity to meet in our normal lives. The relatively open access of Twitter also creates problems. Strangers feel that they are on a familiar basis with those they follow—which is not so very different from celebrity stalkers who are deluded in thinking that they share a life with their victims.

Karl Quinn, an Australian journalist, pointed out that Twitter is perfect for mob nastiness. It enables individuals to make cruel comments and then pass them on: "Many of us are in two minds about whether celebrities are flesh-and-blood human beings or merely life-sized piñatas in need of a damned good whacking."[18] The trouble is that as soon as a victim is identified most of us are more willing to join in with the bullying than we imagine. Remember how that worked in the playground? It was easier than standing up to the mob. The same is true for Twitter—people join in with the mob rule. Also, with the problem of polarization (discussed shortly) that is endemic in social networking sites, attitudes and opinions will naturally shift toward more extremism as those who seem to agree with us egg us on or we feel the need to be more judgmental. With their combination of distorted opinions, rapid communication without the time for reflection, and the perceived distance and anonymity, social networks are a perfect platform for us to behave in a way that we would not in real life.

This raises an important point with regards to the difference between online and offline selves. If we behave differently when we are online, then where is the true self if the self really does exist? Can we draw a real difference between thoughts and actions? If our actions are virtual and anonymous, are they any less representative of our true self? One could argue that because social rules and the pressure to conform in real life are so powerful for many, offline activities do not reflect our true attitudes and thoughts. If they can only be expressed online in the absence of the threat of any repercussions or social rejection, what kind of true self is that? That's one reason why we need to be reminded that the self is an illusion if we believe that it can exist independently of the different contexts and influences of others. One might counter that there is only one self that behaves differently depending on the situation but that is the heart of the illusion. We are far more under the influence of contexts and others than we appreciate. Just like the alcoholic who thinks she can control her drinking, our self illusion prevents us from seeing just how far we are at the mercy of influences outside of our control.

But I am sure you want to hear more about Helen Mirren. What's she like? What does she eat for breakfast? Sadly, I was deluding myself with my own self-importance. When I looked at her profile, it was clear that with only 216 followers, my Helen Mirren was most definitely a "troll." Trolls are individuals who take delight in disrupting social networking sites by posting offensive comments or pretending to be someone else. I don't even know if Helen Mirren is on Twitter but, if she is, I have no doubt she has thousands of followers. For one tantalizing moment that morning, my heart skipped a beat as I thought that my adolescent crush was taking an interest in me. That would have been an enormous boost to my ego, but why would a great British actress like Helen bother with a lowly egghead like me? There again, even celebrity actresses are sometimes intrigued by the mundane lives of mere mortals. She is human, after all.

■ The Human Borg?

Some commentators have expressed anxiety over the rapid rise of social networks and have predicted a breakdown in human civilization. We have heard similar prophets of doom decrying all media from books to radio to television. One fear is that we are allowing the brains of our children to be destroyed forever as they lose the skills necessary to interact with others in real life and pass through a critical period of psychological development that is essential for healthy socialization.[19] As the plasticity of their frontal neural circuits hardens, we are told that they will be forever locked out of normal social development and grow up into retarded adults. The claim is that they may never acquire the adequate attention spans that are stimulated by real-life social interaction. Social networking sites and online activity in general are depriving them of normal social environments. More alarming is the suggestion that the rise in childhood autism may be linked to increased online activity.

The scientific evidence for such claims is sparse, to say the least, and, indeed, the Internet is arguably beneficial for those who find normal social communication difficult.[20] Also, critical periods are restricted to total deprivation at a very early age. Remember the Romanian orphans and the critical first 6 months? There are very few children using the Web before their first birthday! Also, as developmental neuropsychologist Dorothy Bishop pointed out, the claim that online activity causes autism is ludicrous as the condition appears well before school age and the use of computers.[21] When it comes to social development, the human brain is incredibly resilient and resourceful. So long as there is *some* social interaction then all should be fine. Just like language, humans are wired for social interaction but incredibly flexible in the actual way they do it. Yes, children may not learn the same Ps and Qs of social etiquette that their parents acquired during real interactions, but they will develop their own ways of interacting both on- and offline. Consider one example of how children communicate using abbreviations in texting such as LOL ("laugh out loud"), OMG ("oh my God"), SNM ("say no more"), BRB ("be right back"), GTG ("got to go"), or ROFL ("roll on the floor laughing"). This is a highly effective strategy for transmitting phrases in an optimal way. This was not deliberately invented and handed down by the custodians of social networks but, like much of the etiquette on the Web, emerged in a bottom-up fashion. Left to their own devices, the kids will be all right.

In fact, there are arguments that rather than threatening the future of human psychological development, the new social media is returning us to the situation that existed before the old media of print, radio, and television infiltrated all of our lives. One of the gifted prophets of this new social revolution, June Cohen from the TED organization, makes this counterintuitive point.[22] For much of human civilization, she argues, media was what happened between people in the exchange of news, stories, myths, jokes, education, and art. We mostly communicated with one another around the Serengeti campfires. Up to a few hundred years ago, very few of us could actually read. Then the old media of books, radio, and television appeared. If all of human history were compressed into a single 24-hour day, these old media only emerged in the last 2 minutes before midnight. But this media was different from the village gossip we used to spend our time engaged in. Unlike normal communication, which flows in both directions, the media that entered our homes was one-directional. We read the news, listened to the radio, and watched the television. We stopped communicating with each other. As Cohen puts it, "TV created a global audience, but destroyed the village in the process."

Then Tim Berners-Lee invented the Web, providing a different kind of social experience. This new media, which by the same analogy appeared just seconds ago on the clock of human history, is much more democratized, decentralized, and interactive. Cohen believes that we are returning to a point in human development at which we really can communicate with each other again, only this time we are not restricted to the physical size and location of our village.

This may be true but there are some cautionary tales that we must bear in mind. We are interacting once again, but the Web is very different to the campfire or garden fence. We are unlikely to become socially retarded, but the way we construct our sense of self will be affected. The process won't stop, only the way we go about it. This is because the Web is changing the way we live our lives. It is not just the amount and range of readily accessible information or the way we do business or find entertainment. It is the very way we behave toward one another. After all, interaction with one another through a computer is not natural. Then again, neither are telephone conversations, and the telephone hardly reshaped our social development. The real difference is the power of each of us to communicate simultaneously with the group as a whole. That's a first.

Never in the history of humankind have we had the ability to communicate rich information with practically anyone on the planet instantaneously. Each new innovation from the printing press to the telephone and eventually the computer has been regarded as a milestone in human technological advancement, but the invention of the Web will outstrip them all in terms of its impact on the human race. Now we can potentially communicate with anyone. We can harness the collective power of multiples brains. Many of us are amazed by what computers and software can do. For example, there is more technology and power in today's programmable microwave oven than was needed to put a man on the moon. Moore's Law tells us that computer power doubles approximately every 2 years, which is one of the reasons I always seem to delay replacing computers in anticipation of the more powerful model just around the corner. Eventually, we will reach a technical limit to Moore's Law and require a new type of computing. But the Web is different. The Web will not be so limited. This is because the Web is primarily a medium for sharing knowledge and ideas generated by brains.

Every normal human brain is more powerful than any computer so far built. By connecting them together through the Web, we have the potential to harness the collective thinking of millions of individual brains that are constantly checking and rechecking material on the Web. In 2005, the premier science journal *Nature* declared that the online encyclopedia "Wikipedia," created entirely of voluntary contributions from Web users, was as accurate as the *Encyclopaedia Britannica*, the multivolume traditional source of knowledge produced by teams of paid experts and first published at the end of the 18th century. Web users were simply motivated to distribute their knowledge free of charge and, to this day, Wikipedia is funded almost entirely from public donation.

Consider decision-making and the problem of analysis paralysis, which occurs when there are too many choices. Much of that problem is solved for us on the Web. When was the last time you made a purchase online and ignored the ratings and comments left by others? When did you choose the third or fourth rated item on a list? I expect never. Whether it is choosing a book, movie, hotel, or microwave, we ignore the expert review and pay more attention to other users' feedback, as we trust their experience as being more honest. They have no vested reason to lie. We are invited everywhere on the Web to give our opinion with gladiatorial thumbs up or down to make pronouncements. According to the 2010 Neilson report mentioned earlier, up to one in five Web users regularly provides feedback on movies, books, television, music, services, and consumer products. The collective experience of multiple users produces a consensus of opinion that shapes our decisions. Of course, you are the one making the choice, but it is a decision based on what others think.

This hive mind process is not flawless, however, as we tend to follow the herd mentality (as evidenced by stampeding), but this compliance effect is much reduced on the Web. There is more honesty and dissent when we can remain anonymous online. Of course, there are always those who attempt to subvert the process with false recommendations and condemnations, but they are eventually rumbled with time. Last year, there was an almighty hullabaloo in academia when eminent British historian Orlando Figes was accused of trashing other historian's books on Amazon in the guise of an anonymous reviewer who simply called himself "Historian." Figes threatened to take legal action, only to discover to his embarrassment that it was his own wife who had been writing the reviews to discredit her husband's competition.[23] Some would call that charming wifely support.

With all its benefits, the spread of the Web will be relentless. Over the next few years, accessing the Web will no doubt improve in ease, efficiency, speed, and volume as platforms increase our ability to interact with each other. We may even one day make the unsettling transition of being integrated to the Web through biologically compatible interfaces, but the basic fundamental change that is most important to human civilization is that, in the West, we are all now potentially connected to each other. We can benefit from the wisdom of the crowd—the collective power of billions of brains. We have become the human equivalent of the Borg—the science fiction race of cyborgs from the *Star Trek* series who are all simultaneously interconnected. But we are not drones. We are independent autonomous individuals—or at least that's what we think.

■ Mining the Mountain of Data

The march of the Web may be relentless but there is a big problem with it—literally. Natural selection tells us that when something increases in size it becomes inefficient. In the case of the Web, it is becoming too big—too unwieldy. Cisco Systems, the worldwide leader in networking, estimates how much data are generated and stored on the Web. According to their Chief Futurist, Dave Evans, one of the guys who plans the future strategy of the company, "Humans generated more data in 2009 than in the previous 5,000 years combined."[24] With numbers like that, you might as well say the whole history of humankind. There is simply too much information out there to process. Most of it is junk—nuggets of gossip or titillation. As social media scientist danah boyd (she avoids capitalizing her name for some reason) has commented, "If we're not careful, we're going to develop the psychological equivalent of obesity. We'll find our selves consuming content that is least beneficial for our selves or society as a whole."[25] Much of what is on the Web is the equivalent of information junk food, so search engines like Google sift the knowledge for the relevant information using clever modeling algorithms. Whenever we look for information, search engines analyze Web pages that have been viewed by other users seeking similar information and then rank the most relevant pages for review. It harnesses the power of the crowd to establish what we are looking for. This is wonderful. We can use the collective knowledge of others to mine through the impossible mountain of data to filter out what is not relevant to us.

The problem is that filtering excludes information. Every time we surf the Web, the search engines are recording what we do and what information we provide about our selves. It's not evil. It's not spying or an attempt to control our behavior. The machines are simply trying to provide us with the most relevant information. However, Eli Pariser thinks this is a big problem. In his book, *The Filter Bubble: What the Internet Is Hiding from You*, he explains why search engines are potentially dangerous.[26] Try this out for your self. Log on to Google and search for information about "Egypt." Then call up a relative or friend in a different part of the country and ask him or her to do exactly the same thing. What Eli noted was that his friends received totally different lists of links.[27] This difference is important because most people only look at the first page of links. In other words, they are not being allowed to see the full picture.

The reason for this discrepancy is that Google produces a personalized search result tailored for each user by using a filter. According to an unknown engineer from Google to whom Pariser spoke, the filter is based on a profile created from 57 variables known about the user. (One wonders if the engineer was pulling Eli's leg given the famous Heinz marketing ploy of 57 varieties!) Eli noted how personalization was distorting the sorts of information that were being retrieved for him. For example, in an attempt to broaden his view on issues, Eli had deliberately followed Conservatives on his Facebook account even though he mostly had Liberal friends. However, after a while, he noticed that the Facebook software was deliberately filtering out the postings from the Conservatives because these were deemed less relevant than the majority of his Liberal friends. Filtering software was encapsulating him inside a bubble of ignorance about contrasting views. This was the filter bubble.

■ Birds of a Feather

The vision of being connected to everyone on the Web to get a broad perspective on life is false. The software that is necessary for sifting through the impossible volumes of information is only showing us what it thinks we want to see. But we can't blame the software. In real life, we also filter whom we pay attention to. People tend to social network with like-minded individuals who share the same values and opinions and reciprocate communications. We tend to befriend those who are most like us. We tend to read the same newspapers, like the same TV shows, and enjoy the same pastimes. This homophily may lead to increased group cohesion but it also isolates us from other groups who share different values. In other words, it fosters increasing polarization. For example, in one study on attitudes about global warming, Republicans shifted from 49% who believed the planet was warming up in 2001 to 29% in 2010. In contrast, Democrats increased from 60% to

70% who believed it was a problem over the same period.[28] It was if they were living on different planets.

One might think that the Web should counter this tendency of homophily and broaden our minds to different viewpoints. Indeed, Twitter activity encourages total strangers to become connected. If your followers like or dislike what they hear, they can comment or communicate by "mentioning" you in an open post. That way you can tell whether anyone is paying attention to you. Twitter users "retweet" messages and links they like. It's like saying, "Hey everybody, look at what this person over here is saying," thereby spreading the influence from someone they follow to other users not directly connected to them. If you say something influential, it can spread more rapidly across the "Twittersphere" than conventional channels. This is how Twitter users were made aware of the top secret U.S. assault on Osama Bin Laden's complex as it was happening in May 2011: one Twitter user, Sohaib Athar a.k.a. @reallyvirtual, who lived near Bin Laden, live-tweeted the raid without realizing what was going on. He later tweeted, "Uh oh, now I'm the guy who liveblogged the Osama raid without knowing it." Prior to the raid, Sohaib had 750 people following him. After the raid, he had over 90,000. No wonder Twitter makes surfing blogs and the Web look boring and long-winded. You don't even have to be at a computer terminal as these social networking sites are now all accessible on mobile phones. Twitter is the crack cocaine of social networking.

Despite the ease of Twitter connectivity, it leads to homophily, with people of the same age, race, religion, education, and even temperament tending to follow each other and unfollow those with different views. For example, in one study of over 102,000 Twitter users who produced a combined 129 million tweets in 6 months, researchers analyzed their posting on measures of positive or negative content.[29] Upbeat tweets were things like,

"Nothing feels like a good shower, shave and haircut...love it," or "thanks for your follow, I am following you back, great group of amazing people." Those of a more miserable disposition posted tweets such as "She doesn't deserve the tears but I cry them anyway" or "I'm sick and my body decides to attack my face and make me break out!! WTF." When the researchers analyzed the social networking of the group they found that those who clustered together shared the same dispositions. Happy users are connected to other happy users and unhappy users are connected to other miserable sods. It was as if there was emotional contagion between Twitter users, like the mimicry of the mirror system we encountered earlier, only this time the transfer was entirely virtual. Of course, this type of clustering increases polarization. An analysis of 250,000 tweets during the U.S. congressional midterm elections in 2010 revealed that liberals and conservatives significantly retweeted partisan messages consistent with party line, but not those from the opposing camp.[30]

Furthermore, the promise of communication with thousands of users is not fulfilled because of one major stumbling block—our evolved human brain. When the tweets of 1.7 million users over 6 months were analyzed, the researchers made a remarkable discovery.[31] As the number of followers increase, the capacity to interact with others becomes more difficult in this "economy of attention." We cannot have meaningful exchanges with unlimited numbers of other people. There simply is not enough time and effort available to respond to everyone. It turns out that within this vast ocean of social networking the optimum number at which reciprocal communication can be maintained peaks at somewhere between 100 and 200 followers. Likewise, on Facebook, the average user has 130 friends. Does that number seem familiar? It should. It's close to Dunbar's number, which describes the relationship between the primate cortex and social group size. It turns out accurately to predict our social activity in the virtual world of social networking sites as much as the real world.

■ Time for Our Self

Technology was supposed to liberate us from the mundane chores in life. It was supposed to make us happier. Twentieth-century advertisements promised a world of automaticity and instant gratification. When the computer first came along in the 1960s, and then into many Western households during the 1980s and 1990s, we were told that we would have increased freedom to pursue leisure and entertainment. We were supposed to have more time for each other. The computer has certainly made many tasks easier, but paradoxically many of us spend more time alone at our computers than engaging with the people with whom we live and work. My colleague, Simon Baron-Cohen, an expert on autism, has estimated that he answers 50 e-mails a day and has spent over 1,000 hours a year doing so.[32] I think that my online time is much worse. I don't get as many e-mails as Simon, but I am online every day and cannot remember the last time I had a day offline. Even on holiday or trips, I am connected.

If I am not researching articles or preparing teaching material, then I am keeping in contact with people through social networking sites. I e-mail, write a blog, tweet on Twitter, talk on Skype, have a LinkedIn profile, and drop in and out of Facebook. I have joined Google+, the latest development in social networking. I surf the Web relentlessly. I can do this via my office computer, portable laptop, iPad, or smartphone. I am all wired up. Even when I watch some important event on television, I have my social network feed running so I can keep track of what other people's opinions are of the same broadcast. I estimate that I spend at least half of my waking day online from 7 a.m. to midnight. That's well over 3,000 hours per year—excessive by anyone's standards. I know that this level of Web presence is not typical and probably not healthy but, if my teenage daughters are anything to go by, many people in the West are increasingly becoming immersed in their online involvement. Some argue that excessive dependence on Web activity should be considered like any other addiction, although psychiatrists are not in agreement that it really constitutes a well-defined disorder.

My addiction to the Web began in 2009, when I started my online presence and social networking at the request of the publisher of my first book. Initially, I was asked to write a blog—a website where you write stories and hope that people visit and read what you write. From the outset, I thought that blogging was a self-indulgent activity but I agreed to give it a whirl to help promote my book. In spite of my initial reluctance, I soon became addicted to feedback. Readers could leave comments about each posting and, as an administrator of my site, I could see who and how many people were visiting. It was not enough to post blogs for some unseen audience. I needed the validation from visitors that my efforts and opinions were appreciated. These were recorded as "hits"—the number of times people visited my site. This feedback process is supercharged by the accelerated nature of communication on the Web. Unlike peer-reviewed scientific papers or critics' reviews of your books that can take ages and are unpredictable, social networking sites can create instantaneous gratification from feedback. If the public responds positively to something we have written by increasing traffic or leaving kind comments, this makes us feel very good indeed. It justifies our efforts.

We know the reason for this pleasure from experiments on conditioning behavior. Conditioning was originally discovered in the 1890s, by Russian physiologist Ivan Pavlov, who noted that the dogs he had been studying learned to anticipate feeding time because they would salivate before the food arrived.[33] He then presented the sound of a buzzer (not a bell as popular culture portrays it) with the food, so that eventually just the sound elicited salivation. The dog had learned to associate the sound with the food. This was an important discovery. The experimenter could shape the behavior of the dogs to respond to a variety of different stimuli. They could be trained or conditioned by reward. Conditioning was soon developed into a whole school of psychological theory called Behaviorism, championed in the United States by individuals like J. B. Watson and B. F. Skinner, who claimed that any complex behavior could be shaped by rewards and punishments.[34] In fact, we now know that it is not the rewards that strengthen behaviors but rather the anticipation of rewards, which is so satisfying.

This is because deep inside our brain, close to the brain stem, is a reward system that is invigorated by a cluster of around 15,000–20,000 dopamine neurons that send out long fibers to other regions of the brain. Given the billions of neurons in the brain, it is remarkable that this tiny population is the pleasure center critical in controlling our behavior. These neurons enable us to predict and anticipate rewards and punishment.[35] Without them, we would be hopelessly inept in decision-making, and our behavior would be erratic. When an animal in a conditioning experiment learns that pressing a lever or pecking a disc will deliver a reward, anticipatory dopamine is released, which reinforces the behavior rather than does the actual reward. We know this because rats with electrodes implanted in the pleasure center connected to a current will continue to self-stimulate in the absence of any food reward—to the point of starvation.[36] The dopamine rush alone is sufficient to condition the behavior. When patients have electrodes implanted in this same brain region for the treatment of intractable epilepsy, they report feeling pleasure. Like many addictive behaviors from gambling to sex, it's the thrill of expectation that gives us the best buzz.

What's more, the best way to strengthen behavior is to only reward it occasionally—this is called *intermittent reinforcement*. This is because our brains are always seeking out patterns in the environment. Although information and feedback from the environment is often fragmented and incomplete, our brains allow for such inconsistency. When we do something that seems to cause some form of positive reward, we then repeat the action in an attempt to recreate the pleasure. If this reward is only intermittent, we will persist for much longer repeating our attempts. This is the reinforcement principle behind gambling. We gamble more and for longer periods just waiting for that occasional reward.[37] Slot machines only need to pay out every so often on an intermittent reinforcement schedule for players to persist in pumping more coins into them. It's that dopamine hit of anticipation that perpetuates our behavior.

In the same way, conditioning explains our online behavior. We are compelled to check our e-mails or look for approval from our online community just in case something really important or juicy comes along. Every time I checked my e-mail or hit activity on my blog, I was like a rat in one of Skinner's conditioning experiments. At first, the numbers were only a handful but every week they increased. Within a month, I was checking activity every day—thrilled when there was a peak or a kind comment, depressed by the dips and disparaging remarks. Most days there was nothing but every so often, I would be rewarded. The dopamine spurt triggered by associated anticipation had become my drug of choice, and I had become a numbers junkie looking for more and more hits.

So, the Internet can become addictive and it can also be dangerous, especially in the case of *immersive gaming*, in which individuals can play for hours in fantasy worlds. In

2010, South Korea had a greater proportion of its population online than any other nation (81% of 46 million). Most Koreans spend their online time in Internet cafés that provide fast but cheap connections. This can have devastating consequences. Many of them develop serious medical conditions related to hours of online activity at the cost of offline inactivity. Their joints swell up. They develop muscular pain. Sometimes it's others that get hurt. In the same year, a South Korean couple who met online married in real life, but unfortunately had a sickly premature baby.[38] But then they decided to continue their lives online in the café across the road in a game in which they raised a virtual baby. They only returned to the house once a day to feed their own real baby. This lack of care meant that their own child eventually died of severe dehydration and malnutrition. Undoubtedly, this is an extreme case, and many children raised in poverty are neglected, but it highlights the compulsion of the Web. I recently hosted a highly educated academic family visiting from the United States and after the initial social conversation and exchange of anecdotes over dinner; we soon dispersed to check our e-mail, Facebook, and other online lives. It was not only the adults in the group, but the children as well. At one point, I looked up from my laptop and saw everyone else in the room silently immersed in their own Web. Whereas we once used to compartmentalize our lives into the working day and time with the family, the Web has destroyed those boundaries forever. Most of us are connected, and we like it that way. Just like drug addiction, many of us get withdrawal symptoms of anxiety and irritability when we are denied our Web access.

We have become shaped and controlled by our technology in a way predicted by Marshall McLuhan when he introduced phrases such as the "global village" and "the medium is the message."[39] Even in the 1960s, before the invention of the Web, McLuhan predicted that society would change to become dependent and shaped by our communications technology. He understood that we extend our self out to others and in doing so, become influenced by their reciprocal extensions. To this extent, we are intricately interrelated to each other through the mediums by which we communicate. Likewise, Sherry Turkle, the MIT sociologist, has also described this shift from face-to-face interaction to terminal-to-terminal interaction in her recent book, *Alone Together*.[40] As we spend more time online, we are necessarily less offline, which means that we will cease to live the same lives shaped by our immediate others. Rather, who we are will increasingly become shaped by the mediums in which we exist. Some people find this scary. For many it is liberating.

■ We All Want a Second Life

What do you do if you are unemployed, overweight, and living off benefits with no prospect of escaping the poverty trap? Since 2003, there has been another world you can live in—a world where you can get a second chance. This is Second Life, a virtual online world where you reinvent your self and live a life among other avatars who never grow old, have perfect bodies, never get ill, have fabulous homes, and lead interesting lives.

David Pollard and Amy Taylor are two individuals who separately wanted to escape the dreariness of their mundane lives.[41] Both of them lived in Newquay, a seaside resort in southwest England that has become a Mecca for drunken teenagers who come in their hordes to party away the summer. The town is far from idyllic, and I would imagine living there, without a job and prospects, must be depressing. To escape the drudgery, David and Amy (who initially met in an online chatroom) joined Second Life, where they became "Dave Barmy" and "Laura Skye" (see Figure 8.1). Dave Barmy was in his mid-20s, 6-foot-4-inch, slim, with long dark hair, and was a nightclub owner who lived in a sprawling villa. He had a penchant for smart suits and bling. In reality, David Pollard was 40, overweight at 160 kg, balding, and living off worker's compensation benefits in a small apartment. He wore T-shirts and sweatpants.

Laura Skye was an equally exotic character. She was also in her mid-20s, a slim 6-foot with long, dark hair, living in a large house. She liked the country-and-western look of tight denim blouses and boots. In reality, Amy Pollard was an overweight, 5-foot-4-inch redhead who was also living off benefits. The contrast between reality and fiction could hardly have been greater (see Figure 8.2).

When the couple met online as Dave Barmy and Laura Skye, they fell in love and married in Second Life. But they also met up in real life, with Amy moving in with David in Newquay. After 2 years, they married for real—just like the Korean couple. However, as in real life, that's when things started to go wrong. Laura (Amy) suspected Dave was playing around in Second Life so she hired a virtual detective to check up on her virtual husband. At one point, she discovered Dave Barmy having sex with a call girl in the game. In real life, David apologized and begged for forgiveness. The final straw came when Amy caught her

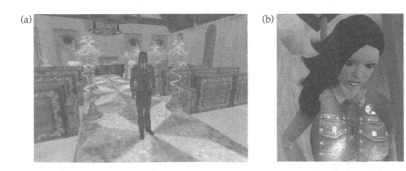

(a)   (b)

FIGURE 8-1   Dave Barmy and Laura Skye. Used with permission of South West News Service, LTD.

FIGURE 8-2   The real Dave Barmy and Laura Skye. Used with permission of South West News Service, LTD.

real husband in front of the computer in their small flat watching his avatar cuddling affectionately on a couch with another Second Life character, Modesty McDonnell— the creation of Linda Brinkley, a 55-year-old twice-divorcee from Arkansas, in the United States. Amy was devastated. She filed for divorce on the grounds of unreasonable behavior even though Dave had not actually had sex or an affair in real life. Soon after, Dave proposed to Modesty online and in real life, even though the couple had never met.

When the world discovered that a couple was divorcing on the grounds of make-believe unreasonable behavior, the press flocked to Newquay. However, in what can only be described as reality imitating art, imitating reality, the Cornish couple initially declined to give interviews and would not answer the door. Then something very odd happened. Two enterprising journalists from the *South West News* hit on the bright idea of going into Second Life to secure an interview. From their offices miles away in Bristol, Jo Pickering and Paul Adcock created virtual ace reporters "Meggy Paulse" and "Jashly Gothley" to seek out Dave Barmy and Laura Skye for an interview.

Jo still works on *South West News*, and she told me that she got the idea after speaking to a colleague who had been using avatars to attend online courses. As Meggy Paulse, Jo found Laura Skye in Second Life. She told me that the online Laura Skye was much more approachable and confident than the real-life Amy. Eventually, Meggy Paulse persuaded Amy to logoff, go downstairs, and open the door to speak to the reporters camped on her doorstep. They eventually got their story.

Jo explained that Amy had felt that the betrayal online was far worse than betrayal in real life because both she and David had created these perfect selves and still that was not good enough. In real life, we are all flawed and often put up with each other's weaknesses, but in Second Life there were supposed to be no weaknesses. That's why the online betrayal hurt. As Jo says, "She had created this perfect version of herself—and even that wasn't good enough for him."

I asked Jo about what finally happened to the couple. Apparently, Dave did eventually meet up with Linda Brinkley, but reality must have kicked in when it came to having a real marriage when you are both poor and live on different continents. When online Dave Barmy met online Modesty McDonnell for real, David Pollard and Linda Brinkley got real. What this morality tale tells us is that the boundaries between reality and fantasy can sometimes become blurred. Paul Bloom tells of a research assistant who was asked by her professor to do some research on these virtual communities.[42] Apparently, the young woman never came back. Like some electronic cult, she preferred life in a virtual world compared to the real one. If the urge to live a life online is so compelling, it does make you wonder what the future holds. Surely, something has to give, as one cannot be in two places at the same time even between virtual and real worlds. Both require the limited resource of time, and that is something that cannot be easily divided.

■ When Online Behavior Is Off

Some individuals in power seek out sexual gratification by engaging in risky encounters. They step over the boundaries of decent behavior. The Web has made this type of transgression all too easy. With what must be the most unfortunate of surnames, U.S. Republican Congressman Anthony Weiner found himself at the center of a career-destroying scandal in 2011, when he was forced to resign after confessing to sending pictures of his penis to women whom he followed on Twitter.[43] "Weinergate," as it became known, was just another example of high-profile men using the Web to send naked images of themselves to women. In the past, men exposed themselves for sexual gratification in public places but, with the advent of social networking sites, offline flashing has moved online and is much more common.

Indeed, some argue that one of the main uses of the Internet is for sex. A 2008 survey of more than 1,280 teenagers (13–20 years) and young adults (20–26 years) revealed that one in five teenagers and one in three young adults had sent nude or semi-nude photographs of themselves over the Internet.[44] One online dating site, Friendfinder. com, estimates that nearly half of its subscribers are married. Either they are looking for new partners or the opportunity to flirt.[45] Probably one of the most remarkable cases was U.S. Army Colonel Kassem Saleh, who had simultaneously wooed over 50 women online and made marriage proposals to many of them, despite the fact that he was already married.

"Sexting" is a relatively new phenomenon in which individuals use technology to engage in sexual activities at a distance. Susan Lipkins, a psychologist from Port Washington, New York, reports that in her online survey of 13- to 72-year-olds, two-thirds of the sample had sent sexually explicit messages. The peak activity was in the late teenagers and young adults. What was interesting was that this behavior was associated with personality measures of power such as assertiveness, dominance, and aggression in those over the age of 27. Power was not a factor in the younger group but was significantly related to sexting in the older men.[46] The ease and speed of the Web, as well as the perceived dissociation and distance from reality, lead to an escalation of brazen activity. This can easily slide into moral indiscretions that are unregulated by social norms when compared to real life. Just like bullying, the apparent anonymity, distance, and remoteness of being online allows us to not be our self as we would behave in the real world.

■ The Cyber Rape by Mr. Bungle the Clown

When it comes to the boundaries between reality and fantasy and between moral and immoral acts, probably the most poignant tale that reveals the blurring in these situations is the story of Mr. Bungle the Clown. Mr. Bungle was a cyber character who inhabited the virtual world of LamdaMOO—one of the first online communities back in the early 1990s where multiple players create and control virtual characters. Mr. Bungle was a particularly nasty piece of work. In one notorious event one evening in a virtual room in a virtual mansion, he violated members of his fellow online community using software subroutines (sections of code designed for a particular task in computer programming) to make the other characters perform perverted sexual acts.[47]

Of course, this terrifying vision of Mr. Bungle was all in the user's mind. He didn't really exist. If you logged on to LamdaMOO back in these early days of virtual communities, you simply accessed a database stored somewhere inside a Xerox Corporation research computer in Silicon Valley that presented the user with scrolling lines of description. The environment, objects, and all the characters were just subroutines of text—fairly basic stuff compared to the rich visual environments that are expected in today's technologically advanced online communities. LamdaMOO was nothing compared to the graphical 3D visual worlds of Second Life or World of Warcraft, but then human imagination doesn't require very much to generate a vivid impression.

Mr. Bungle was the disturbed creation of a young hacker logging on from New York University. He had managed to hack the system's software to produce a subroutine that presented other users with unsolicited text. During the event in question, several female users were online when they were presented with text describing how their characters inserted various utensils and derived sexual pleasure as Mr. Bungle watched, laughing sadistically. Again, it was all in the mind as the whole attack was played out as a series of scrolling texts.

Afterwards, one female user from Seattle whose character, called "Legba," had been virtually abused, publicly posted her assault on the LambdaMOO's community chatboard and called for Mr. Bungle's castration. Months later, she told the reporter who had first covered the story that as she wrote those words, "posttraumatic tears were streaming down her face." Clearly, this was no longer a virtual incident in her mind—as a victim, she had taken it to heart. The assault had crossed the boundary of imagination to affect the real-life emotions of those concerned.

They say words can never harm you but for the self illusion, words from other people can be everything. The case of Mr. Bungle raises so many interesting issues about identity, the self, and the way these operate in online communities. Everything that happened, the characters, the assault, the reaction, and the eventual retribution were nothing more than words, the frenetic typing of cyber geeks on their keyboards. But why the outrage? Why did people feel emotionally upset? No physical contact had ever taken place. Clearly, the players were not deluded into believing that a real assault had happened, but psychologically the users felt violated. In the minds of the players, it had gone beyond role-playing. Their indignation was real. Ostracism and the pain of social rejection can be so easily triggered by simple computer simulations of communities that are a sufficient substitute for reality. That's because they stimulate our deep-seated need for social interaction.

So, where is the real self in these different examples of online communities and virtual worlds? Most of us believe that we are not hypocrites or duplicitous. We like to think we have integrity. If the self is a coherent, integrated entity, then one would predict that the way we behave online should accurately mirror the way we behave offline. However, that does not appear to be the case. How people behave depends on the context in which they find themselves. The Web is no different. The way you behave online would never be acceptable offline and vice versa. Online you have to be open, engaging, and willing to share but then you are more likely to tell others what you think of them, flirt, and generally act in a way that would get you into trouble in real life.

Sometimes we surprise our self in the way we behave online as if we have become a different person. Maybe this is why online life is so popular. We get to be a different self. We get to be someone else—maybe someone we aspire to be. At the very least, we get to interact with others who are missing in our daily lives. This need for an online identity that seems so different to our offline self perplexes pre-Web adults, but we need to understand how this need for technological escapism has become integrated into human psychological development. Because the Web will eventually swallow up everyone on the planet, it is important to consider how it may influence and change the next generation. We are not likely to become like the Borg, but we do seem to shift effortlessly between our online and offline selves. Consequently, the Web dramatically reveals the extent to which the notion of a core self is an illusion.

9 ■

Why You Can't See Your Self in Reflection

When I was a graduate student working on visual develop-ment in very young babies some 20 years ago, I studied how they move their eyes. Babies don't speak, but their eyes are windows into their brain. Where they look and for how long reveals what their brain is paying attention to. Where is the self in this decision? If you think about it, for the most part, we do this unconsciously. But who is moving our eyes? Who decides? Does a newborn have a self in con-trol? Working with newborn babies, sometimes only min-utes old, I never really asked this sort of question. I was more concerned with what newborn babies looked at.

It seemed obvious to me that babies look at things that they can see most clearly and that this is determined by what is out there in the world to look at. As far as I was concerned, it seemed unlikely that they had models of the world already encoded in their brains that predicted where they would look next. Rather, at the very beginning, everything must be driven by what existed already in the environment to be seen. It is the properties of the external world that compete for the attention of the eye movement systems in the babies brain. There was no need for a self in control. Newborns don't really make decisions about where to look. Rather, the brain mechanisms they are born with have evolved to seek out information from the external world and then keep a record of those experiences. It was this early insight into the mind of an infant that opened my eyes to the self illusion.

As the brain develops, it builds up more complex models of the world—expectations about where and what should happen. We develop an increasing flexibility to apply those models to understand and make predictions. Twenty years ago, I appreciated that development was the integration of internal mechanisms working in conjunction with information in the world. That fundamental principle works all the way up the nervous system from simple eye movements to the full repertoire of human thoughts and behaviors—the same activities that give rise to the self. This is why the self is an illusion. It did not suddenly manifest one day inside our head on our second or third birthday. It has been slowly emerging—sculpted out of the richness of human activity and interaction. Our self is a product of our mind, which in turn is a product of our brain working in conjunction with other brains. As the brain develops, so does the self. As the brain deteriorates, then so must the self.

Why did we evolve the self illusion? Like every other illusion our brain generates, it serves a useful purpose. If you think about the "I" and the "me" that we usually refer to as the self, it provides a focal point to hang experiences together both in the immediate here and now, as well as to join those events over a lifetime. Experiences are fragmented episodes unless they are woven together in a meaningful narrative. This is why the self pulls it all together. Without a focus, the massive parallel processing in our brain means that we would be overwhelmed by the sheer volume of computations if we ever had to deal with them individually. Rather, we get a summarized headline that relates all the outputs from these unconscious processes. Sometimes we can delve into the details of the story a little more closely if we scrutinize the content, but very often much of it is hidden from us.

The self illusion depends on stored information that has been acquired during a lifetime. These are our memories that are constructed as we interpret the world. That interpretation is guided by mechanisms that seek out certain information in the world but also by those around us who help us to make sense of it all. In this way, we are continually shaped by those around us. As the species with the longest proportion of life spent as juveniles dependent on others, human children are particularly evolved for social interaction, and much of what our brains compute appears to be dedicated to socially relevant information. In the absence of social interaction early in development, children can be permanently socially disabled even though their intellect may be intact. Certainly, the formative years leave a legacy of how we interact with others for the rest of our lives. It is through this social interaction with others that we construct our sense of identity and ultimately our sense of self.

We have not evolved to think about others as a bundle of processes. Rather, we have evolved to treat others as individual selves. It is faster, more economical, and more efficient to treat others as a self rather than as an extended collection of past histories, hidden agendas, unresolved conflicts, and ulterior motives. Treating humans as selves optimizes our interactions. We fall in love and hate individuals, not collections. We cannot abandon our morality simply because we decompose the individual self into its myriad of influences. Punishment and praise is heaped on the individual, not on the multitude of others who shaped the self. Those who reject the notion of a self in control of destiny, lead sadder, less satisfying lives. Those who embrace the self illusion feel fulfilled and purposeful.

Why is it so difficult to see through the illusion? The answer may have something to do with reflections in one form or another that have popped up throughout this book. Think back over all the examples:

Babies and animals recognizing themselves in mirrors
Brain-damaged adults with mirror misidentification
Mirroring behavior of others
Mirror-touch synesthesia, in which some actually feel another's pain
Mirror neurons that map one mind directly onto another
Not stealing candy or cheating when there is a mirror in the room
Guards wearing mirror shades to dehumanize prisoners
Looking in the mirror for self affirmation

What is it about a mirror that is so central to the notion of the self? When we look at the mirror, we see the outward appearance of our self but we believe that the image is simply the outer shell of the body we occupy. We believe there is so much more to our self on the inside. This is what we feel and know. Others cannot have access to this inner self, and so they are forever cut off from knowing our true self. But what if we have got it the wrong way round? What if we are a looking glass self that is created by the environment about us—an environment that is predominantly populated by others?

Consider all the different influences that there have been on your life up to this point in time from your parents, your schooling, your hobbies, your first adult relationships, your spouse, your children, your job, your colleagues, and your political views to every other sphere of influence that has touched your life. Imagine how they have impressed upon you. Like the illusory square we saw in the Prologue of this book, our self is constructed just like the imaginary white circle you can plainly see in Figure 9.1.

You only exist as a pattern made up of all the others things in your life that shape you. If you take each away, "you" would eventually cease to exist. This does not mean that you do not exist at all, but rather that you exist as a combination of all the others who complete your sense of self. These are the memories and experiences that shape you. The problem, as we have seen, however, is that these memories are not always that reliable and so the self that is constructed is not necessarily an accurate or consistent version. It is continually shifting and reshaping as the contexts change. We are so willing to accommodate others that we adapt to each role in a continuous, dynamic, shape-shifting ballet.

This visual metaphor also makes a fundamental point about the nature of reality and illusion. The shape of "you" may be an illusion but our brains use illusions to recreate the world. Everything is processed and abstracted, with the brain putting in a large amount of effort to organize,

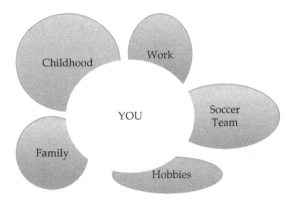

FIGURE 9-1   The self illusion is an emergent property from the cluster of external influences.

interpret, and fill in missing information based on past experience. For example, we know that there are circuits of the brain that are firing as if the illusory circle in the diagram was really there. That's why you see the invisible circle. What this means is that the brain considers the arrangement and decides that the only sensible explanation for the way each sphere seems to be missing a piece is because of the "you" circle in the middle. In other words, the brain hallucinates the experience of "you" by stimulating its own neural circuits to create that impression. It may be an illusion, but it is real as far as the brain is concerned. It's not magic—it's just basic neurophysiology describing how the pattern-seeking structures of the brain prefer order and create explanations.

So, why can't you see that you are a reflected self? For one thing, that view is inconsistent with the narrative that our brain generates. Many of our thoughts and actions that we think reflect our self are not what they seem. We believe we have freedom to choose, but, in many instances, the choices occur in the absence of any deliberation and often under the influence of others. We are so dependent on maintaining our social inclusion that we readily conform to the will of the group. Because we are our brains, which create our sense of self, we have no privileged access to this invisible process from an outsider's perspective.

One final mirror demonstration may leave you convinced that we are blind to how our brain creates our experience. Take a good hard look at your self in a mirror. Focus your gaze on your left eye and have a good look at it. Now switch and focus your gaze on your right eye. Notice anything odd? If you alternate your focus of gaze from the left eye to the right eye and back again, you cannot see your own eye movements from the left to the right and back again. Your eyes are moving—you just cannot see them move. Ask someone else to do the same thing. Now you can easily see their eyes moving but, like you, they cannot see their own movements in the reflection in the mirror. This is because our brains deliberately wipe out the visual experience of seeing the world every time we move our eyes. You may be surprised to discover that you are effectively blind for about an average of 2 hours on every waking day, but you would never know this.

This simple biological quirk is just one of the many different ways that our brain hides its true operations from our consciousness. We think we see a stable visual world but, in fact, it is constructed every time we move our eyes. In fact, unless you are paying close attention, we could switch objects in the world and you would never notice the change. This is because we assume that the world is stable, but that is an illusion. The self is the same. We cannot be aware of the underlying processes that create it and yet we feel it is coherent. You never see that you are a reflection of the others around you because you cannot easily see how you change. And we don't easily see our self switching from one to another until it is pointed out to us by those around us or we recognize that the context has changed.

At the danger of overextending the metaphor, if we were able to see the world during our eye movements, we would become nauseous because it would become unstable and we would experience motion sickness. The world would smear as the visual input stimulated the neurons that process the light. Here, too much information can be a bad thing. So, our brain protects us from the true nature of the situation. Maybe this is why we do not see the cognitive illusions that create the self. Cognitive dissonance protects us from ruminating over failed goals, positive biases keep us motivated, free will gives us grounds for praise and blame, decision-making gives us the illusion of control. Without these cognitive illusions, we would not be able to function because we would be overwhelmed by the true complexity of the hidden processes and mechanisms that control us. And that, in the end, is a good thing.

What of the future of this self illusion? It's unlikely to disappear. It is an evolved adaptation after all—but it may have to change. Currently, the world's population is just under 7 billion. Within the next generation, the United Nations estimates that the majority of us will be living in a megacity—metropolitan areas with a density of at least 2,000 people per square kilometer and at least 10 million inhabitants. The expansion of the Internet means that the majority of the world's population will have the potential to communicate with each other. Instantaneous language translation is just round the corner and will further erode another barrier to communication. These developments are a far cry from the Serengeti savannahs where our ancestors first appeared. One can speculate how changes will impact upon the individual's identity, but it would seem that in an ever more crowded future, we are going to need a pretty strong sense of self to survive.

Notes ■

Prologue: The Reflected Self

1. N. Dietrich, *The Amazing Howard Hughes* (London: Hodder Fawcett, 1972).

2. The notion of the 'I' and the 'me' comes from William James's *Principles of Psychology* (NY: Henry Holt & Company, 1890).

3. P. Ricoeur, *Oneself as Another* (Chicago, IL: University of Chicago Press, 1992).

4. G. Strawson, "The self," *Journal of Consciousness*, 4 (1997), 405–428.

5. D. Hume, *A Treatise of Human Nature*, Book 1, part 4, section 6.

6. D. Parfit, "Divided minds and the nature of persons," in C. Blakemore and S. Greenfield (eds.), *Mindwaves* (Oxford: Blackwell, 1987), 19–26.

7. D. Chalmers, "Facing up to the problem of consciousness," *Journal of Consciousness Studies*, 3 (1995), 200–219.

8.   D. C. Dennett, *Consciousness Explained* (Boston, MA: Little, Brown and Co., 1991).

9.   C. H. Cooley, *Human Nature and the Social Order* (New York: Scribner's, 1902).

10.   D. T. Gilbert and P. S. Malone, The correspondence bias. *Psychological Bulletin,* 117 (1995), 21–38.

CHAPTER 1: THE MOST WONDROUS ORGAN

1.   F. A. C. Azevedo, L. R. B. Carvalho, L. T. Grinberg, J. M. Farfel, E. E. L. Ferretti, R. E. P. Leite, W. Jacob Filho, R. Lent, and S. Herculano-Houzel, "Equal numbers of neuronal and nonneuronal cells make the human brain an isometrically scaled-up primate brain," *Journal of Comparative Neurology,* 513 (2009), 532–541. This is the most recent analysis of the human neural architecture. They estimated that there were 85 billion non-neuronal cells and 86 billion neuronal cells.

2.   C. E. Shannon, "A mathematical theory of communication," *Bell System Technical Journal,* 27 (1948), 379–423 and 623–656.

3.   Binary code was first introduced by the German mathematician and philosopher Gottfried Wilhelm Leibniz during the 17th century. Binary code works well because it works with only two states—"on" and "off"—which is ideally suited for electrical systems.

4.   E. Ruppin, E. L. Schwartz, and Y. Yeshurun, "Examining the volume-efficiency of the cortical architecture in a multi-processor network model," *Biological Cybernetics,* 70:1 (1993), 89–94.

5.   M. Abeles, *Corticonics: Neural Circuits of the Cerebral Cortex* (Cambridge: Cambridge University Press, 1991).

6.   M. A. Arib, *The Handbook of Brain Theory and Neural Networks* (Cambridge, MA: MIT Press, 2002).

7.   The number of atoms in the observable universe is estimated to be around 10^{81}. I am indebted to Dan Wolpert for providing me with this bizarre mathematical comparison.

8.   W. Penfield, *The Mystery of the Mind* (Princeton, NJ: Princeton University Press, 1975).

9.   P. MacLean, *The Triune Brain in Evolution: Role of Paleocerebral Functions* (New York: Plenum, 1990).

10.   Azevedo et al. (2009).

11.   J. Atkinson, *The Developing Visual Brain* (Oxford: Oxford University Press, 2000).

12.   B. M. Hood, "Shifts of visual attention in the human infant: A neuroscientific approach," in L. Lipsitt and C. Rovee-Collier (eds.), *Advances in Infancy Research*, vol. 9 (Norwood, NJ: Ablex, 1995), 163–216.

13.   A. Diamond, "Neuropsychological insights into the meaning of object concept development," in S. Carey and R. Gelman (eds.), *The Epigenesis of Mind: Essays on Biology and Cognition* (Cambridge, MA: MIT Press, 1991), 433–472.

14.   F. Bertossa, M. Besa, R. Ferrari, and F. Ferri, "Point zero: A phenomenological inquiry into the seat of consciousness," *Perceptual and Motor Skills*, 107 (2008), 323–335.

15.   P. Rakic, "Intrinsic and extrinsic determinants of neo-cortical parcellation: A radial unit model," in M. H. Johnson, Y. Munakata, and R. Gilmore (eds.), *Brain Development and Cognition: A Reader* (2nd ed., Oxford: Blackwell, 2002), 57–82.

16.   Y. Brackbill, "The role of the cortex in orienting: Orienting reflex in an anencephalic human infant," *Developmental Psychology*, 5 (1971), 195–201.

17.   A. J. DeCasper and M. J. Spence, "Prenatal maternal speech influences newborns" perception of speech sounds," *Infant Behavior and Development*, 9 (1986), 133–50; J. A. Mennella, C. P. Jagnow, and G. K. Beauchamp, "Prenatal and postnatal flavor learning by human infants," *Pediatrics* 107:6 (2001), E88; P. G. Hepper, "An examination of fetal learning before and after birth," *Irish Journal of Psychology*, 12:2 (1991), 95–107.

18.   M. H. Johnson, *Developmental Cognitive Neuroscience* (Oxford: Wiley-Blackwell, 2011).

19. J. L. Conel, *The Postnatal Development of the Human Cerebral Cortex*, Vols. I–VIII (Cambridge, MA: Harvard University Press, 1939–1967).

20. W. T. Greenough and J. E. Black, "Induction of brain structures by experience: Substrates for cognitive development," in M. Gunnar and C. Nelson (eds.), *Minnesota Symposium on Child Psychology: Vol. 24. Developmental Behavioral Neuroscience* (Hillsdale, NJ: Erlbaum, 1992, 155–200).

21. P. R. Huttenlocher, C. de Courten, L. G. Garey, and H. Van der Loos, "Synaptogenesis in human visual cortex. Evidence for synapse elimination during normal development," *Neuroscience Letters*, 33 (1982), 247–252.

22. J. Zihl, D. von Cramon and N. Mai, "Selective disturbance of movement vision after bilateral brain damage," *Brain*, 106 (1983), 313–340.

23. D. H. Hubel, *Eye, Brain and Vision*, Scientific American Library Series (New York: W. H. Freeman, 1995).

24. J. Atkinson, *The Developing Visual Brain* (Oxford: Oxford University Press, 2002).

25. W. T. Greenough, J. E. Black, and C. S. Wallace, "Experience and brain development," *Child Development*, 58: 3 (1987), 539–559.

26. Konrad Lorenz, *King Solomon's Ring*, trans. Marjorie Kerr Wilson (London: Methuen, 1961).

27. S. Pinker, *The Language Instinct* (Harmondsworth: Penguin, 1994).

28. J. S. Johnson and E. L. Newport, "Critical period effects in second language learning: The influence of maturational state on the acquisition of English as a second language," *Cognitive Psychology* 21 (1989), 60–99.

29. J. Werker, "Becoming a native listener," *American Scientist*, 77 (1989), 54–69.

30. The "Mozart effect" is the claim popularized by Don Campbell in his 1997 book (*The Mozart Effect: Tapping the Power of Music to Heal the Body, Strengthen the Mind, and*

Unlock the Creative Spirit) that listening to classical music increases your IQ. Such was the power of this disputed claim that Zell Miller, the governor of Georgia, announced that his proposed state budget would include $105,000 a year to provide every child born in Georgia with a tape or CD of classical music. To make his point, Miller played legislators some of Beethoven's "Ode to Joy" on a tape recorder and asked, "Now, don't you feel smarter already?"

31. J. T. Bruer, *The Myth of the First Three Years: A New Understanding of Early Brain Development and Lifelong Learning* (New York: Free Press, 1999).

32. F. J. Zimmerman, D. A. Christakis, and A. N. Meltzoff, "Associations between media viewing and language development in children under age two years," *Journal of Pediatrics*, 51 (2007), 364–368.

33. Azevedo et al. (2009).

34. S. Herculano-Houzel, B. Mota, and R. Lent, "Cellular scaling rules for rodent brains," *Proceedings of the National Academy of Sciences of the United States of America*, 103 (2006), 12138–12143.

35. R. I. M. Dunbar, "The social brain hypothesis," *Evolutionary Anthropology*, 6 (1998), 178.

36. R. Sapolsky, *"The uniqueness of humans."* http://www.ted.com/talks/robert_sapolsky_the_uniqueness_of_humans.html (TED talk, 2009).

37. R. I. M. Dunbar and S. Shultz, "Evolution in the social brain," *Science*, 317 (2007), 1344–1347.

38. S. R. Ott and S. M. Rogers, "Gregarious desert locusts have substantially larger brains with altered proportions compared with the solitarious phase," *Proceedings of the Royal Society, B*, 277 (2010) 3087–3096.

39. Personal communication with Dunbar.

40. A. Whiten and R. W. Byrne, *Machiavellian Intelligence: Social Expertise and the Evolution of Intellect in Monkeys, Apes and Humans.* (Oxford: Oxford University Press, 1988).

41. M. Gladwell, *The Tipping Point. How Little Things Can Make a Big Difference* (London: Little, Brown and Co., 2000).

42. T. Nagel, "What is it like to be a bat?," *Philosophical Review*, 83 (1974), 433–450.

43. This anecdote is relayed by A. Gopnik, *The Philosophical Baby: What Children's Minds Tell Us About Truth, Love, and the Meaning of Life* (New York: Farrar, Strauss and Giroux, 2009).

Chapter 2: The Machiavellian Baby

1. J. M. Baldwin, *Development and Evolution* (Boston, MA: Adamant Media Corporation, 1902/2002).

2. J. Locke, *An Essay Concerning Human Understanding* (London, 1690).

3. W. James, *Principles of Psychology* (New York: Henry Holt, 1890).

4. A. Gopnik, *"What are babies really thinking?"* http://blog.ted.com/2011/10/10/what-are-babies-really-thinking-alison-gopnik-on-ted-com/ (TED talk, 2011).

5. R. Byrne and A. Whiten, *Machiavellian Intelligence* (Oxford: Oxford University Press, 1988).

6. N. Kanwisher, J. McDermott, and M. Chun, "The fusiform face area: A module in human extrastriate cortex specialized for the perception of faces," *Journal of Neuroscience*, 17 (1997), 4302–4311. Actually, there is now some dispute whether the area is specific to faces or any special category of well-known objects. Given that faces are the most common diverse objects that we encounter, this suggests that the area probably evolved primarily for faces.

7. M. H. Johnson, S. Dziurawiec, H. Ellis, and J. Morton, "Newborns' preferential tracking for face-like stimuli and its subsequent decline," *Cognition*, 40 (1991), 1–19.

8. O. Pascalis, M. de Haan, and C. A. Nelson, "Is face processing species-specific during the first year of life?," *Science*, 296(2002), 1321–1323.

9. Y. Sugita, "Face perception in monkeys reared with no exposure to faces," *Proceedings of the National Academy of Science, USA*, 105 (2008), 394–398.

10. R. Le Grand, C. Mondloch, D. Maurer, and H. P. Brent, "Early visual experience and face processing," *Nature*, 410 (2001), 890.

11. M. Heron-Delaney, G. Anzures, J. S. Herbert, P. C. Quinn, and A. M. Slater, "Perceptual training prevents the emergence of the other race effect during Infancy," *PLoS ONE*, 6:5 (2011), e19858, doi:10.1371/journal.pone.0019858

12. A. N. Meltzoff and M. K. Moore, "Imitation of facial and manual gestures by human neonates," *Science*, 198 (1977), 75–78.

13. P. F. Ferrari, E. Visalberghi, A. Paukner, L. Fogassi, A. Ruggiero, and S. J. Suomi, "Neonatal imitation in rhesus macaques," *PLoS Biology*, 4:9 (September 2006), e302, doi:10.1371/journal.pbio.0040302

14. J. Panksepp, *Affective Neuroscience: The Foundations of Human and Animal Emotions* Series in Affective Science. (New York: Oxford University Press, 1998).

15. D. Leighton and C. Kluckhohn, *Children of the People; the Navaho Individual and His Development*. (Cambridge, MA: Harvard University Press, 1947/1969).

16. A. B. Fries, T. E. Ziegler, J. R. Kurian, S. Jacoris, and S. D. Pollack, "Early experience in humans is associated with changes in neuropeptides critical for regulating social interaction," *Proceedings of the National Academy of Sciences of the United States of America*, 102 (2005), 17237–17240.

17. F. Strack, L. L. Martin, and S. Stepper, "Inhibiting and facilitating conditions of the human smile: A nonobtrusive test of the facial feedback hypothesis," *Journal of Personality and Social Psychology*, 54 (1988), 768–777.

18. R. E. Kraut and R. E. Johnston, "Social and emotional messages of smiling: An ethological account," *Journal of Personality and Social Psychology*, 37(1979), 1539–1553.

19.   O. Epstein, G. D. Perkin, and J. Cookson, *Clinical Examination* (Edinburgh: Elsevier Health Sciences, 2008), 408.

20.   S. H. Fraiberg, "Blind infants and their mothers: An examination of the sign system," in M. Lewis and L. Rosenblum (eds.), *The effect of the Infant on Its Caregiver* (New York: Wiley, 1974), 215–232.

21.   C. Darwin, *The Expression of the Emotions in Man and Animals* (London: John Murray, 1872).

22.   V. Frankl, *Man's Search for Meaning* (New York: Simon and Schuster, 1959), 54–56.

23.   T. Anderson, *Den of Lions* (New York: Ballantine Books, 1994).

24.   R. R. Provine, *Laughter: A Scientific Investigation* (New York: Penguin 2001).

25.   J. Panksepp and J. Burgdorf, "'Laughing'" rats and the evolutionary antecedents of human joy?," *Physiology and Behavior*, 79 (2003), 533–547.

26.   L. Weiskrantz, J. Elliott, and C. Darlington, "Preliminary observations on tickling oneself," *Nature*, 230 (1971), 598–499.

27.   S. J. Blakemore, D. M. Wolpert, and C. D. Frith, "Central cancellation of self-produced tickle sensation," *Nature Neuroscience*, 1 (1990), 635–640.

28.   S. J. Blakemore, D. M. Wolpert, and C. D. Frith, "Why can't you tickle yourself?," *NeuroReport*, 11 (2000), R11–16.

29.   J. M. S. Pearce, "Some neurological aspects of laughter," *European Neurology*, 52 (2004), 169–171.

30.   There is a vast literature on newborn preferences for their mothers. On smell: J. M. Cernack and R. H. Porter, "Recognition of maternal axillary odors by infants," *Child Development*, 56 (1985), 1593–1598. On face: I. M. Bushnell, F. Sai, and J. T. Mullen, "Neonatal recognition of the mother's face," *British Journal of Developmental Psychology*, 7 (1989), 3–15. On voice: A. J. DeCasper and M. J. Spence, "Prenatal maternal speech influences newborns'

perception of speech sounds," *Infant Behavior and Development*, 9 (1986), 133–150.

31. W. C. Roedell and R. G. Slaby, "The role of distal and proximal interaction in infant social preference formation," *Developmental Psychology*, 13 (1977), 266–273.

32. C. Ellsworth, D. Muir, and S. Han, "Social-competence and person-object differentiation: An analysis of the still-face effect," *Developmental Psychology*, 29 (1993), 63–73.

33. L. Murray, A. Fiori-Cowley, R. Hooper, and P. Cooper, "The impact of postnatal depression and associated adversity on early mother-infant interactions and later infant outcome," *Child Development*, 67 (1996), 2512–2526.

34. H. R. Schaffer, *The Child's Entry into a Social World* (London, Academic Press, 1984).

35. M. Lewis, "Social development," in A. M. Slater and M. Lewis (eds.) *Introduction to infant development* (Oxford: Oxford University Press, 2007), 233–252. This provides a good overview of early social development.

36. K. Lorenz, "Die Angebornen Formen mogicher Erfahrung," *Zeitschrift fur Tierpsychologie*, 5 (1943), 233–409.

37. W. Fullard and A. M. Reiling, "An investigation of Lorenz's babyness," *Child Development*, 50 (1976), 915–922.

38. S. E. Taylor, *The Tending Instinct* (New York: Henry Holt, 2001).

39. S. Levine, D. F. Johnson, and C. A. Gonzalez, "Behavioral and hormonal responses to separation in infant rhesus monkeys and mothers," *Behavioral Neuroscience*, 99 (1985), 399–410.

40. M. C. Larson, M. R. Gunnar, and L. Hertsgaard, "The effects of morning naps, car trips and maternal separation on adrenocortical activity in human infants," *Child Development*, 62 (1991), 362–372.

41. P. S. Zeskind and B. M. Lester, "Analysis of infant crying," in L. T. Singer and P. S. Zeskind (eds.),

Biobehavioral Assessment of the Infant (New York: Guilford, 2001), 149–166.

42. *Baby It's You: The First Three Years,* Emmy Award-winning series produced by Wall to Wall for UK's Channel 4 (1994).

43. J. Bowlby, *Attachment and Loss, Vol. 1 Attachment* (London: Hogarth Press 1969).

44. R. A. Spitz, "Motherless infants," *Child Development,* 20 (1949), 145–155.

45. M. D. S. Ainsworth. *Infancy in Uganda: Infant Care and the Growth of Love.* (Baltimore, MD: John Hopkins University Press, 1967).

46. M. D. S. Ainsworth, M. C. Blehar, E. Waters, and S. Wall, *Patterns of Attachment: A Psychological Study of the Strange Situation* (Hillsdale, NJ: Erlbuam, 1978).

47. M. H. van IJzendoorn and P. M. Kroonenberg, "Cross-cultural patterns of attachment: A meta-analysis of the strange situation," *Child Development,* 59 (1988), 147–156.

48. J. Kagan, "Temperament and the reactions to unfamiliarity," *Child Development,* 68 (1997), 139–143.

49. C. Hazan and P. Shaver, "Romantic love conceptualized as an attachment process," *Journal of Personality and Social Psychology,* 52 (1987), 511–524.

50. J. A. Simpson, "Influence of attachment style on romantic relationships," *Journal of Personality and Social Psychology,* 59 (1990), 971–980.

51. H. Lane, *The Wild Boy of Aveyron* (Cambridge, MA: Harvard University Press, 1979).

52. J. M. G. Itard, *An Historical Account of the Discovery and Education of a Savage Man or of the First Developments, Physical and Moral of the Young Savage Caught in the Woods Near Aveyron in the Year* 1798 (London: Richard Phillips, 1802), 17.

53. G. Bremner, *Infancy* (2nd ed., Oxford: Wiley-Blackwell, 2004), 2.

54.   P. E. Jones, "Contradictions and unanswered questions in the Genie case: A fresh look at the linguistic evidence," *Language and Communication*, 15 (1995), 261–280.

55.   U. Firth, *Autism: Explaining the Enigma* (2nd ed., Oxford: Wiley-Blackwell, 2003).

56.   Alvin Powell, interview with Chuck Nelson, "Breathtakingly awful," *Harvard Gazette* (5 October 2010).

57.   D. E. Johnson, D. Guthrie, A. T. Smyke, S. F. Koga, N. A. Fox, C. H. Zeanah, and C. A. Nelson, "Growth and associations between auxology, caregiving environment, and cognition in socially deprived Romanian children randomized to foster vs ongoing institutional care," *Archives of Pediatrics and Adolescent Medicine*, 164 (2010), 507–516.

58.   M. Rutter, T. G. O'Connor, and the English and Romanian Adoptees (ERA) Study Team, "Are there biological programming effects for psychological development? Findings from a study of Romanian adoptees," *Developmental Psychology*, 40 (2004), 81–94.

59.   H. F. Harlow and M. L. Harlow, "The affectional systems," in A. M. Schrier, H. F. Harlow, and F. Stollnitz (eds.), *Behavior of Nonhuman Primates, Vol.* 2 (New York: Academic Press, 1965).

60.   T. Field, M. Hernandez-Reif, and J. Freedman, "Stimulation programs for preterm infants," *Social Policy Report*, 18 (2004), 1–19.

61.   D. O. Hebb, "The effects of early experience on problem solving at maturity," *American Psychologist*, 2 (1947), 306–307.

62.   J. T. Cacioppo, J. H. Fowler, and N. A. Christakis, "Alone in the crowd: The structure and spread of loneliness in a large social network," *Journal of Personality and Social Psychology*, 97 (2009), 977–991.

63.   H. Ruan and C. F. Wu, "Social interaction-mediated lifespan extension of *Drosophila* Cu/Zn superoxide dismutase mutants," *Proceedings of the National Academy of*

Sciences of the United States of America, 105: 21 (2008), 7506–7510.

64.   R. S. Kempe and C. H. Kempe, *Child Abuse* (Cambridge, MA: Harvard University Press, 1978).

65.   D. G. Dutton and S. Painter, "Emotional attachments in abusive relationships. A test of traumatic bonding," *Violence and Victims*, 8 (1993), 105–120.

66.   G. A. Morgan and H. N. Ricciuti, "Infants' responses to strangers during the first year," in B. M. Foss (ed.), *Determinants of Infant Behavior, Vol. 4* (London: Methuen, 1967).

67.   A. N. Meltzoff, P. K. Kuhl, J. Movellan, and T. J. Sejnowski, "Foundations for a new science of learning," *Science*, 325 (2009), 284–288.

68.   A. N. Meltzoff, "Infant imitation and memory: Nine-month-olds in immediate and deferred tests," *Child Development*, 59 (1988), 217–225.

69.   G. Gergely, H. Bekkering, and I. Király, "Rational imitation of goal directed actions in preverbal infants," *Nature*, 415 (2002), 755.

70.   A. N. Meltzoff and R. Brooks, "Self-experience as a mechanism for learning about others: A training study in social cognition," *Developmental Psychology*, 44 (2008), 1257–1265.

71.   S. Itakura, H. Ishida, T. Kanda, Y. Shimada, H. Ishiguro, and K. Lee, "How to build an intentional android: Infants" imitation of a robot's goal-directed actions," *Infancy*, 13 (2008), 519–532.

72.   V. Gallese, L. Fadiga, L. Fogassi, and G. Rizzolatti, "Action recognition in the premotor cortex," *Brain*, 119 (1996), 593–609.

73.   V. Gallese, M. A. Gernsbacher, C. Heyes, G. Hickok, and M. Iacoboni, "Mirror Neuron Forum," *Perspectives on Psychological Science*, 6 (2011), 369–407.

74.   This claim was made by the eminent neuroscientist Vilayanur Ramachandran and is related in C. Keysers,

The Empathic Brain (Los Gatos, CA: Smashwords e-book, 2011).

75. D. T. Neal and T. L. Chartrand, "Embodied emotion perception: Amplifying and dampening facial feedback modulates emotion perception accuracy," *Social Psychological and Personality Science* (2011), doi:10.1177/1948550611406138

76. S.-J. Blakemore, D. Bristow, G. Bird, C. Frith, and J. Ward, "Somatosensory activations during the observation of touch and a case of vision-touch synaesthesia," *Brain*, 128 (2005), 1571–1583.

77. J. Ward, *The Frog Who Croaked Blue: Synesthesia and the Mixing of the Senses* (London: Routledge, 2008).

78. M. J. Richardson, K. L. Marsh, R. W. Isenhower, J. R. L. Goodman, and R. C. Schmidt, "Rocking together: Dynamics of intentional and unintentional interpersonal coordination," *Human Movement Science*, 26 (2007), 867–891.

79. M. S. Helt, I.-M. Eigsti, P. J. Snyder, and D. A. Fein, "Contagious yawning in autistic and typical development," *Child Development*, 81 (2010), 1620–1631.

80. T. J. Cox, "Scraping sounds and disgusting noises," *Applied Acoustics*, 69 (2008), 1195–1204.

81. O. Sacks, *The Man Who Mistook His Wife for a Hat* (New York: Harper Perennial, 1987), 123.

CHAPTER 3: THE LOOKING GLASS SELF

1. C. H. Cooley, *Human Nature and the Social Order* (New York: Scribner's, 1902).

2. N. Breen, D. Caine, and M. Coltheart, "Mirrored-self misidentification: Two cases of focal onset dementia," *Neurocase*, 7 (2001), 239–254.

3. J. Cotard, *Etudes sur les Maladies Cerebrales et Mentales* (Paris: Bailliere, 1891).

4. E. C. M. Hunter, M. Sierra, and A. S. David, "The epidemiology of depersonalisation and derealisation:

A systematic review," *Social Psychiatry Psychiatric Epidemiology*, 39 (2004), 9–18.

5.   A. J. Barnier, R. E. Cox, M. Connors, R. Langdon, and M. Coltheart, "A stranger in the looking glass: Developing and challenging a hypnotic mirrored-self misidentification delusion," *International Journal of Clinical and Experimental Hypnosis*, 59 (2011), 1–26.

6.   G. B. Caputo, "Strange-face-in-the-mirror illusion," *Perception*, 39 (2010), 1007–1008.

7.   G. G. Gallup, "Chimpanzees: Self-recognition," *Science*, 167 (1970), 86–87.

8.   B. I. Bertenthal and K. W. Fischer, "Development of self-recognition in the infant," *Developmental Psychology*, 14 (1978), 44–50.

9.   P. Rochat, *Others in Mind: Social Origins of Self-Consciousness* (Cambridge: Cambridge University Press, 2009).

10.   D. Bruce, A. Dolan, and K. Phillips-Grant, "On the transition from childhood amnesia to the recall of personal memories," *Psychological Science*, 11 (2000), 360–364.

11.   M. J. Eacott, "Memory for the events of early childhood," *Current Directions in Psychological Sciences*, 8 (1999), 46–49.

12.   D. Wearing, *Forever Today: A Memoir of Love and Amnesia* (London: Doubleday, 2005).

13.   Wearing (2005), 158.

14.   J. Piaget, *The Child's Construction of Reality* (London: Routledge and Kegan Paul, 1955).

15.   C. Rovee and D. T. Rovee, "Conjugate reinforcement of infant exploratory behavior," *Journal of Experimental Child Psychology*, 8 (1969), 33–39.

16.   D. B. Mitchell, "Nonconscious priming after17 years: Invulnerable implicit memory?," *Psychological Science*, 17 (2006), 925–929.

17.   E. Tulving, *Elements of Episodic Memory* (Oxford: Clarendon Press, 1983).

18. M. A. Conway and C. W. Pleydell-Pearce, "The construction of autobiographical memories in the self-memory system," *Psychological Review*, 107 (2000), 261–288.

19. H. L. Roediger III and K. B. McDermott, "Tricks of memory," *Current Directions in Psychological Science*, 9 (2000), 123–127.

20. F. C. Bartlett, *Remembering* (Cambridge, England: Cambridge University Press, 1932).

21. E. F. Loftus, "Leading questions and eyewitness report," *Cognitive Psychology*, 7 (1975), 560–572.

22. E. F. Loftus, "Lost in the mall: Misrepresentations and misunderstandings," *Ethics and Behavior*, 9 (1999), 51–60.

23. The story of Piaget's false memory can be found in C. Tavris, "Hysteria and the incest-survivor machine," *Sacramento Bee*, Forum section (17 January 1993).

24. K. A. Wade, M. Garry, J. D. Read, and D. S. Lindsay, "A picture is worth a thousand lies: Using false photographs to create false childhood memories," *Psychonomic Bulletin and Review*, 9 (2002), 597–603.

25. Loftus' recollection of this incident is found in J. Neimark, "The diva of disclosure, memory researcher Elizabeth Loftus," *Psychology Today*, 29 (1996), 48.

26. D. J. Simons and C. F. Chabris, "What people believe about how memory works: A representative survey of the US population," *PLoS ONE*, 6: 8 (2011), e22757, doi:10.1371/journal.pone.0022757

27. W. L. Randall, "From compost to computer: Rethinking our metaphors for memory," *Theory Psychology*, 17 (2007), 611–633.

28. Simons, quoted in K. Harmon, "4 things most people get wrong about memory," *Scientific American* (4 August 2011), http://blogs.scientificamerican.com/observations/2011/08/04/4-things-most-people-get-wrong-about-memory

29. P. K. Dick, "We can remember it for you wholesale," *Magazine of Fantasy and Science Fiction* (April 1966).

30. *Total Recall* (1990), directed by Paul Verhoeven.

31. K. Tustin and H. Hayne, "Defining the boundary: Age-related changes in childhood amnesia," *Developmental Psychology*, 46 (2010), 1049–1061.

32. M. L. Howe and M. L. Courage, "On resolving the enigma of infantile amnesia," *Psychological Bulletin*, 113 (1993), 305–326.

33. Rochat (2009).

34. D. Premack and G. Woodruff, "Does the chimpanzee have a theory of mind?," *Behavioral and Brain Sciences*, 1 (1978), 515–526.

35. The story of Binti is told in S. Budiansky, "Still red tooth and claw," *Wall Street Journal* (12 March 1978).

36. Studies of gaze following indicate that this is present early and may even be innate. See, for example, B. M. Hood, J. D. Willen, and J. Driver, "An eye direction detector triggers shifts of visual attention in human infants," *Psychological Science*, 9 (1998), 53–56.

37. A. Phillips, H. M. Wellman, and E. S. Spelke, "Infants' ability to connect gaze and emotional expression to intentional action," *Cognition*, 85 (2002), 53–78.

38. B. M. Repacholi and A. Gopnik, "Early reasoning about desires: Evidence from 14- and 18-month-olds," *Developmental Psychology*, 33 (1997), 12–21.

39. D. J. Povinelli and T. J. Eddy, *What Chimpanzees Know about Seeing*, Monographs of the Society of Research in Child Development 61:2:247 (Boston, MA: Blackwell, 1996).

40. D. Dennett, "Beliefs about beliefs," *Behavioral and Brain Sciences*, 1 (1978), 568–570.

41. A. Gopnik and J. W. Astington, "Children's understanding of representational change and its relation to the understanding of false belief and the appearance reality distinction," *Child Development*, 59 (1988), 26–37.

42. H. Wimmer and J. Perner, "Beliefs about beliefs: Representations and constraining function of wrong

beliefs in young children's understanding of deception," *Cognition*, 13 (1983), 103–128.

43. A. Gopnik, *The Philosophical Baby: What Children's Minds Tell Us About Truth, Love, and the Meaning of Life* (NY: Farrar, Straus & Giroux, 2009).

44. A. McAlister and C. Peterson, "A longitudinal study of child siblings and theory of mind development," *Cognitive Development*, 22 (2007), 258–270.

45. C. Keysers, *The Empathic Brain* (Los Gatos, CA: Smashwords e-book, 2011).

46. C. J. Newschaffer, L. A. Croen, and J. Daniels et al., "The epidemiology of autism spectrum disorders," *Annual Review of Public Health*, 28 (2007), 235–258.

47. U. Frith, *Autism: Explaining the Enigma* (2nd ed., Oxford: Wiley-Blackwell, 2003).

48. S. Baron-Cohen, *Mindblindness: An Essay on Autism and Theory of Mind* (Cambridge, MA: MIT Press, 1995).

49. A. Gopnik, "Mindblindness" (Unpublished essay. Berkeley: University of California, 1993).

50. M. S. Helt, I. Eigsti, P. J. Snyder, and D. A. Fein, "Contagious yawning in autistic and typical development," *Child Development*, 81 (2010), 1620–1631.

51. T. Grandin, *The Way I See It* (2nd ed., Arlington, TX: Future Horizons, 2011).

52. O. Sacks, *An Anthropologist on Mars: Seven Paradoxical Tales* (New York: Vintage, 1996).

53. A. Bailey, A. Le Couteur, I. Gottesman, P. Bolton, E. Simonoff, E. Yuzda, and M. Rutter, "Autism as a strongly genetic disorder: Evidence from a British twin study," *Psychological Medicine*, 25 (1995), 63–77.

54. J. H. Pfeifer, M. Iacoboni, J. C. Mazziotta, and M. Dapretto, "Mirroring others' emotions relates to empathy and interpersonal competence in children," *Neuroimage*, 15 (2008), 2076–2085; M. Dapretto, M. S. Davies, J. H. Pfeifer, M. Sigman, M. Iacoboni, S. Y. Bookheimer, et al.,

"Understanding emotions in others: Mirror neuron dysfunction in children with autism spectrum disorders," *Nature Neuroscience*, 9 (2006), 28–30.

55. J. A. Bastiaansen, M. Thioux, L. Nanetti, C. van der Gaag, C. Ketelaars, R. Minderaa, and C. Keysers, "Age-related increase in inferior frontal gyrus activity and social functioning in autism spectrum disorder," *Biological Psychiatry*, 69 (2011), 832–838.

56. J. M. Allman, K. K. Watson, N. A. Tetreault, and A. Y. Hakeem, "Intuition and autism: A possible role for Von Economo neurons," *Trends in Cognitive Sciences*, 9 (2005), 367–373.

57. A. L. Beaman, E. Diener, and B. Klentz, "Self-awareness and transgression in children: Two field studies," *Journal of Personality and Social Psychology*, 37 (1979), 1835–1846.

58. D. Elkind, "Egocentrism in adolescence," *Child Development*, 38 (1967), 1025–1034.

59. S.-J. Blakemore, "The social brain in adolescence," *Nature Reviews Neuroscience*, 9 (2008), 267–277.

60. J. Pfeifer, M. Lieberman, and M. Dapretto, "'I know you are but what am I?': Neural bases of self and social knowledge retrieval in children and adults," *Journal of Cognitive Neuroscience*, 19:8 (2007), 1323–1337.

61. S.-J. Blakemore, H. den Ouden, S. Choudhury, and C. Frith, "Adolescent development of the neural circuitry for thinking about intentions," *Social Cognitive and Affective Neuroscience*, 2:2 (2007), 130–139.

62. S. Burnett, G. Bird, J. Moll, C. Frith, and S.-J. Blakemore, "Development during adolescence of the neural processing of social emotion," *Journal of Cognitive Neuroscience*, 21:9 (2009), 1736–1750.

63. L. Steinberg, "A neurobehavioral perspective on adolescent risk taking," *Developmental Review*, 28 (2008), 78–106.

64. The story of Storm can be found at J. Poisson, "Parents keep child's gender secret," *Star* (21 May 2011), www.thestar.com/article/995112

65. E. E. Maccoby, *The Two Sexes: Growing Up Apart, Coming Together* (Cambridge, MA: Belknap Press, 1998).

66. C. L. Martin and D. Ruble, "Children's search for gender cues: Cognitive perspectives on gender development," *Current Directions in Psychological Science*, 13 (2004), 67–70.

67. A. S. Rossi, "A biosocial perspective on parenting," *Daedalus*, 106 (1977), 1–31.

68. J. Condry and S. Condry, "Sex differences: A study of the eye of the beholder," *Child Development*, 47 (1976), 812–819.

69. C. Smith and B. Lloyd, "Maternal behavior and perceived sex of infant: Revisited," *Child Development*, 49 (1978), 1263–1265.

70. D. Fisher-Thompson, "Adult toy purchase for children: Factors affecting sex-typed toy selection," *Journal of Applied Developmental Psychology*, 14 (1993), 385–406.

71. J. L. R. Delk, R. B. Madden, M. Livingston, and T. T Ryan, "Adult perceptions of the infant as a function of gender labeling and observer gender," *Sex Roles*, 15 (1986), 527–534.

72. A. Pomerleau, D. Bolduc, G. Malcuit, and L. Cossette, "Pink or blue: Environmental gender stereotypes in the first two years of life," *Sex Roles*, 22 (1990), 359–367.

73. S. K. Thompson, "Gender labels and early sex-role development," *Child Development*, 46 (1975), 339–347.

74. S. A. Gelman, M. G. Taylor, and S. P. Nguyen, *Mother-child Conversations about Gender*, Monographs of the Society for Research in Child Development, 69:1:275 (Boston, MA: Blackwell, 2004).

75. J. Dunn, I. Bretherton, and P. Munn, "Conversations about feeling states between mothers and their young children," *Developmental Psychology*, 23 (1987), 132–139.

76. K. Crowley, M. A. Callanan, H. R. Tenenbaum, and E. Allen, "Parents explain more often to boys than to girls during shared scientific thinking," *Psychological Science*, 12 (2001), 258–261.

77. M. Sadker and D. Sadker, *Failing at Fairness: How America's Schools Cheat Girls* (New York: Scribner's, 1994).

78. K. C. Kling, J. S. Hyde, C. J. Showers, and B. N. Buswell, "Gender differences in self-esteem: A meta-analysis," *Psychological Bulletin*, 125 (1999), 470–500.

79. D. F. Halpern, "A cognitive-process taxonomy for sex differences in cognitive abilities," *Current Directions in Psychological Science*, 13 (2004), 135–139.

80. R. L. Munro, R. Hulefeld, J. M. Rodgers, D. L. Tomeo, and S. K. Yamazaki, "Aggression among children in four cultures," *Cross-Cultural Research*, 34 (2000), 3–25.

81. T. R. Nansel, M. Overpeck, R. S. Pilla, W. J. Ruan, B. Simons-Morton, and P. Scheidt, "Bullying behaviors among US youth: Prevalence and association with psychosocial adjustment," *Journal of the American Medical Association*, 285 (2001), 2094–2100.

82. P. A. Jacobs, M. Brunton, M. M. Melville, R. P. Brittain, and W. F. McClemont, "Aggressive behavior, mental sub-normality and the XYY male," *Nature*, 208 (1965), 1351–1352.

83. M. C. Brown, "Males with an XYY sex chromosome complement," *Journal of Medical Genetics*, 5 (1968), 341–359.

84. H. A. Witkin et al., "Criminality in XYY and XXY men," *Science*, 193 (1976), 547–555.

85. A. Caspi, J. McClay, T. E. Moffitt, J. Mill, J. Martin, I. W. Craig, A. Taylor, and R. Poulton, "Role of genotype in the cycle of violence in maltreated children," *Science*, 297 (2002), 851–854.

86. E. Yong, "Dangerous DNA: The truth about the 'warrior gene,'" *New Scientist* (7 April 2010).

87. G. Naik, "What's on Jim Fallon's mind? A family secret that has been murder to figure out," *Wall Street Journal* (30 November 2009).

88. Interview with Jim Fallon by Claudia Hammond for *All in the Mind*, BBC Radio 4 (26 April 2011).

89. B. D. Perry, "Incubated in terror: Neurodevelopmental factors in the 'Cycle of Violence,'" in J. Osofsky (ed.), *Children, Youth and Violence: The Search for Solutions* (New York: Guilford Press, 1997), 124–148.

90. W. Mischel, *Personality and Assessment* (New York: Wiley, 1968).

91. W. Mischel, Y. Shoda, and M. L. Rodriguez, "Delay of gratification in children," *Science*, 244 (1989), 933–938.

92. Y. Shoda, W. Mischel, and P. K. Peake, "Predicting adolescent cognitive and social competence from preschool delay of gratification: Identifying diagnostic conditions," *Developmental Psychology*, 26 (1990), 978–986; W. Mischel and O. Ayduk, "Willpower in a cognitive-affective processing system: The dynamics of delay of gratification," in R. F. Baumeister and K. D. Vohs (eds.), *Handbook of Self-Regulation: Research, Theory, and Applications* (New York: Guilford, 2004), 99–129.

93. P. H. Wender, *ADHD: Attention-Deficit Hyperactivity Disorder in Children and Adults* (Oxford: Oxford University Press, 2002).

94. M. Strock, *Attention Deficit Hyperactivity Disorder* (London: National Institute of Mental Health, 1996), available at http://www.nimh.nih.gov/health/publications/adhd/nimhadhdpub.pdf

95. G. Kochanska, K. C. Coy, and K. T. Murray, "The development of self-regulation in the first four years of life," *Child Development*, 72 (2001), 1091–1111.

96. D. Parfit, *Reason and Persons* (Oxford: Oxford University Press, 1986).

97. S. Gelman, *The Essential Child: Origins of Essentialism in Everyday Thought* (Oxford: Oxford University Press, 2003).

98. P. Bloom, *How Pleasure Works: The New Science of Why We Like What We Like* (New York: W. W. Norton and Company, 2010).

CHAPTER 4: THE COST OF FREE WILL

1. G. M. Lavergne, *A Sniper in the Tower: The Charles Whitman Murders* (Denton, TX: University of North Texas Press, 1997).

2. J. M. Burns and R. H. Swerdlow, "Right orbitofrontal tumor with pedophilia symptom and constructional

apraxia sign," *Archives of Neurology*, 60 (2003), 437–440.

3.   D. M. Eagleman, *Incognito: The Secret Lives of the Brain* (Edinburgh: Canongate, 2011).

4.   N. Levy, *Neuroethics: Challenges for the 21st Century* (Cambridge: Cambridge University Press, 2007).

5.   B. de Spinoza, *A Spinoza Reader: The Ethics and Other Works*, ed. and trans. E. Curley (Princeton: Princeton University Press, 1994).

6.   Dennett is quoted in E. Taylor, *Mind Programming: From Persuasion and Brainwashing, to Self-Help and Practical Metaphysics* (San Diego, CA: Hay House, 2009).

7.   E. R. Macagno, V. Lopresti, and C. Levinthal, "Structure and development of neuronal connections in isogenic organisms: Variations and similarities in the optic system of Daphnia magna," *Proceedings of the National Academy of Sciences of the United States of America*, 70 (1973), 57–61.

8.   H. Putnam, "Psychological predicates," in W. H. Capitan and D. D. Merrill (eds.), *Art, Mind, and Religion* (Pittsburgh, PA: University of Pittsburgh Press, 1967), 37–48.

9.   This example comes from Gazzaniga's Gifford lecture where he introduced the work of neurophysiologist Eve Marder to demonstrate the principle of Putnam's multiple realizability; J. M. Goaillard, A. L. Taylor, D. J. Schulz, and E. Marder, "Functional consequences of animal-to-animal variation in circuit parameters," *Nature. Neuroscience*, 12 (2009), 1424–1430.

10.   B. Libet, C. Gleason, E. Wright, and D. Pearal, "Time of unconscious intention to act in relation to onset of cerebral activity (readiness-potential)," *Brain*, 106 (1983), 623–642.

11.   C. S. Soon, M. Brass, H.-J. Heinze, and J.-D. Haynes, "Unconscious determinants of free decisions in the human brain," *Nature Neuroscience*, 11 (2008), 543–545.

12.   G. Ryle, *The Concept of Mind* (London: Peregrine, 1949), 186–189.

13.   F. Assal, S. Schwartz, and P. Vuilleumier, "Moving with or without will: Functional neural correlates of alien hand syndrome," *Annals of Neurology*, 62 (2007), 301–306.

14.   See M. S. Gazzaniga, "Forty-five years of split-brain research and still going strong," *Nature Reviews Neuroscience*, 6:8 (August 2005), 653–659, for Gazzaniga's reflection of his work in split-brain research.

15.   F. Lhermitte, "Human autonomy and the frontal lobes. Part II: Patient behavior in complex and social situations: The 'environmental dependency syndrome,'" *Annals of Neurology*, 19 (1986), 335–343.

16.   F. Lhermitte, "'Utilization behavior' and its relation to lesions of the frontal lobes," *Brain*, 106 (1983), 237–255.

17.   D. Wegner, *The Illusion of Conscious Will* (Cambridge, MA: MIT Press, 2002).

18.   D. Wegner, "Self is magic," in J. C. Kaufman and R. F. Baumeister (eds.), *Are We Free? Psychology and Free Will* (New York: Oxford University Press, 2008).

19.   J. Cloutier and C. N. Macrae, "The feeling of choosing: Self-involvement and the cognitive status of things past," *Consciousness and Cognition*, 17 (2008), 125–135.

20.   L. M. Goff and H. L. Roediger III, "Imagination inflation for action events: Repeated imaginings lead to illusory recollections," *Memory and Cognition*, 26 (1998), 20–33.

21.   L. Lindner, G. Echerhoff, P. S. R. Davidson, and M. Brand, "Observation inflation: Your actions become mine," *Psychological Science*, 21 (2010), 1291–1299.

22.   E. R. Hilgard, *Hypnotic Suggestibility* (New York: Harcout Brace and World, 1965).

23.   Hilgard (1965).

24.   P. Rainville, R. K. Hofbauer, T. Paus, G. H. Duncan, M. C. Bushnell, and D. D. Price, "Cerebral mechanisms of hypnotic induction and suggestion," *Journal of Cognitive Neuroscience*, 11 (1999), 110–122.

25.   T. R. Sarbin, "Contributions to role-taking. I. Hypnotic behavior," *Psychological Review*, 57 (1950), 255–270.

26.   S. Vyse, *Believing in Magic: The Psychology of Superstition* (Oxford: Oxford University Press, 1997).

27.   K. Ono, "Superstitious behavior in humans," *Journal of the Experimental Analysis of Behavior*, 47 (1987), 261–271.

28.   *Daily Mail* (27 January 2009).

29.   B. Malinowski, "Fishing in the Trobriand Islands," *Man*, 18 (1918), 87–92.

30.   S. S. Dickerson and M. E. Kemeny, "Acute stressors and cortisol responses: A theoretical integration and synthesis of laboratory research," *Psychological Bulletin*, 130 (2004), 355–391.

31.   G. Keinan, "The effects of stress and desire for control on superstitious behavior," *Personality and Social Psychology Bulletin*, 28 (2002), 102–108.

32.   *Independent* (9 April 2007).

33.   The primatologist Josep Call told the author about this phenomenon.

34.   M. M. Robertson and A. E. Cavanna, "The disaster was my fault," *Neurocase*, 13 (2007), 446–451.

35.   I. Osborn, *Tormenting Thoughts and Secret Rituals: The Hidden Epidemic of Obsessive-Compulsive Disorder* (New York: Dell, 1998).

36.   T. E. Oltmanns, J. M. Neale, and G. C. Davison, *Case Studies in Abnormal Psychology* (3rd ed., New York: Wiley, 1991).

37.   A. M. Graybiel and S. L. Rauch, "Toward a neurobiology of obsessive-compulsive disorder," *Neuron*, 28 (2000), 343–347.

38.   M. Field, "Impulsivity, restraint and ego depletion in heavy drinkers," Presentation at the Bristol Psychopharmacology Research Network: Workshop 3, Bristol Institute for Advanced Studies (1 December 2010).

39.   N. L. Mead, J. L. Alquist, and R. F. Baumeister, "Ego depletion and the limited resource model of self-control," in R. R. Hassin, K. N. Ochsner and Y. Trope (eds.), *Self*

Control in Society, Mind and Brain (Oxford: Oxford University Press, 2010), 375–388.

40.   R. F. Baumeister, *The Self in Social Psychology* (Philadelphia: Psychology Press, 1999).

41.   M. Muraven and R. F. Baumeister, "Self-regulation and depletion of limited resources: Does self-control resemble a muscle?," *Psychological Bulletin*, 126 (2000), 247–259.

42.   J. Rotton, "Affective and cognitive consequences of malodorous pollution," *Basic Applied Social Psychology*, 4 (1983), 171–191; B. J. Schmeichel, K. D. Vohs, and R. F. Baumeister, "Intellectual performance and ego depletion: Role of the self in logical reasoning and other information processing," *Journal of Personality and Social Psychology*, 85 (2003), 33–46; G. W. Evans, "Behavioral and physiological consequences of crowding in humans," *Journal of Applied Social Psychology*, 9 (1969), 27–49; D. C. Glass and J. E. Singer, *Urban Stress: Experiments on Noise and Social Stressors* (New York: Academic Press, 1972).

43.   D. Kahan, J. Polivy, and C. P. Herman, "Conformity and dietary disinhibition: A test of the ego-strength model of self control," *International Journal of Eating Disorders*, 32 (2003), 165–171; M. Muraven, R. L. Collins, and K. Neinhaus, "Self-control and alcohol restraint: An initial application of the self-control strength model," *Psychology of Addictive Behaviors*, 16 (2002), 113–120; K. D. Vohs, R. F. Baumeister, B. J. Schmeichel, J. M. Twenge, N. M. Nelson, and D. Tice, "Mating choices impairs subsequent self-control: A limited resource account of decision making, self-regulation, and active initiative," *Journal of Personality and Social Psychology*, 94 (2008), 883–898.

44.   K. D. Vohs, R. F. Baumeister, and N. J. Ciarocco, "Self-regulation and self-presentation: Regulatory resource depletion impairs impression management and effortful self-presentation depletes regulatory resources," *Journal of Personality and Social Psychology*, 88 (2005), 632–657.

45.   N. J. Ciarocco, K. Sommer, and R. F. Baumeister, "Ostracism and ego depletion: The strains of silence," *Personality and Social Psychology Bulletin*, 27 (2001), 1156–1163.

46. M. T. Gailliot, R. F. Baumeister, C. N. DeWall, J. K. Maner, E. A. Plant, D. M. Tice, L. E. Brewer, and B. J. Schmeichel, "Self-control relies on glucose as a limited energy source: Willpower is more than a metaphor," *Journal of Personality and Social Psychology*, 92 (2007), 325–336.

47. I. W. Hung and A. A. Labroo, "From firm muscles to firm willpower: Understanding the role of embodied cognition in self-regulation," *Journal of Consumer Research*, 37 (2011), 1046–1064.

48. D. R. Carney, A. J. C. Cuddy, and A. J. Yap, "Power posing: Brief nonverbal displays affect neuroendocrine levels and risk tolerance," *Psychological Science*, 21 (2010), 1363–1368.

49. L. W. Barsalou, "Grounded cognition," *Annual Review of Psychology*, 59:1 (2008), 617–645.

50. M. Tuk, D. Trampe, and L. Warlop, "Inhibitory spillover: Increased urination urgency facilitates impulse control in unrelated domains," *Psychological Science*, 22 (2011), 627–633.

51. J. Baggini, *The Ego Trick* (London: Granta, 2011).

52. H. Rachlin, "Teleological behaviorism and the problem of self-control," in R. R. Hassin, K. N. Ochsner, and Y. Trope (eds.), *Self Control in Society, Mind, and Brain* (Oxford: Oxford University Press, 2010), 506–521.

53. V. Job, C. S. Dweck, and G. M. Walton, "Ego depletion— is it all in your head? Implicit theories about willpower affect self-regulation," *Psychological Science*, 21 (2010), 1686–1693.

54. C. M. Mueller and C. S. Dweck, "Intelligence praise can undermine motivation and performance," *Journal of Personality and Social Psychology*, 75 (1998), 33–52.

55. K. D. Vohs and J. W. Schooler, "The value of believing in free will: Encouraging a belief in determinism increases cheating," *Psychological Science*, 19 (2008), 49–54.

56. T. F. Stillman, R. F. Baumeister, K. D. Vohs, N. M. Lambert, F. D. Fincham, and L. E. Brewer, "Personal

philosophy and personnel achievement: Belief in free will predicts better job performance," *Social Psychological and Personality Science*, 1 (2010), 43–50.

CHAPTER 5: WHY OUR CHOICES ARE NOT OUR OWN

1. F. Presbrey, "1855–1936. The history and development of advertising," *Advertising and Society Review*, 1:1 (2000).

2. The phrase "subliminal advertising" was coined in 1957 by U.S. market researcher James Vicary, who said he could get moviegoers to "drink Coca-Cola" and "eat popcorn" by flashing those messages onscreen for such a short time that viewers were unaware. Vicary later admitted he had fabricated his results.

3. J. N. Axelrod, "Advertising measures that predict purchase," *Journal of Advertising Research*, 8 (1968), 3–17.

4. Both von Helmholtz and Freud wrote about the unconscious processes that shape our behaviors: H. von Helmholtz, "Concerning the perceptions in general," in *Treatise on Physiological Optics, Vol. III*, trans J. P. C. Southall (New York: Dover, 1925/1962); S. Freud, *The Interpretation of Dreams*, trans. A. A. Brill (New York: Macmillan, 1913).

5. P. Johansson, L. Hall, S. Sikström, and A. Olsson, "Failure to detect mismatches between intention and outcome in a simple decision task," *Science*, 310:5745 (2005), 116–119.

6. L. Hall, P. Johansson, B. Tärning, S. Sikström, and T. Deutgen, "Magic at the marketplace: Choice blindness for the taste of jam and the smell of tea," *Cognition*, 117 (2010), 54–61.

7. S. Pinker, *The Blank Slate: The Modern Denial of Human Nature* (New York: Viking, 2002).

8. L. Festinger, *A Theory of Cognitive Dissonance* (Stanford, CA: Stanford University Press, 1957).

9. V. V. Bapeswara Rao and M. Bhaskara Rao, "A three-door game show and some of its variants," *Mathematical Scientist*, 17 (1992), 89–94.

10.   E. Langer, "The illusion of control," *Journal of Personality and Social Psychology*, 32 (1975), 311–328.

11.   D. Salsburg, *The Lady Tasting Tea: How Statistics Revolutionized Science in the Twentieth Century* (New York: Holt, 2002).

12.   G. Gigerenzer, *Reckoning with Risk* (Harmondsworth: Penguin, 2003).

13.   G. Gigerenzer, "Dread risk, September 11, and fatal traffic accidents," *Psychological Science*, 15 (2004), 286–287.

14.   M. E. P. Seligman and S. F. Maier, "Failure to escape traumatic shock," *Journal of Experimental Psychology*, 74 (1967), 1–9.

15.   M. E. P. Seligman, *Helplessness: On Depression, Development, and Death* (San Francisco: W. H. Freeman, 1975).

16.   G. W. Brown and T. Harris, *Social Origins of Depression* (New York: Free Press, 1978).

17.   S. F. Maier and L. R. Watkins, "Stressor controllability, anxiety and serotonin," *Cognitive Therapy Research*, 22 (1998), 595–613.

18.   T. V. Salomons, T. Johnstone, M.-M. Backonja, and R. J. Davidson, "Perceived controllability modulates the neural response to pain," *Journal of Neuroscience*, 24 (2004), 7199–7203.

19.   S. Botti and A. L. McGill, "The locus of choice: Personal causality and satisfaction with hedonic and utilitarian decisions," *Journal of Consumer Research*, 37 (2011), 1065–1078.

20.   B. Schwartz, *The Paradox of Choice: Why More is Less* (London: Harper Collins, 2005).

21.   D. Ariely, *Predictably Irrational* (New York: Harper, 2008).

22.   D. Kahneman, "The riddle of experience vs money," TED Talk (February 2010), *TED* website, www.ted.com/talks/daniel_kahneman_the_riddle_of_experience_vs_memory.html

23.   D. A. Redelmeier, J. Katz and D. Kahneman, "Memories of colonoscopy: A randomized trial," *Pain*, 104 (2003), 187–194.

24. D. Ariely and G. Loewenstein, "The heat of moment: The effect of sexual arousal on sexual decision making," *Journal of Behavioral Decision Making*, 19 (2006), 87–98.

25. W. James, *Principles of Psychology* (New York: Henry Holt, 1890).

26. P. Kanngiesser, N. L. Gjersoe, and B. M. Hood, "The effect of creative labor on property-ownership transfer by preschool children and adults," *Psychological Science*, 21 (2010), 1236–1241.

27. B. M. Hood and P. Bloom, "Children prefer certain individuals to perfect duplicates," *Cognition*, 106 (2008), 455–462.

28. B. M. Hood, K. Donnelly, U. Leonards, and P. Bloom, "Implicit voodoo: Electrodermal activity reveals a susceptibility to sympathetic magic," *Journal of Culture and Cognition*, 10 (2010), 391–399.

29. D. J. Turk, K. van Bussel, G. D. Waiter, and C. N. Macrae, "Mine and me: Exploring the neural basis of object ownership," *Journal of Cognitive Neuroscience* 23 (2011), 3657–3668.

30. S. J. Cunningham, D. J. Turk, and C. N. Macrae, "Yours or mine? Ownership and memory," *Consciousness and Cognition*, 17 (2008), 312–318.

31. "Settlement reached over Auschwitz suitcase," *Auschwitz-Birkenau Memorial and Museum* website (June 2009), http://en.auschwitz.org/m/index.php?option=com_content&task=view&id=630&Itemid=8

32. M. Carroll, "'Junk' collections among mentally retarded patients," *American Journal of Mental Deficiency*, 73 (1968), 308–314.

33. P. Sherwell, "Hoarder killed by collapsing clutter," *Daily Telegraph* (22 January 2006).

34. R. W. Belk, "Possession and the extended self," *Journal of Consumer Research*, 15 (1988), 139–168.

35. R. Thaler, "Toward a positive theory of consumer choice," *Journal of Economic Behavior and Organization*, 1 (1980), 39–60.

36. D. Kahneman, J. L. Knetsch, and R. H. Thaler, "Anomalies: The endowment effect, loss aversion and status quo bias," *Journal of Economic Perspectives*, 5 (1991), 193–206.

37. E. van Dijk and D. van Knippenberg, "Trading wine: On the endowment effect, loss aversion, and the comparability of consumer goods," *Journal of Economic Psychology*, 19 (1998), 485–495; J. L. Knetsch, "The endowment effect and evidence of non-reversible indifference curves," *American Economic Review*, 79 (1989), 1277–1284.

38. J. R. Wolf, H. R. Arkes, and W. A. Muhanna, "The power of touch: An examination of the effect of duration of physical contact on the valuation of objects," *Judgment and Decision Making*, 3 (2008), 476–482.

39. B. Knutson, G. E. Wimmer, S. Rick, N. G. Hollon, D. Prelec, and G. Loewenstein, "Neural antecedents of the endowment effect," *Neuron*, 58 (2008), 814–822.

40. A. Kogut and E. Kogut, "Possession attachment: Individual differences in the endowment effect," *Journal of Behavioral Decision Making* (20 April 2010), doi:10.1002/bdm.698

41. M. Wallendorf and E. J. Arnould, "'My favorite things': A cross-cultural inquiry into object attachment, possessiveness, and social linkage," *Journal of Consumer Research*, 14 (1988), 531–547.

42. C. L. Apicella, E. M. Azevedo, N. Christakis, and J. H. Fowler, "Isolated hunter-gatherers do not exhibit the endowment effect bias" Invited talk: New York University for Neuroeconomics, New York.

43. M. H. Kuhn and T. S. McPartland, "An empirical investigation of self-attitude," *American Sociological Review*, 19 (1954), 68–76.

44. W. M. Maddux, H. Yang, C. Falk, H. Adam, W. Adair, Y. Endo, Z. Carmon, and S. J. Heine, "For whom is parting with possessions more painful? Cultural differences in the endowment effect," *Psychological Science*, 21 (2010), 1910–1917.

45. A. P. Bayliss, A. Firschen, M. J. Fenske, and S. P. Tipper, "Affective evaluations of objects are influenced by observed gaze direction and emotional expression," *Cognition*, 104 (2007), 644–653.

Chapter 6: How the Tribe Made Me

1. R. C. Kessler, P. Berglund, O. Demler, R. Jin, and E. E. Walters, "Lifetime prevalence and age-of-onset distributions of DSM-IV disorders in the National Comorbidity Survey Replication," *Archives of General Psychiatry*, 62 (2005), 593–602.

2. R. B. Zajonc, "Social facilitation," *Science*, 149 (1965), 269–274.

3. G. Porter, B. M. Hood, T. Troscianko, and C. N. Macrae, "Females, but not males, show greater pupillary response to direct than deviated gaze faces," *Perception*, 35 (2006), 1129–1136.

4. J. W. Michaels, J. M. Blommel, R. M. Brocato, R. A. Linkous, and J. S. Rowe, "Social facilitation and inhibition in a natural setting," *Replications in Social Psychology*, 2 (1982), 21–24.

5. S. J. Karau and K. D. Williams, "Social loafing: A meta-analytic review and theoretical integration," *Journal of Personality and Social Psychology*, 65 (1993), 681–706.

6. S. Moscovici and M. Zavalloni, "The group as a polarizer of attitudes," *Journal of Personality and Social Psychology*, 12 (1969), 125–135.

7. I. Janis, *Groupthink* (New York: Houghton Mifflin Company, 1982).

8. "DJ condemned for playing Van Halen's Jump as woman leaps from bridge," *Daily Mail* (18 January 2010).

9. L. Mann, "The baiting crowd in episodes of threatened suicide," *Journal of Personality and Social Psychology*, 41 (1981), 703–709.

10. T. Postmes and R. Spears, "Deindividuation and antinormative behavior: A meta-analysis," *Psychological Bulletin*, 123 (1998), 238–259.

11.   M. Bateson, D. Nettle, and G. Roberts, "Cues of being watched enhance cooperation in a real-world setting," *Biology Letters*, 2:3 (2006), 412–414.

12.   E. Diener and M. Wallbom, "Effects of self-awareness on antinormative behavior," *Journal of Research in Personality*, 10 (1976), 107–111.

13.   V. Bell, "Riot psychology," blog posted on the *Mind Hacks* website (2011), www.mindhacks.com

14.   T. Postmes and R. Spears, "Deindividuation and antinormative behavior: A meta-analysis," *Psychological Bulletin*, 123 (1998), 238–259.

15.   P. Rochat, *Others in Mind* (Cambridge: Cambridge University Press, 2010).

16.   National Institutes of Health, "Bullying widespread in US schools, survey finds," National Institutes of Health press release (24 April 2001), www.nichd.nih.gov/news/releases/bullying.cfm

17.   N. R. Crick and J. K. Grotpeter, "Relational aggression, gender, and social-psychological adjustment," *Child Development*, 66 (1995), 710–722.

18.   N. I. Eisenberger, M. D. Lieberman, and K. D. Williams, "Does rejection hurt? An FMRI study of social exclusion," *Science*, 302 (2003), 290–292.

19.   R. F. Baumeister, C. N. Dewall, N. J. Ciarocco, and J. M. Twenge, "Social exclusion impairs self-regulation," *Journal of Personality and Social Psychology*, 88 (2005), 589–604.

20.   K. D. Williams and S. A. Nida, "Ostracism: consequences and coping," *Current Directions in Psychology*, 20 (2011), 71–75.

21.   M. Gruter and R. D. Masters (eds.), "Ostracism: A social and biological phenomenon," *Ethology and Sociobiology*, 7 (1986), 149–395.

22.   K. D. Williams, "Ostracism: A temporal need-threat model," in M. Zanna (ed.), *Advances in Experimental Social Psychology* (New York: Academic Press, 2009), 279–314.

23. W. A. Warburton, K. D. Williams, and D. R. Cairns, "When ostracism leads to aggression: The moderating effects of control deprivation," *Journal of Experimental Social Psychology*, 42 (2006), 213–220.

24. M. R. Leary, R. M. Kowalski, and L. Smith, "Case studies of the school shootings," *Aggressive Behavior*, 29 (2003), 202–214.

25. Telegram to the Friar's Club of Beverly Hills, as recounted in G. Marx, *Groucho and Me* (New York: B. Geis, 1959), 321.

26. A. Bandura, B. Underwood, and M. E. Fromson, "Disinhibition of aggression through diffusion of responsibility and dehumanization of victims," *Journal of Research in Personality*, 9 (1975), 253–269.

27. H. Tajfel, M. G. Billig, R. P. Bundy, and C. Flament, "Social categorization and intergroup behavior," *European Journal of Social Psychology*, 1 (1971), 149–178.

28. W. Peters, *A Class Divided, Then and Now* (Expanded ed., New Haven, CT: Yale University Press, 1987).

29. M. B. Brewer, "The social self: On being the same and different at the same time," *Personality and Social Psychology Bulletin*, 17 (1991), 475–482.

30. S. E. Asch, "Studies of independence and conformity: 1. A minority of one against a unanimous majority," *Psychological Monographs: General and Applied*, 70 (1956), 1–70.

31. D. K. Campbell-Meiklejohn, D. R. Bach, A. Roepstorff, R. J. Dolan, and C. D. Frith, "How the opinion of others affects our valuation of objects," *Current Biology*, 20 (2010), 1165–1170; J. Zaki, J. Schirmer and J. P. Mitchell, "Social influence modulates the neural computation of value," *Psychological Science*, 22 (2011), 894–900.

32. P. Zimbardo, *The Lucifer Effect: How Good People Turn Evil* (London: Random House, 2007).

33. S. Reicher and S. A. Haslam, "Rethinking the psychology of tyranny: The BBC prison study," *British Journal of Social Psychology*, 45 (2006), 1–40.

34. *Cool Hand Luke* (1967), directed by Stuart Rosenberg, Warner Brothers.

35. S. Milgram, "Behavioral study of obedience," *Journal of Abnormal and Social Psychology*, 67 (1963), 371–378.

36. C. L. Sheridan and R. G. King, "Obedience to authority with an authentic victim," *Proceedings of the Annual Convention of the American Psychological Association*, 7: 1 (1972), 165–166.

37. C. K. Hofling, E. Brotzman, S. Dalrymple, N. Graves, and C. M. Pierce, "An experimental study in nurse-physician relationships," *Journal of Nervous and Mental Disorder*, 143 (1966), 171–180.

38. The hoax strip-search scam and Zimbardo's involvement are documented in his book, Zimbardo (2007).

39. C. Borge, "The science of evil," *Primetime*, ABC News (3 January 2007), http://abcnews.go.com/Primetime/story?id=2765416andpage=1

40. E. Brockes, "What happens in war happens," interview with Lynndie England, *Guardian* (3 January 2009), www.guardian.co.uk/world/2009/jan/03/abu-ghraib-lynndie-england-interview

41. H. Arendt, *Eichmann in Jerusalem: A Report on the Banality of Evil* (London: Faber and Faber, 1963).

42. A. Dijksterhuis and A. van Knippenberg, "The relation between perception and behavior, or how to win a game of 'Trivial Pursuit,'" *Journal of Personality and Social Psychology*, 74 (1998), 865–877.

43. T. L. Chartrand and J. A. Bargh, "The chameleon effect: The perception-behavior link and social interaction," *Journal of Personality and Social Psychology*, 76 (1999), 893–910.

44. J. N. Cappella and S. Panalp, "Talk and silence sequences in informal conversations: III. Inter-speaker influence," *Human Communication Research*, 7 (1981), 117–132.

45. R. B. van Baaren, L. Janssen, T. L. Chartrand and A. Dijksterhuis, "Where is the love? The social aspects of

mimicry," *Philosophical Transactions of the Royal Society B*, 364 (2009), 2381–2389.

46.   R. B. van Baaren, W. W. Maddux, T. L. Chartrand, C. DeBouter, and A. van Knippenberg, "It takes two to mimic: behavioral consequences of self-construals," *Journal of Personality and Social Psychology*, 84 (2003), 1093–1102.

47.   R. B. van Baaren, R. W. Holland, K. Kawakami, and A. van Knippenberg, "Mimicry and pro-social behavior," *Psychological Science*, 15 (2004), 71–74.

48.   R. B. van Baaren, R. W. Horgan, T. L. Chartrand, and M. Dijkmans, "The forest, the trees and the chameleon: Context-dependency and mimicry," *Journal of Personality and Social Psychology*, 86 (2004), 453–459.

49.   R. B. van Baaren, R. W. Holland, B. Steenaert, and A. van Knippenberg, "Mimicry for money: Behavioral consequences of imitation," *Journal of Experimental Social Psychology*, 39 (2003), 393–398.

50.   D. Wigboldus, M. van Gaal, R. Dotsch, and R. B. van Baaren, "Virtual mimicry: Implicit prejudice moderates the effects of mimicking" (in preparation).

51.   W. C. Roedell and R. G. Slaby, "The role of distal and proximal interaction in infant social preference formation," *Developmental Psychology*, 13 (1977), 266–273.

52.   L. Murray, A. Fiori-Cowley, R. Hooper and P. Cooper, "The impact of postnatal depression and associated adversity on early mother-infant interactions and later infant outcome," *Child Development*, 67 (1996), 2512–2526.

53.   H. R. Schaffer, *Social Development* (Oxford: Blackwell, 1996).

54.   S. S. Wiltermuth and C. Heath, "Synchrony and cooperation," *Psychological Science*, 20 (2009), 1–5.

55.   J. A. Bargh, M. Chen, and L. Burrows, "Automaticity of social behavior: Direct effects of trait construct and stereotype activation on action," *Journal of Personality and Social Psychology*, 71 (1996), 230–244.

56.   Dijksterhuis and van Knippenberg (1998).

57.   C. M. Steele and J. Aronson, "Stereotype threat and the intellectual test performance of African Americans," *Journal of Personality and Social Psychology*, 69 (1995), 797–811.

58.   M. Shih, T. L. Pittinsky, and N. Ambady, "Stereotype susceptibility: Identity salience and shifts in quantitative performance," *Psychological Science*, 10 (1999), 80–83.

59.   N. P. Leander, T. L. Chartrand, and W. Wood, "Mind your mannerisms: Behavioral mimicry elicits stereotype conformity," *Journal of Experimental Social Psychology*, 47 (2011), 195–201.

60.   R. E. Nisbett, *The Geography of Thought* (London: Nicholas Brealey, 2003).

61.   H. C. Triandis, "The self and social behavior in differing cultural contexts," *Psychological Review*, 96 (1989), 269–289.

62.   S. D. Cousins, "Culture and self-perception in Japan and the United States," *Journal of Personality and Social Psychology*, 56 (1989), 124–131.

63.   S. Kitayama, S. Duffy, T. Kawamura, and J. T. Larsen, "Perceiving an object and its context in different cultures: A cultural look at the New Look," *Psychological Science*, 14 (2003), 201–206.

64.   S. Duffy, R. Toriyama, S. Itakura, and S. Kitayama, "Development of cultural strategies of attention in North American and Japanese children," *Journal of Experimental Child Psychology*, 102 (2008), 351–359.

65.   T. Masuda and R. E. Nisbett, "Attending holistically vs. analytically: Comparing the context sensitivity of Japanese and Americans," *Journal of Personality and Social Psychology*, 81 (2001), 922–934.

66.   M. W. Morris and K. Peng, "Culture and cause: American and Chinese attributions for social physical events," *Journal of Personality and Social Psychology*, 67 (1994), 949–971.

67.   H. F. Chua, J. E. Boland, and R. E. Nisbett, "Cultural variation in eye movements during scene perception," *Proceedings of the National Academy of Sciences of the United States of America*, 102 (2005), 12629–12633.

68. W. James, *Principles of Psychology* (New York: Henry Holt, 1890).

69. A. Fernald and H. Morikawa, "Common themes and cultural variations in Japanese and American mothers' speech to infants," *Child Development*, 64 (1993), 637–656.

70. A. Gopnik and S. Choi, "Do linguistic differences lead to cognitive differences. A cross-linguistic study of semantic and cognitive development," *First Language*, 10 (1990), 199–215.

71. W. L. Gardener, S. Gabriel, and A. Y. Lee, "'I' value freedom but 'we' value relationships: Self-construal priming mirrors cultural differences in judgment," *Psychological Science*, 10 (1999), 321–326.

72. Y.-Y. Hong, C.-Y. Chiu, and T. M. Kung, "Bringing culture out in front: Effects of cultural meaning system activation on social cognition," in K. Leung, Y. Kashima, U. Kim, and S. Yamaguchi (eds.), *Progress in Asian Social Psychology, Vol.* 1 (Singapore: Wiley, 1997), 135–146.

CHAPTER 7: THE STORIES WE LIVE BY

1. A. Gatton, "Twin Towers 'survivor' a lonely imposter," *Herald Sun* (14 September 2008).

2. J. E. LeDoux, "Brain mechanisms of emotion and emotional learning," *Current Opinion in Neurobiology*, 2 (1992), 191–197.

3. R. Brown and J. Kulik, "Flashbulb memories," *Cognition*, 5 (1977), 73–99.

4. S. Galea, J. Ahern, H. Resnick, D. Kilpatrick, M. Bucuvalas, J. Gold, et al., "Psychological sequelae of the September 11 terrorist attacks in New York City," *New England Journal of Medicine*, 346 (2002), 982–987.

5. G. Vaiva, F. Ducrocq, K. Jezequel, B. Averland, P. Lestavel, A. Brunet, and C. R. Marmar, "Immediate treatment with propranolol decreases posttraumatic stress disorder two months after trauma," *Biological Psychiatry*, 54 (2003), 947–949; R. K. Pitman, K. M. Sanders, R. M. Zusman, A. R. Healy, F. Cheema, N. B. Lasko, L. Cahill, et al., "Pilot

study of secondary prevention of posttraumatic stress disorder with propranolol," *Biological Psychiatry*, 51 (2002), 189–192.

6.   R. M. Henig, "The quest to forget," *New York Times Magazine* (4 April 2004), 32–37. Also Leon Kass, former chair of the President's Council on Bioethics is quoted as saying that such a pill would be a "morning-after pill for just about anything that produces regret, remorse, pain or guilt." N. Levy, *Neuroethics: Challenges for the 21st Century* (Cambridge: Cambridge University Press, 2007).

7.   *The 9/11 Faker*, Channel 4 (September 2008).

8.   D. Parfitt, "Divided minds and the nature of persons," in C. Blakemore and S. Greenfield (eds.), *Mindwaves* (Oxford: Blackwell, 1987), 19–26; C. Priest, *The Prestige* (New ed., London: Gollancz, 2005).

9.   J. Locke, *Essay Concerning Human Understanding*, ed. P. H. Nidditch (Oxford: Clarendon Press, 1690/1975), Book 2, Chapter 27.

11   L. J. Rips, S. Blok, and G. Newman, "Tracing the identity of objects," *Psychological Review*, 113 (2006), 1–30.

12.   B. Hood and P. Bloom, "Children prefer unique individuals over perfect duplicates," *Cognition*, 106 (2008), 455–462.

13.   N. L. Gjersoe, B. M. Hood, and P. Bloom, "The development of mind-body dualism through early childhood." Poster presented at the Society for Research into Child Development biannual conference (Boston, USA, 2009).

14.   O. Sacks, *The Man Who Mistook His Wife for a Hat* (New York: Harper Perennial, 1987), 108.

15.   M. S. Gazzaniga, J. E. Bogen, and R. W. Sperry, "Some functional effects of sectioning the cerebral commissures in man," *Proceedings of the National Academy of Sciences of the United States of America*, 48 (1962), 1765–1769.

16.   M. S. Gazzaniga, personal communication.

17.   D. P. McAdams, *The Stories We Live By: Personal Myths and the Making of the Self* (New York: Guilford Press).

18. J. Campbell, *The Hero with a Thousand Faces* (Princeton, NJ: Princeton University Press, 1949).

18. A. Greenwald, "The totalitarian ego: Fabrication and revision of personal history," *American Psychologist*, 35 (1980), 603–618.

19. B. R. Forer, "The fallacy of personal validation: A classroom demonstration of gullibility," *Journal of Abnormal and Social Psychology*, 44 (1949), 118–123.

20. D. H. Dickson and I. W. Kelly, "The 'Barnum Effect' in personality assessment: A review of the literature," *Psychological Reports*, 57 (1985), 367–382.

21. Theophrastus, *The Characters of Theophrastus*, trans. J. M. Edmonds (London: William Heinemann (1929).

22. R. R. McCrae and O. P. John, "An introduction to the five-factor model and its application," *Journal of Personality*, 60 (1992), 329–361.

23. U. Schimmack, P. Radhakrishnan, S. Oishi, V. Dzokoto, and S. Ahadi, "Culture, personality, and subjective well-being: Integrating process models of life-satisfaction," *Journal of Personality and Social Psychology*, 82 (2002), 582–593; L. A. Jensen-Campbell, R. Adams, D. G. Perry, K. A. Workman, J. Q. Furdella, and S. K. Egan, "Agreeableness, extraversion, and peer relations in early adolescence: Winning friends and deflecting aggression," *Journal of Research in Personality*, 36 (2002), 224–251; D. D. Danner, D. A. Snowdon, and W. V. Friesen, "Positive emotions in early life and longevity: Findings from the nun study," *Journal of Personality and Social Psychology*, 80 (2001), 804–813; M. R. Barrick, M. K. Mount, and R. Gupta, "Meta-analysis of the relationship between the Five Factor model of personality and Holland's occupational types," *Personnel Psychology*, 56 (2003), 45–74.

24. K. M. Sheldon, R. M. Ryan, L. J. Rawsthorne, and B. Ilardi, "Trait self and true self: Cross-role variation in the Big-Five personality traits and its relations with psychological authenticity and subjective well-being," *Journal of Personality and Social Psychology*, 73 (1997), 1380–1393.

25. J. M. Darley and C. D. Batson, "From Jerusalem to Jericho: A study of situational and dispositional variables in helping behavior," *Journal of Personality and Social Psychology*, 27 (1973), 100–119.

26. S. E. Taylor, *Positive Illusions: Creative Self-deception and the Healthy Mind* (New York: Basic Books, 1989).

27. E. Langer, "The illusion of control," *Journal of Personality and Social Psychology*, 32 (1975), 311–328.

28. J. Kruger and J. Burrus, "Egocentrism and focalism in unrealistic optimism (and pessimism)," *Journal of Experimental Social Psychology*, 40 (2004), 332–340.

29. Q. Wang, "Autobiographical memory and culture," *Online Readings in Psychology and Culture, Unit 5* (May 2011), http://scholarworks.gvsu.edu/orpc/vol5/iss2/2

30. Q. Wang, "Earliest recollections of self and others in European American and Taiwanese young adults," *Psychological Science*, 17 (2006), 708–714.

31. Q. Wang, "Relations of maternal style and child self-concept to autobiographical memories in Chinese, Chinese immigrant, and European American 3-year-olds," *Child Development*, 77 (2006), 1794–1809.

32. K. Nelson and R. Fivush, "The emergence of autobiographical memory: A social cultural developmental theory," *Psychological Review*, 111 (2004), 486–511.

33. Q. Wang, M. D. Leichtman, and K. I. Davies, "Sharing memories and telling stories: American and Chinese mothers and their 3-year-olds," *Memory*, 8 (2000), 159–177.

34. F. C. Bartlett, *Remembering: A Study in Experimental and Social Psychology* (Cambridge: Cambridge University Press, 1932), 296.

35. "The man with ten personalities," *Time* (23 October 1978), www.astraeasweb.net/plural/milligan-1978.html

36. R. Carter, *Multiplicity: The New Science of Personality* (New York: Little, Brown and Co. 2008).

37. B. Waldvogel, A. Ullrich, and H. Straburger, "Sighted and blind in one person. A case report and conclusions on the psychoneurobiology of vision," *Nervenarzt*, 78 (2007), 1303–1309 (in German).

38. Katherine Morris, personal communication.

39. P. Gebhard, "Fetishism and sadomasochism," in J. H. Masserman (ed.), *Dynamics of Deviant Sexuality* (New York: Grune and Stratton, 1969), 71–80.

CHAPTER 8: CAUGHT IN THE WEB

1. Personal witness account from the mother of Peter Moskos retrieved from his blog, P. Moskos, "Crowd stampede at Netherlands WWII ceremony," *Cop in the Hood* website (5 May 2010), www.copinthehood.com/2010/05/crowd-stampede-at-netherlands-wwii.html

2. N. Christakis, "The hidden influence of social networks," TED talk (May 2010), www.youtube.com/watch?v=2U-tOghblfE

3. For an overview see T. Gilovich, D. Keltner and R. E. Nisbett, *Social Psychology* (New York: W. W. Norton, 2006).

4. N. A. Christakis and J. H. Fowler, "The spread of obesity in a large social network over 32 years," *New England Journal of Medicine*, 357:4 (2007), 370–379.

5. J. H. Fowler, J. E. Settle, and N. A. Christakis, "Correlated genotypes in friendship networks," *Proceedings of the National Academy of Sciences of the United States of America*, 108 (2011), 1993–1997.

6. P. Ekman, "Lie catching and micro expressions," in C. Martin (ed.), *The Philosophy of Deception* (Oxford: Oxford University Press, 2009).

7. J. Sundén, *Material Virtualities* (New York: Peter Lang, 2003), 3.

8. L. E. Buffardi and W. K. Campbell, "Narcissism and social networking web sites," *Personality and Social Psychology Bulletin*, 34 (2008), 1303–1314.

9.   Results of a survey of 3,000 British parents especially commissioned to mark the launch of a TV series, *Tarrant Lets the Kids Loose,* on the Watch channel: Taylor Herring, "On the subject of traditional careers," *Taylor Herring* website (6 October 2009), www.taylorherring.com/blog/index.php/tag/traditional-careers

10.   Association of Teachers and Lecturers (UK), press release (March 2008), http://news.bbc.co.uk/1/hi/7296306.stm

11.   Nielsen, "What Americans do online: Social media and games dominate activity," *Nielsenwire* website (2 August 2010), http://blog.nielsen.com/nielsenwire/online_mobile/what-americans-do-online-social-media-and-games-dominate-activity

12.   Nielsen, "Nielsen and McKinsey form joint venture to help companies use social media intelligence for superior business performance," Press release (14 June 2010), www.mediainsight.nl/media/nm_incite_pressrelease.pdf

13.   M. Ito et al., *Hanging Out, Messing Around and Geeking Out,* The John D. and Catherine T. MacArthur Foundation Series on Digital Media and Learning (Cambridge, MA: MIT Press, 2011).

14.   Ofcom, *The Communications Market Report United Kingdom: A Nation Addicted to Smartphones* (London: Ofcom, 4 August 2011), http://stakeholders.ofcom.org.uk/market-data-research/market-data/communications-market-reports/cmr11/uk

15.   R. Epstein, "The myth of the teen brain," *Scientific American Mind* (April 2007).

16.   M. Gardner and L. Steinberg, "Peer influence on risk-taking, risk preference, and risky decision-making in adolescence and adulthood: An experimental study." Developmental Psychology, 41 (2005), 625–635.

17.   R. B. Cialdini, R. J. Borden, A. Thorne, M. R. Walker, S. Freeman, and L. R. Sloan, "Basking in reflected glory. Three Football Field Studies." *Journal of Personality & Social Psychology,* 34(1976), 366–375.

18. K. Quinn, "Anonymous online tweets: It's just bullying in 140 letters," *Age* (21 February 2011).

19. F. Swain, "Susan Greenfield: Living online is changing our brains," *New Scientist* (3 August 2011).

20. D. Bavelier, C. S. Green, and W. G. Dye, "Children, wired: For better and for worse," *Neuron*, 67 (2010), 692–701.

21. D. Bishop, "An open letter to Baroness Susan Greenfield," *BishopBlog* website (4 August 2011), http://deevybee. blogspot.com/2011/08/open-letter-to-baroness-susan. html; see also T. McVeigh, "Research linking autism to internet use is criticised," *Guardian* (6 August 2011), www.guardian.co.uk/society/2011/aug/06/research-autism-internet-susan-greenfield

22. J. Cohen, "The rise of social media is really a reprise," in J. Brockman (ed.), *Is the Internet Changing the Way You Think? The Net's Impact on Our Minds and Future* (New York: Harper Perennial, 2011).

23. "The professor, his wife, and the secret, savage book reviews on Amazon," *Guardian* (20 April 2010).

24. A. Jeffries, "A sensor in every chicken: Cisco bets on the internet of things," *Read Write Web* website (2010), www. readwriteweb.com/archives/cisco_futurist_predicts_ internet_of_things_1000_co.php

25. d. m. boyd, "Streams of content, limited attention: The flow of information through social media," presentation at "Web2.0 Expo," New York (17 November 2009).

26. E. Pariser, *The Filter Bubble: What the Internet Is Hiding from You* (New York: Penguin, 2011).

27. E. Pariser, "Beware online 'filter bubbles,'" TED Talk, *TED* website (March 2011), www.ted.com/talks/eli_ pariser_beware_online_filter_bubbles.html

28. A. M. McCright and R. E. Dunlap, "The politicization of climate change and polarization in the American public's views of global warming 2001–2010," *Sociological Quarterly*, 52 (2011), 155–194.

29. J. Bollen, B. Gonçalves, G. Ruan, and H. Mao, "Happiness is assortative in online social networks," *Artificial Life*, 17 (2011), 237–251.

30. M. D. Conover, J. Ratkiewicz, M. Francisco, B. Gonçalves, A. Flammini, and F. Menczer, "Political polarization on Twitter," Proceedings of International Conference on Weblogs and Social Media 2011 (2011), http://truthy. indiana.edu/site_media/pdfs/conover_icwsm2011_ polarization.pdf

31. B. Goncalves, N. Perra, and A. Alessandro Vespignani, "Modeling user activity on Twitter networks: Validation of Dunbar's number," *PLoS ONE*, 6:8 (2011), e22656, doi:10.1371/journal.pone.0022656

32. S. Baron-Cohen, "1000 hours a year," in J. Brockman (ed.), *Is the Internet Changing the Way You Think? The Net's Impact on Our Minds and Future* (New York: Harper Perennial, 2011).

33. I. P. Pavlov, *Conditioned Reflexes* (Oxford: Oxford University Press, 1927).

34. J. B. Watson, "Psychology as the behaviorist views it," *Psychological Review*, 20 (1913), 158–177; B. F. Skinner, *The Behavior of Organisms: An Experimental Analysis* (New York: Appleton-Century-Crofts, 1938).

35. R. Montague, *Why Choose This Book? How We Make Decisions* (New York: Dutton, 2006).

36. J. Olds, "Pleasure center in the brain," *Scientific American*, 195 (October 1956), 105–116.

37. L. Sharpe, "A reformulated cognitive-behavioral model of problem gambling: A biopsychosocial perspective," *Clinical Psychology Review*, 22 (2002), 1–25.

38. "South Korean couple starved child while raising virtual baby," *CNN News* (2010).

39. M. McLuhan, *Understanding Media: The Extensions of Man* (New York: McGraw Hill, 1964).

40. S. Tuckle, *Alone Together: Why We Expect More from Technology and Less from Each Other* (New York: Basic Books, 2011).

41. S. Morris, "How South West News got its divorce scoop in Second Life," *Guardian* (14 November 2008).

42. P. Bloom, "First person plural," *Atlantic Magazine* (8 November 2008).

43. C. Cuomo, C. Vlasto, and D. Dwyer, "Rep. Anthony Weiner: "The Picture Was of Me and I Sent It," *ABC News* website (6 June 2011), http://abcnews.go.com/Politics/rep-anthony-weiner-picture/story?id=13774605

44. National Campaign to Prevent Teen and Unplanned Pregnancy, *Sex and Tech: Results from a Survey of Young Teens and Adults* (Washington, DC: National Campaign to Prevent Teen and Unplanned Pregnancy, 10 December 2008), www.thenationalcampaign.org/sextech/PDF/SexTech_Summary.pdf

45. J. M. Albright, "How do I love thee and thee and thee: Self presentation, deception, and multiple relationships online," in M. T. Whitty, A. J. Baker, and J. A. Inman (eds.), *Online Matchmaking* (London: Palgrave Macmillan, 2007), 81–96.

46. S. Lipkins, J. Levy, and B. Jerabkova, "Sexting… Is it all about power?," *Real Psychology* website (n.d.), http://realpsychology.com/content/tools-life/sextingis-it-all-about-power

47. "Evil clown is a scary success," *Orange News* (13 April 2010), http://web.orange.co.uk/article/quirkies/Evil_clown_is_a_scary_success; J. Dibbell, "A rape in cyberspace: How an evil clown, a Haitian trickster spirit, two wizards, and a cast of dozens turned a database into a society," *Village Voice* (23 December 1993).

ACKNOWLEDGMENTS ■

This was a difficult book to write for a number of reasons. It covers a vast array of different areas that have a long history dating back to the dawn of human self-reflection. I expect that it will annoy many for failing to fully acknowledge all those who have gone before and who have tackled this issue and for leaving out critical points or not considering all variations of the arguments. That would have been an impossible book to read, let alone write. I have tried to synthesize an account that brings this vast volume of work into an easily understandable format with one simple claim: I believe I have distilled what are the main issues that are relevant to cognitive neuroscience.

The most difficult aspect of writing the book was that it forced me to confront my own self illusion and the way I have lived my life. It made me uncomfortably aware of my own weaknesses, vanity, insecurity, lack of integrity, lack of cohesion, and all the other negative things that few of us admit, but that a self illusion can conceal. It is a thesis that does not, and will not, sit easily with those who regard their self as real. However, I do believe that questioning the nature of our self on a regular basis is a necessary process to get the most out of life.

I am indebted to those who understand this and have helped me shape the book. I would particularly like to thank my agent, Robert Kirby, not only for his professional input, but also for his support during my moments of doubt. Also I would like to thank my U.S. agent Zoë Pagnamenta for taking on a difficult task. My U.K. editor Andreas Campomar ignited the idea and has been enthusiastically supportive. I hope it does not blow up in our faces. Joan Bossert (Oxford University Press, U.S.) gave me some great ideas to develop, and Jim Gifford (Harper Collins, Canada) pointed out the dangers of my boyish tendencies. I would like to thank the friends, colleagues, and students who have read earlier drafts and provided invaluable feedback and support. These include (in alphabetical order) Sara Baker, Sue Blackmore, Paul Bloom, Katy Donnelly, Teobesta Tesfa Endrias, Iain Gilchrist, Nathalia Gjersoe, Shoji Itakura, Monica Jensen, Pat Kanngiesser, Cristine Legare, Kate Longstaffe, George Newman, Arnoud Van Voorst, and Jan Woike.

I would like to acknowledge the support of the various funding agencies that have supported me and my research over the past 3 years and have enabled me to write this book. These include the Economic and Social Research Council of the United Kingdom, the Leverhulme trust, the Bial foundation, and the Perrott-Warwick Fund. This book is dedicated to Kim who has had to endure this particular chaotic bundle. Without her, I would have come apart years ago.

INDEX ■